PRAISE FOR
SOCIAL ENTREPRE
AND INNOVATION

'I believe this collection of stories of passion and impact will leave people hungering for more and will inspire more than a few readers to explore their passions and translate them into incremental stories of meaningful change.'
Alex Moen, Vice President of Explorer Programs, National Geographic

'This important, timely book gives the reader an invaluable insight into the workings of the world of social entrepreneurship. It is a must-read for students, practitioners, policy makers and anyone with a passing interest in how to work for the greater good.'
Professor Klaus Schwab, Founder of the World Economic Forum and Co-Founder of the Schwab Foundation for Social Entrepreneurship

'The world's most challenging problems are being taken on by people motivated by their personal passions, informed by their deep understanding of local realities and shaped by their frustration with inadequate solutions. Ken Banks and the other remarkable innovators here offer inspiration and insight into building practical solutions while calling into question established wisdom about social innovation. This is a must-read book for anyone who wants to solve problems with global implications through local knowledge and involvement.'
Ethan Zuckerman, Director of the Centre for Civic Media, MIT

'These real – occasionally raw – stories do more to capture the life of the committed social entrepreneur than anything else I've read. Inspiring, yes, but even better, it works as a real world case-based manual for how to create change for the better.'
Kevin Starr, Managing Director, Mulago Foundation

'This book is a refreshing antidote to pessimism about the potential of individuals influencing "social change". The author of each chapter has a personal story to tell, but each in such a way that it helps us to better understand the different ways it is possible to make that change happen.'
Dr Elizabeth Harrison, Reader in Anthropology and Head of International Development, University of Sussex

'The case studies in Ken's book show that we really can all learn from everyone, anywhere, and often it's the stories from countries or areas of expertise we don't know that draw us in the most. But the common traits of belief in a vision, of using data to build evidence for that vision and of altruism and helping others, which drives these innovators far more than the motive to persuade a consumer to upgrade their gadget to the latest model, make it a practical book you can apply to whatever your country or area of work might be.'
Laurie Lee, Chief Executive, CARE International UK

'This book is required reading for any student or anyone interested in technology-based invention to improve peoples' lives, and social innovation as a potential life path. Its honest stories of unforeseen challenges and unexpected opportunities from the people encountering them both are an inspiration and refreshing reality check.'
Joshua Schuler, Executive Director, Lemelson–MIT Program

Social Entrepreneurship and Innovation

Social
Entrepreneurship
and Innovation
International case studies and practice

Edited by Ken Banks

KoganPage

LONDON PHILADELPHIA NEW DELHI

First published in Great Britain and the United States in 2016 by Kogan Page Limited

2nd Floor, 45 Gee Street
London
EC1V 3RS
United Kingdom

1518 Walnut Street, Suite 1100
Philadelphia PA 19102
USA

4737/23 Ansari Road
Daryaganj
New Delhi 110002
India

ISBN   978 0 7494 75918
E-ISBN 978 0 7494 75925

British Library Cataloguing-in-Publication Data

A CIP record for this book is available from the British Library.

Library of Congress Control Number

2016932618

Typeset by Graphicraft Limited, Hong Kong
Print production managed by Jellyfish
Printed and bound by CPI Group (UK) Ltd, Croydon CR0 4YY

CONTENTS

02   Closing Latin America's 'digital divide'   45

CDI – Rodrigo Baggio

03   Patent wars: fighting big pharma to enable access to drugs for all   67

I-MAK – Priti Radhakrishnan

04   Data science, technology and design for social justice   81

Visualizing Impact – Jessica Anderson and Joumana al Jabri

05   Bringing the Silicon Valley revolution in technology and business to global health   109

Magpi – Joel Selanikio

06   Food waste meets food poverty: closing the loop   133

FoodCycle – Kelvin Cheung and Michael Norton

07   Innovation in Africa's Silicon Savannah   147

Ushahidi – Erik Hersman

08   Touch-based treatment for autism   165

QSTI (Qigong Sensory Training Institute) – Louisa Silva

09   Reconnecting the disconnected: a story of technology, refugees and finding lost family   185

Refugees United – David and Christopher Mikkelsen

13   Power to the people: reengineering democracy   255

GovRight – Tarik Nesh Nash

ABOUT THE EDITOR

Ken Banks, Founder of kiwanja.net, devotes himself to the application of mobile technology for positive social and environmental change, and has spent the past two decades working on projects in Africa. His early research resulted in the development of FrontlineSMS, an award-winning text message communication system today powering thousands of social change projects in over one hundred and seventy countries around the world.

Ken graduated from Sussex University with honours in Social Anthropology with Development Studies, was awarded a Stanford University Reuters Digital Vision Fellowship in 2006 and was named a Pop!Tech Social Innovation Fellow in 2008. In 2009 he was named a Laureate of the Tech Awards, an international awards programme which honours innovators from around the world who are applying technology to benefit humanity. He was named a National Geographic Emerging Explorer in May 2010 and an Ashoka Fellow in 2011, and was the recipient of the 2011 Pizzigati Prize for Software in the Public Interest. That summer he won the Curry Stone Design Prize for his pioneering work with FrontlineSMS, and was selected as a member of the UK Prime Minister's delegation to Africa. In 2012 the Cambridge business community presented Ken with a Special Achievement Award for his work as a social entrepreneur. Later that year he was made a Fellow of the Royal Society of Arts. In 2013 he was nominated for the TED Prize, and in 2015 he was invited to RMIT University in Melbourne, Australia, as a Visiting Fellow.

Ken represents Sussex University as their Ambassador for International Development, and is a founding member of the Digital Advisory Board of British Government's Department for International Development. In late 2015 Ken was appointed CARE International's first Entrepreneur in Residence. In addition to his own work, Ken mentors early-stage entrepreneurs through Pop!Tech and the Unreasonable Institute, and more seasoned entrepreneurs in the Ashoka network.

When he's not working, Ken spends much of his time being bossed around by his young son, Henry, and twins Madeleine and Oliver.

FOREWORD
By Peter Gabriel, musician

It is far easier to imagine and talk through grand ideas that change the world than it is to actually get out there and do it. What is inspiring about Ken's work is that his focus is on those that have discovered a very real need and in turn created very practical solutions that address them.

Traditionally most attempts at improving things were rolled out in a top-down fashion. What makes the projects that Ken highlights in his book so significant is that they all flip this model upside down. These projects begin on the ground and prove so effective that their influence and their model spread out around the world from there.

I used to be a bit of a pyromaniac as a kid and would always light little fires around the farm where I grew up. I would often watch as big bonfires had sump oil from the tractors casually thrown over them to try to help the wet branches and leaves burn, but this often failed. But I also noticed if you started on the ground and made a little fire you could build it up slowly, maintaining the intensity of heat and ash. By working with it directly at this level you could respond to the needs of the fire while instantly responding to the changing circumstances – things like the types of wood, how wet it was, the structure of the fire and the changing winds.

I am convinced we are going to see new platforms that will facilitate this ground-up revolution in social innovation. The old concept of aid will be replaced by new means of empowering people directly with solutions that are free-flowing, faster-moving and highly responsive, all the time generating comprehensive and useful data, which in turn can be fed back in to allow for improvements. The closer these feedback learning loops are to where the action is, the more the system can become smarter and more effective. Small, smart and responsive is the way to go.

The digital revolution and the ubiquity of mobile phones are shrinking the huge opportunity gap between the haves and the have-nots. With access available to information, tools, mentoring, funding and with knowledge from those with similar goals or experience available on tap, we have a far more open playing field than ever before. Power really is in the hands of the people. Many of the key elements that are fundamental to social transformation are now within reach. The cost of smartphones is plummeting and it is becoming harder by the day to find places in the world that are offline. What we're still lacking, however, is a unifying, easy-to-use visual platform that can help the many ground-up initiatives connect to everything they need to flourish. If this can be meshed into the world of big data then we have a real engine of accelerated transformation.

When Ken Banks approached me and asked if I'd be interested in writing the foreword to the book you are now holding – sharing the stories of some of the organizations included and its focus in the process – my answer was a definite Yes.

It's full of hope, of obstacles conquered and dreams realized. The innovators in this book are what I'd call the gardeners of dreams for a better world.

Today, fewer people than ever have an excuse to not know what's going on around the world, and fewer people than ever lack the tools to contribute to that news sharing and generation. These tools transcend all social change boundaries, contributing to solutions to how we stay healthy, how we feed ourselves, how we protect our planet and how we better educate our children, as well as how we fight for dignity and basic human rights. The advance in technology combined with advances in human awareness, and passionate idealistic young people emerging everywhere, determined more than ever to leave the world in better shape than when they entered it, gives us an unprecedented opportunity for change.

I've been extremely fortunate over the years to work and campaign with some truly amazing people, especially those involved in the Elders who have lives that I have found particularly inspiring – people like Archbishop Desmond Tutu, Mary Robinson, Jimmy Carter, Gro Bruntland, Kofi Annan, Ela Bhatt, Marti Ahtisaari and the late Nelson Mandela.

Part of the dream with the Elders was to create real links between those doing the powerful and practical work on the ground and those with international influence who can call up any head of state. A link between young and old that could act like a pincer movement on the middle-aged in power.

But while leadership at the top is critical in addressing some of the bigger challenges facing us and the planet, it would count for little were it not connected to the work of millions of unsung heroes, like those featured in this book, who tirelessly fight each and every day for justice and a better life for everyone. As my good friend Archbishop Tutu so eloquently reminds us, 'Do your little bit of good wherever you are, for it's those little bits of good put together that overwhelm the world.' We all indeed have a contribution to make, and history shows us that if we do, even the greatest of problems can be overcome.

Social entrepreneurship, seen as one of the most promising ways to create change, is often viewed by outsiders as an effortless and almost romantic pursuit, yet in reality it is far from it. Social entrepreneurs and social innovators around the world often have to make considerable sacrifices, sacrifices that often test their passion and commitment to the limit. On their journey, many have had plenty of opportunities to give up, but they didn't. They also hit many dead ends, but found ways around them. It is this tenacity and, if you like, stubbornness which perhaps more than anything separates them from everyone else.

When people ask me about the kind of people most likely to succeed in music, they assume I will reply that it is the most talented. But it's clear that the ones who succeed are actually those with the most bloody-minded determination. The same stubbornness and strength of character will regularly leap out at you as you flick through the pages of this book, and it is clearly a testament to what is good and effective in the human spirit.

Through the campaigning organizations I have been a part of, I have witnessed the power of that spirit. Individuals *can* and *do* make a difference if they stand up for what they believe in, and through the new world of mobile phones and the internet we have a whole new set of tools to turn passion into real results, to connect and learn from those who can advise, teach and fund our dreams for a better world. A new ground-up movement for change is being grown in wonderful ways all around the world.

Social Entrepreneurship and Innovation: International case studies and practice shines a light on some of the people creating the kind of change we all want to see in the world, sharing their very personal stories of success, and what they went through in order to get there. For those seeking inspiration and belief that change is possible, or those building their own social change projects to tackle all manner of problems, this is a book that will inspire – inspire your trust and faith in the possible.

FOREWORD
By Bill Drayton, Founder and CEO, Ashoka

Some months ago, one of Pakistan's best social entrepreneurs and an Ashoka Fellow – and friend of ten years – shared with me a story. I love it. Because it shows how close we are to a far, far better world – if only we will each give ourselves (and everyone else) permission to be changemakers for the good.

Ali's story represents the newest proof of his core belief – that all young people, very much including the disadvantaged, will change their world if that's what you expect of them, thereby breaking the chains of disbelief. Last year he challenged 6,000 poor students across 74 charity government vocational schools to create ventures within a month. He went to them and said, 'I believe in you. You can all start businesses and citizen groups and you can all succeed.' He said this to all the students in all the schools, none coming from privilege.

He helped them organize into peer teams and get started sharing ideas, helping each other, building things together. He banished training sessions because they are 'where someone tells you what to do'. His Youth Engagement Service provided the seed capital to each group, and would take all the loss or profit. A month later he had achieved an 83 per cent profit. (Ali is now working with 1,200 educational and technical institutions and a hundred leading colleges across Pakistan.)

The problem isn't young people – it's us. We create a poisonous atmosphere when we tell young people 'You can't' in so many subtle and not-so-subtle ways. They can – and they must. So, ultimately, can we all.

Like Ali, almost all of the roughly 1,000 Ashoka Fellows (out of 3,300) who are focused on children and young people do more than just believe in them. They put them in charge. So do 200 Ashoka Changemaker Schools and 35 Ashoka-affiliated colleges and universities. The results are dramatic and marvellous – once changemaking has become the norm, and not a very difficult, counterculture exception.

Once a teen has had a dream, built a team and changed her world, she will be a changemaker for life, contributing again and again to whatever problem needs solving. She has her power. She will never be afraid. And she will be in great demand. We live in a world where the demand for those who can adapt to and contribute to change is accelerating exponentially, even as the demand for repetitive work is falling just as fast.

For many, many centuries the game was efficiency in repetition (think assembly lines and law firms). You were educated in a particular skill, be it as a barber or a banker, which you would then apply within walls for life. A very few orchestrated the many. Life was guided by rules. In today's change-driven environment, all of those old ways are going through a new, mass extinction. Success now goes to fast-morphing teams of teams – all of whose members are observing, adapting, spotting opportunities and helping build and serve new teams of teams around these newly identified goals.

Anyone who cannot play this game is out. You can't play the change-game unless you are a changemaker.

How many schools, education reformers or parents know that they are failing unless their young people are practising being changemakers? And that the most important educational metric has become: 'What percentage of any school's students know they are changemakers?'

Education reform that is about equal access to an obsolete system ensures at best a generation of failure. Trying to solve youth unemployment by 'giving young people needed skills' is a chimera.

Major turning points always catch societies by surprise. And this is the big one. It changes the most basic structures of society. It is far bigger than any technology-based revolution.

It leads to a wonderful place. An 'everyone a changemaker' world is one:

- where problems cannot outrun solutions
- that is structurally far more equal because everyone is powerful
- where everyone, not just the fortunate elites, can express love and respect in action – the root cause of happiness and health.

The alternative is a deeply divided, angry world.

The challenge for leaders – and all of us – is to recognize and welcome the fact that we are at a turning point, and now must change everything from how we grow up to how we lead.

Students, and those who remain open, increasingly realize that they need to become ever-more skilled changemakers, both to succeed in society and to live the deep satisfaction of contributing importantly to the good of all.

Where can they look for help?

Ken Banks, an Ashoka Fellow and a leader in our community, wrote this book to help you get to the essence of what it means to be a social entrepreneur. The decades of creating, listening and changing, and creating again as both your idea and the world keep wriggling and changing. The fact that, given that you are seeking both to be a pattern-changing entrepreneur and to serve the good of all, you have both the great satisfaction and competitive advantage of focusing on all and also the personal challenge of having to do so, unlike your friends in narrow, walled and therefore far easier (and more boring) professional boxes.

As the world has already entered a turning point, during which our mindsets and society's arrangements are rapidly reorienting away from repetition and towards change, a growing number of universities, schools, consultants, writers and others are responding to this need to explain our field. There is much that is useful here.

However, this book does what many of these scholars and others cannot. Ken does not look at us as a Martian exploring a very foreign Earth would. He is very much one of us. Moreover, he has refocused his entrepreneurial drive to helping you and your friends grasp this historical moment, to see the resulting opportunities, and to open the way for everyone to become key contributors in this new world. Success for him is *you* becoming a changemaker.

This book is a big step towards that 'everyone a changemaker' world.

Introduction

KIWANJA.NET – KEN BANKS

I shall pass this way but once. Any good that I can do or any kindness I can show to any human being, let me do it now. Let me not defer nor neglect it, for I shall not pass this way again.

ETIENNE DE GRELLET, QUAKER MISSIONARY

While the term 'social entrepreneurship' is relatively new, social entrepreneurs are not. Florence Nightingale, the founder of modern nursing in the 1800s, was a social entrepreneur. Dr Maria Montessori, who developed the Montessori approach to early childhood education in the early 1900s, was also a social entrepreneur. Social entrepreneurship, as a specific term to describe those driven, persistent, ambitious individuals working on innovative solutions to society's most pressing social problems – people such as Florence and Maria – only began to appear in social change literature as recently as the 1960s and 1970s.

The discipline found one of its early champions in Bill Drayton, who founded the Ashoka network in 1980 (Bill, who wrote one of the forewords to this book, is often described as the 'grandfather of social entrepreneurship'). Ashoka became one of the first organizations dedicated to specifically supporting and promoting social entrepreneurship, and today it is one of the largest global networks of what it refers to as 'innovators for the public'. Seminal publications such as Charles Leadbeater's *The Rise of the Social Entrepreneur* in 1997 went on to help the practice gain further traction and attention.

Whilst the term has become mainstream over recent years, particularly in academic circles, there remains confusion and concern around both definition and the struggle for sustainability in many social entrepreneurship activities. Indeed, in my work over the past two decades – the last five as an Ashoka Fellow – I find some of the most heated debates centre on the question of definition, with the only thing everyone agreeing on being that it's problematic. While it is sometimes useful to have clear definitions – academia is a fan, in particular – given the wide reach and influence of social entrepreneurship it is perhaps more helpful to allow the term to be used more loosely. I, for one, didn't identify myself as a social entrepreneur until I was first approached by Ashoka in 2009, and millions of other innovators and social change agents around the world today would no doubt feel the same. I'm still not sure if I am one, to be honest, but don't think it matters. Actions speak louder than words, and the label attached to a particular activity is unlikely to have much impact on how that activity develops although, admittedly, being labelled a social entrepreneur does seem to open doors to funding and support not available to people not officially labelled or recognized as one. This, in my view, is one thing the sector needs to work on.

If I'm honest, I'm drawn more towards the term 'social innovation' than 'social entrepreneurship'. I prefer the term because, while it also focuses on the social aspect of the work, it doesn't imply the application of business skills or practices to the initiative. Whilst 'innovation' may also be a contentious word – again, definitions are wide and varied – in my view many of the social innovators I meet and work with, including those showcased in this book, have genuinely developed new approaches to often-old problems, and for that alone I see their work as innovative. Business practices – activities you may define as 'entrepreneurship' – are not always present. It is one component of the complex, wider debate if they really need to be or not.

A journey into meaning and empathy

The seeds for what was to become my later life's work were planted at a very young age. Our mother, who brought my brother, two sisters and I up on her own after the death of our father when I was six, encouraged us to be inquisitive, enquiring and curious. My love of nature and the outdoors, which would later lead me to conservation work in Africa, started from spending long days and evenings outside, mixed with country walks collecting insects and flowers, and looking and listening for birds. I was fortunate to spend my childhood and much of my early adulthood in Jersey, where I was born – an island blessed with natural beauty – and my mother drew every last drop of value from it not only while we were growing up but also for herself, right up until her death.

FIGURE 0.1   Early family photo: Ken, second right, with brother and sisters

PHOTO: Joan Banks

My love of writing stemmed from my mother's encouragement to read, and the very tangible support she gave by buying me my first typewriter – a second-hand cast iron Olympus – when I was 10 years old. I would spend hours typing away, making up imaginary exam and quiz papers, writing poetry, and doing homework. The *Amoco Cadiz* oil tanker disaster in March 1978, which threatened the island's beaches, inspired me to write a small book on oil which I still have to this day. My mother encouraged me to reach far and wide for information, and I still treasure the written response I got from the BBC. Later, the poetry I wrote would lead me to win two island-wide competitions, and cement my love of creative writing.

Hacking the code

Thanks to Mr Cooper, who ran a social club on the estate where I grew up, I was exposed to technology early. The large, heavy Commodore PET computers he owned did not fail to spark my curiosity and interest and, while other children used them to play games, I figured out how to hack into the code and break them, kick-starting a career in information technology. I soon began writing teaching programs for children with learning difficulties (the social club doubled up as an education centre), and I was earning pocket money developing software for Mr Cooper, who was also a teacher. Looking back, this was perhaps the early sign of an entrepreneurial flair which would develop and grow as I got older. Earning an income, albeit a small one, at a young age certainly taught me to value money, and it gave me a degree of independence that many friends didn't have. The same applies today, decades later, as I find comfort and success in the freedom of self-employment.

My early flair for computing didn't go unnoticed by the IT teacher at college, who shared the software I was writing there – including a simple word-processing application – with a local technology company. I was offered the opportunity to quit college and start a career in software development, but – unlike Bill Gates – decided to see my education out. To the surprise of many people, to this day I have had no formal training in technology, despite it being a cornerstone of almost all of my efforts to help make the world a better place.

Beating the education system

Sadly, too many of the world's education systems seem to curb many of the early instincts of childhood, and mine was no exception. As results-driven education dominates, creativity often takes a backseat, and our curious, always-questioning young minds slowly become more critical and closed. I fought against this, and as a result was always something of an outsider through much of my childhood. I was described by teachers as 'too thoughtful and sensitive', as if these were negative traits. I left school unhappy, having failed six out of eight exams despite being described as 'intelligent with great potential'. After a spell at college studying business, where I did a little better, I left school and entered the world of work, taking up a position at a merchant bank. Despite my struggles, I was lucky that the finance industry in Jersey was sufficiently buoyant at the time to need as many people as it could get, regardless of qualifications.

Needing new direction

As I settled into work, a cosy career in offshore banking beckoned. Despite this, I even drifted between banks, moving from the bullion delivery team in one, to become the operator of the mainframe computer in another. While banking promised to deliver materially, spiritually it felt far removed from the kinds of things I felt I should be doing. I'd already started taking an interest in global development, something kick-started after watching Live Aid in 1985, a global music event organized in response to the Ethiopian famine.

I struggled to understand how, with all of the money and resources that the international development sector had at its disposal, such inequality could not just exist but appeared to grow across vast swathes of the planet. I also felt a sense of guilt, something I'm not ashamed to admit today, that I was one of the fortunate ones to be born on a side of the world where many of these injustices did not exist. As I read more and took more of an interest, these questions increasingly challenged my 'thoughtful and sensitive' mind.

Africa calling

A chance trip to Zambia in 1993 to help build a school as part of a Jersey government project changed everything for me. For the first time I came face to face with some of the realities of life for people much less fortunate than myself. It was an uncomfortable, but hugely informative few weeks. Whilst there, I sought out a local artist and bought one of his paintings. It turned out he was holding multiple jobs to keep his five sons at school after his wife had died of an HIV/AIDS-related illness a couple of years earlier. I admired him and his determination, and supported him financially on my return home up until his own death, two years later, of a similar illness. Worried that his sons would be forced out of school and, even worse, split up, I made copies of his painting and sold them at a local art market in Jersey. The proceeds, along with those from a barbeque event I organized, helped keep the brothers together and through school. To this day we are still in touch – although it's now through Facebook, of course – and the family are thriving. What happened with Justice Kabango and his family set the tone for everything that followed – a strong, built-in desire to provide people with whatever opportunity I could to help them better themselves and meet their potential.

I followed up the Zambia trip with another Jersey government project in 1995, this time to help build a hospital in northern Uganda. My thirst for knowledge and understanding continued unabated, and I wanted to spend as much time in the field as possible in my quest to understand what life was like for the people I felt a drive to help. On my return I applied to Voluntary Service Overseas (VSO) for a two-year overseas placement, but was turned down. I was devastated, but this turned out to be just the first of a number of major setbacks. My response was to quit my job, sell everything I owned up to that point, and to move to England with just two suitcases to study social anthropology with development studies at Sussex University. Fortunately somebody there believed in me, and the introduction to anthropology turned out to be pivotal to the work I was to do in later years. During my studies I was also introduced to the concept of appropriate technologies, another pivotal moment, and I thrived studying subjects that genuinely interested and inspired me. I graduated in 1999, missing out on a 'First Class' degree by less than 1 per cent.

One step forward, two steps back

The more I read, the more I wrote and the more I studied, the more I realized that life sucked for the vast majority of people on the planet. This continued to trouble me deeply. Despite the enormous scale of the challenges these people faced, figuring out how I could contribute to any kind of solution, however small, became my call to action. But for longer than I remember I struggled to figure out precisely what that action should be. How could I – *me* – contribute to fixing these huge, global injustices? It would have been so much easier not to care, to turn my back, but I did not seem to be wired for such a response.

After graduating, my search continued and I ended up returning to the world of technology. I became a team leader at Cable & Wireless as they accelerated the rollout of digital cable television across the United Kingdom. Fate later took me to Finland where I taught English to senior business executives. I applied to study for a Masters in Development Geography at the University of Helsinki, but was turned down. I still remember burning their refusal letter on my balcony in frustration. I was drifting, and becoming increasingly disillusioned. Jobs in international development were hard to come by, and that seemed the only way to fulfil my ambition and dream. How wrong I turned out to be.

I turned my attention back to voluntary work, and online found a primate sanctuary in Calabar, southern Nigeria in need of a project manager. I met a trustee for coffee in Brighton train station and within a few weeks, after selling all of my belongings once again, I was on my way back to Africa. It was a tough year, spent in suffocating heat and humidity, mixed with the odd bout of malaria. But it was worth it as I continued to learn a huge amount, at first hand, of the problems being faced by communities there. I still didn't know what I could genuinely and meaning-fully do to help, though, and I'd often sit in my room at night with a candle, trying to capture my thoughts in a diary, continually probing while drinking cheap Nigerian beer. As with much of the previous 10 years, I didn't find anything.

From motorbikes to mobile

It took a late night motorcycle accident on a busy road in Calabar for my life to turn. After eight days my leg was finally put back together in a hospital in Jersey. I lay there in pain with no money, no mobility, no job, nowhere to live and still no idea where my life was headed. This was the lowest I was to get. Soon after I received a random phone call from an ex-colleague at Jersey Zoo where I'd previously worked writing their membership system. He offered me the chance to work on a very early mobile-for-development project. I jumped at the chance and upped sticks once more and moved over to England to live. It was January 2003, 10 years after my Zambia trip and the beginning of my search. Figuring out how mobile phones, still rare in number but spreading quickly across the developing world, could help solve some of the more pressing conservation and development problems of our time was a perfect fit for me, blending my passion for technology with a passion for international development and a desire to help people solve their own problems.

My one-year contract turned into two as the work we were doing gained traction. Most of that first year was spent building a conservation portal called wildlive!, where people could download conservation-themed mobile games, animal ringtones and wallpaper images, and get live news from the field, all through their mobile phones. It was groundbreaking, and an exciting time to be working in information and communication technology for development, or ICT4D as it was beginning to be known. 2003 also marked the birth of kiwanja.net, my own organization through which I began openly sharing my work. During the second year I co-authored one of the earliest reports on the potential of mobile technology to help in conservation and development work, and it was during this time that the seeds of an idea for a project of my own were sown.

Disruptive grassroots messaging

During one of our many field trips to Bushbuckridge, an area straddling the eastern border of Kruger National Park in South Africa, I was approached by the park authorities. They were trying to determine whether they could use text messaging to better communicate with the communities living around the park. Phones were far from everywhere, but they were appearing, and mobile coverage in the area was spreading. After some research I was able to find a few messaging tools, but these required internet access and credit cards to work, and neither of these were available to the Kruger staff. I shared the bad news and returned to my regular work.

FIGURE 0.2   Bushbuckridge: The inspiration behind FrontlineSMS

PHOTO: Ken Banks

It wasn't until January of the following year, 2005, that a solution came to me, and it came quite randomly during a Saturday night football show. I wondered whether you could connect a mobile phone with a cable to a laptop computer, and use software to send and receive group messages through the phone, not the internet. I jotted down a few notes, drew a diagram and the following morning jumped online. No 'offline' messaging platforms seemed to exist, and certainly nothing aimed at the kinds of grassroots user I had in mind. A further search revealed the Hayes modem commands needed to instruct a phone to send a message, and further commands showed me how to read messages back. eBay was my last stop, where I found a Nokia 6100 mobile phone for sale from one supplier, and a cable from another. Safely ordered, I got back to what was left of my weekend.

A few days later the packages arrived, as had my moment of truth. Fortunately, I'd previously worked with communications devices so configuring everything was second nature. Once complete, I opened up 'Terminal', a communications program which came with all Windows computers, and asked the phone to respond if it was there. 'OK' appeared boldly on the laptop screen. Good. Next I sent down the three commands needed to tell it to send a text message to my own phone, which sat next to me, and waited. A few seconds later my mobile beeped. It had worked. I replied to the text message, and asked the laptop to request the phone to send up any messages in the inbox through the cable. Up came my reply on the laptop screen. It was a true eureka moment, even though technically it was not difficult at all to do. I began to imagine the possibilities of grassroots NGOs being able to send large numbers of text messages to groups of people, and then handle and sort replies, all through a piece of software I would need to write.

That week I hastily put together a two-page proposal. I didn't need much money, but did need a development laptop and a couple more phones, modems and cables, plus the VisualBasic.NET programming environment in which to write it (and a couple of books to help me figure out what to do). Karen Hayes and Simon Hicks, the friends from Jersey Zoo, helped me secure a little start-up capital from two former Vodafone directors – enough to buy the kit I needed – and by the summer I was ready to start coding. I needed somewhere quiet to focus, so followed my now-wife over to Finland (where she was born) and wrote ProjectSMS while she did a summer job there. Through much trial and error, and plenty of learning on my feet – I'd never written a Windows application before, never mind one which needed to communicate with a mobile phone – I eventually got something not only to work, but to work quite well. I kept refining the software over the following weeks, adding an 'auto-reply' feature after the realization that it might be helpful came to me during a bus journey across London. By the time October 2005 had come, the name had changed to FrontlineSMS, the software was about as good to go as I felt it needed to be, and the website (which I also wrote) was up. I pushed it out to the world and returned to my day job.

FrontlineSMS is unleashed on the world

FrontlineSMS was still a side hobby, as it had been since conception, and my paid work at the time involved testing the operating systems of mobile phones. I was particularly good at finding bugs and crashing the devices, and because of that regularly found myself with time on my hands as the programmers and engineers tried to figure out what I'd done. While I waited, I made good use of the time to search for, and e-mail, anyone I could find online who was interested in, working on or writing about the use of technology – and mobile phones in particular – in conservation and development around the world.

I pitched FrontlineSMS to every single one of them. Some downloaded it and tried it out. Others shared news with potential users they knew. Others blogged and wrote about it. I was relentless in my outreach, something which continued throughout the history of the project. Word travelled quickly, and far and wide. People seemed very quickly to 'get' what FrontlineSMS was all about, and why I had written it. Within two weeks I'd got my first user, a civil society organization in Zimbabwe called Kubatana. They immediately deployed FrontlineSMS to help get news and information to and from communities suffering under the Mugabe regime. For an idea seeded in a national park, I was pleasantly surprised to see it being deployed in activism. That early trend continued, with various forms of activism representing the majority of the more significant uses over the first couple of years.

All manner of interesting uses continued to come in, everything from coffee prices to farmers in Aceh to security alerts for fieldworkers in Afghanistan. I knew what was happening because I'd written the software in a way that meant potential users had to contact me for activation codes before it would fully function. (The activation codes, incidentally, were local names of the places David Livingstone, the famous missionary explorer, had visited on his travels across Africa.) Requiring registration was very unpopular among the dedicated, hardcore software development and activist community, but I realized I had to know who was using it, what for and where if I was to be able to share their stories (assuming they wanted them to be shared), and continue to add useful functionality based on the use cases, and fix bugs. Despite doing it for all the right reasons I was challenged on my approach during those early years, but stood my ground. The project wasn't being funded by anyone, so I didn't have donors or partners to answer to. Remaining 'independent' was key to its eventual success and, as it turned out, my decision on activation codes was vindicated when evidence-hungry donors came on the scene a couple of years later.

And then came the Nigerian elections

In 2007 things stepped up a gear. The year before I had been accepted as a Visiting Fellow at Stanford University, mentoring and supporting other social entrepreneurs working on technology-driven social change. Ironically, they didn't think much of FrontlineSMS when I applied, so I had to continue that work in my own time. That said, the Fellowship itself was somewhat fortunate. A Fellow from the 2005 class, Erik Sundelof, contacted me about my messaging software and, although he didn't end up using it in his work he did think the Reuters Digital Vision Fellows Program he was on was a great fit for me. I agreed, and applied, but was rejected. Not for the first time I was hugely disappointed. I waited a few days, and responded with a carefully crafted e-mail describing how useful I could be to the other Fellows. Stanford changed its mind, and I was on my way. To save money, I lived in a VW camper van on the edge of campus, which became something of a joke as donors came on board. Not only did it allow me to stretch my limited finances – the Fellowship was unpaid – but living in a van somehow kept me focused and 'real'.

By April 2007, FrontlineSMS had a growing number of interesting use cases, but downloads were less than 100 as it approached its two-year anniversary. Suffice to say, it wasn't setting the world on fire. I considered pulling the plug, and started diverting my attention to other projects. But then a phone call in the middle of the night, followed by an e-mail the following day, diverted my attention back. It was from a group calling themselves the Nigerian Mobile Election Monitors (NMEM). The 2007 Nigerian presidential elections were a couple of weeks away, and they were going to use FrontlineSMS to carry out citizen monitoring. A press release followed. My initial reaction, after the excitement had worn off, was that they must be mad. But they were serious. Regardless, if they were going to do this, I thought, the least I could do was help them promote it. After all, the more citizens who got to hear about it, the more would text in their observations (and, in addition, I had something of a soft spot for all things Nigerian after my time there). I pushed the press release out to a few people, including my good friend Bill Thompson who had contacts at the BBC, and he replied. Shortly before the polls opened, FrontlineSMS appeared in an article on the elections on the BBC website. Things would never be the same again.

FIGURE 0.3 The breakthrough moment: FrontlineSMS on the BBC website (via news.bbc.co.uk)

Knock knock

I've always believed that if you do good things, money will follow. And it did. The MacArthur Foundation contacted me as the Nigerian election use gained ground among the mobile and activism communities. They offered me a $200,000 grant to do a major rewrite and build a new, better website, but they first needed evidence that it was finding use beyond Nigeria, and luckily my insistence of collecting information about users meant I could share a number of great case studies with them. It was enough, and the funding came through. I was still at Stanford, though, and MacArthur insisted the funds would have to go through them. I was offered 'Visiting Scholar' status and stayed on another year after the end of my original Fellowship, and ran the FrontlineSMS project from my desk and my van. Stanford took 35 per cent of the money for the privilege of handling the grant, but there was still enough to build a solid new version of FrontlineSMS, and Wieden+Kennedy, the global advertising agency, had already offered to work with me on the project, so at very reduced rates they built and designed a new website, and gave us a fantastic new logo and brand.

The relaunch went well and the user base continued to grow, with a huge variety in deployments. FrontlineSMS was being used in the Azerbaijani elections to help mobilize the youth vote. It was used in Kenya to report breakages in fences caused by elephants, and ran the Overseas Filipino Workers (OFW-SOS) emergency help line, allowing workers to receive immediate assistance in case of personal emergency. It was deployed in the DRC as part of the Ushahidi mapping platform (more in this book later) to collect violence reports via SMS, and was deployed by Grameen Technology Centre in Uganda to communicate with their Village Phone network. Projects in Cambodia and El Salvador used it to help create transparency in agricultural

FIGURE 0.4   The relaunched FrontlineSMS, complete with new logo

PHOTO: Ken Banks

markets, and Survivors Connect made use of it in a number of countries to run anti-trafficking reporting systems among vulnerable communities. The list went on.

The ups and downs of growth

As this growth took hold I found myself with users who were becoming increasingly dependent on me for support, and speaking and writing commitments subsequently rose. For the first time the challenges of financial sustainability came into play. Whereas I had previously handled FrontlineSMS as a side project, it was gradually demanding more and more of my time. Something had to give.

As MacArthur's money ran out, putting any future growth in doubt, Larry Diamond – Professor of Sociology and Political Science at Stanford University, and a senior fellow at the Hoover Institute – wrote to the Hewlett Foundation, who were based just up the road from campus. Larry had become a huge supporter and friend, and he saw FrontlineSMS as a significant innovation in his field. Hewlett later responded and granted the project $400,000. Things were really beginning to move. Hewlett were also happy to give the funds to me directly. Fortunately, a few months earlier I had founded my own 501c3 tax-exempt US foundation in hope, and anticipation, of further funding. I sold my VW van and returned to the United Kingdom in the late summer of 2008 with two years' funding secured.

Over the next few years funding came in as often as the awards and recognition. The Open Society Institute, Rockefeller Foundation and Omidyar Network all contributed support in the region of $1 million dollars. Fellowships and awards came in from PopTech, the Tech Awards, National Geographic, Ashoka, Curry Stone, the Pizzigati Prize, the World Technology Network, Cambridge Business Magazine, the Royal Society of Arts and the University of Sussex. FrontlineSMS was coming of

FIGURE 0.5   Speaking at National Geographic HQ: A career highlight

PHOTO: Ken Banks

age, and was beginning to grow. We had staff, and offices, and were turning into a fully-fledged organization.

Users, users everywhere

As well as the things we'd planned, elsewhere things began happening organically. A student at Stanford, Josh Nesbit, who I met during my time there, had made waves in the mobile health sector after using FrontlineSMS to great effect in a hospital in Malawi. His project grew, becoming FrontlineSMS:Medic and, later, Medic Mobile. Ben Lyon developed a similar adaptation for the mobile money sector, giving rise to FrontlineSMS:Credit. Other variants followed, including FrontlineSMS:Radio, FrontlineSMS:Learn and FrontlineSMS:Legal. It was fascinating to see others building new, sector-specific functionality on top of the core FrontlineSMS platform I had built, and for a while FrontlineSMS seemed to be everywhere.

FIGURE 0.6   FrontlineSMS at St Gabriel's Hospital, Malawi

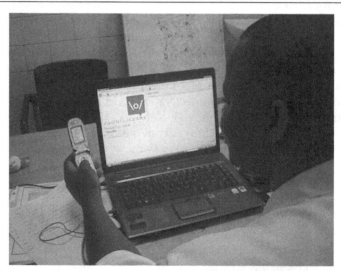

PHOTO: Josh Nesbit

This popularity began to be reflected in the numbers. The number of downloads would soon hit the hundreds of thousands, the number of countries where it was active pass 170, and the number of people benefiting from its use hit upwards of 20 million. Users were beginning to win awards, and funding, for their own use of the platform. What was happening was living proof of something I'd said a couple of years earlier about why I thought FrontlineSMS was special:

> FrontlineSMS provides the tools necessary for people to create their own projects that make a difference. It empowers innovators and organizers in the developing world to achieve their full potential through their own ingenuity.

Growing pains and a time to step back

With success came different kinds of pressure, and by 2011 it was all beginning to change for me. What started out as a desire to innovatively apply technology to grassroots development challenges had become more about running an organization, and this wasn't something I really wanted to do. I didn't think I'd be particularly good at it, either. After an extended handover, where my senior management team effectively ran FrontlineSMS for me, I announced that I'd be stepping back in May 2012. It wasn't a difficult decision.

I've always maintained that it's important to be aware of your limitations just as much as your strengths, and as FrontlineSMS grew its way out of my one-bedroom flat in Cambridge and my VW camper at Stanford University, it became clear that the project needed a whole new set of skills to take it to the next level. In one of my favourite blog posts – 'The Rolling Stones School of Innovation Management' – I wrote about how the Rolling Stones needed three different managers over the course of their careers, each of whom had entirely different skills needed at very different stages of their growth. Funnily enough, FrontlineSMS followed a similar trajectory with different needs at the technological, business and organizational levels. As I wrote back then:

> As The Stones example demonstrates, each phase requires a very different skill set, and it would take an extraordinary individual to be able to manage and deliver successfully on each. While I may have been the right person – in the right place at the right time at the very least – to successfully deliver on Phase One, that doesn't mean I'm the right person for Phase Two, or Three. A large part of building a successful organisation is assembling a talented, diverse team with complementary skill sets. Identifying gaps and being honest about our own strengths and weaknesses is a large part of the process.

The handover was met with a mixture of surprise and enthusiasm. Founders rarely step away from their creations, in some cases dragging them back down in the process, and many people saw what we did at FrontlineSMS as a model for others to follow. As I closed the door behind me, I found myself with a new lease of life. Within months of my departure I had started a new project, Means of Exchange, had ramped up my consultancy services and was planning a new book. I continued to speak and write widely, and advise and mentor a range of organizations. I was invited to be Ambassador for International Development at Sussex University, and was appointed a founding member of the UK Government's Department for International Development's (DFID) 'Digital Advisory Board'. I travelled with the UK Prime Minister during an official visit to Africa, and was nominated for the TED Prize. Those early struggles for meaning and purpose seemed like a long way off.

A few words on empathy

Anyone connected with or interested in social entrepreneurship could not have failed to notice the growing debate around empathy (ie the ability to understand and share the feelings of another). For me and my work, empathy was critical. I only felt remotely qualified to help grassroots non-profits in Africa with their communication problems because I'd spent the best part of 20 years living and working with them. It gave me an understanding and insight – and yes, empathy – which was not only crucial to my solution working for them, but it also gave me credibility among the people I was trying to help.

According to Ashoka's Empathy Initiative:

> Applied empathy encompasses the abilities to feel and understand another's perspective, and then act with a concern for the welfare of others. Consequently, empathy requires a number of different skills and aptitudes: emotional literacy, perspective-taking, self-regulation, communication, problem-solving, and more. For individuals, such skills are correlated with greater success in reasoning, collaboration, and academic and professional performance. For communities, a greater empathetic capacity facilitates a greater likelihood of conflict resolution and cooperation.

Social innovators looking to develop solutions to problems faced by communities in the developing world – and there are plenty of them – have little alternative than to actually get out there and spend time with them. Empathy is critical if any solution is to have a chance of success, and there really are no short cuts. It takes time, and effort.

That said, while we should certainly be encouraging people to take an interest in helping others, we also need to make sure it is done respectfully. I frequently argue that we shouldn't develop solutions to problems we don't understand, that we shouldn't take ownership of a problem that isn't ours, and we certainly shouldn't build solutions from thousands of miles away and then jump on a plane in search of a home for them. This, in the ICT4D world where I spent most of my time, is generally what tends to happen. Good intentions, often poorly executed.

In a recent guest article in the *Stanford Social Innovation Review*, I argued this very point. My argument was well received, but one commenter asked what I suggest all the people who lived far away from the problems of the developing world should do with their passion and time. My response was that there are problems everywhere, including where they lived, and it might be better to try to solve some of those instead. If people really do want to contribute to solving the problems of 'others' then they really need to go and live under the same conditions as them for a while. Each of the social innovators in this book had direct exposure to the problems they decided to solve, and with the people those problems affected.

Problems with the teaching of social entrepreneurship

During my time at Stanford University I became increasingly exposed to social entrepreneurship, social innovation and design thinking as academic disciplines. I found myself meeting increasing numbers of smart young people looking to colleges and universities to equip them with the skills they felt they needed to 'go out and change the world'. I was a bit taken aback. You didn't need qualifications to change the world, did you? Often I'd dig deeper and ask what they wanted to do when they graduated. Answers such as 'I want to be a social entrepreneur' perplexed me. Few people I know in the messy, often frustrating world of social entrepreneurship ever set out with the explicit aim of becoming one. Rather, they stumbled across a problem, a wrong or a market inefficiency which bothered them to such an extent that they decided to dedicate much – if not all – of their lives to putting it right. It was rarely, if ever, part of a wider plan.

Many of the students I met were unlikely to experience that problem, injustice or market inefficiency within the walls of their college or university. Teaching the mechanics of social innovation may be helpful, yes, but only if matched with passion, and a cause, to which people can apply it. Desperately seeking that one thing that switches you on can be a lonely, difficult journey. It took me long enough.

What I was witnessing was the increasing institutionalization of social entrepreneurship. I thought it unhelpful on many fronts, not to mention that it could easily be seen as a barrier by many motivated young people unable to afford further education. Not only that, it implied that social change was a well-thought out process, when in reality it is far messier and more random than that, as many of the case studies in this book testify. You don't *learn* how to be a social entrepreneur in the classroom. You learn by being out *doing* in the world.

Passion and purpose are critical, although it is far easier to learn the mechanics of social entrepreneurship – business plans and elevator pitches among them – than to manufacture a passion or calling in life. You may be the person best-qualified to solve a particular problem, but that's of little use if you don't find it. Finding purpose is often the toughest part of the process, and there are few short cuts other than to leave your comfort zone and get yourself out there. You won't, after all, get to experience 'Third World' maternal care in London, Paris or New York, but you will if you follow Laura Stachel's lead and spend hard time on the ground in maternity wards in West Africa. You can read more about Laura's work later in this book.

While the mechanics of social entrepreneurship dominate, most of the aspiring social innovators I meet want stories. Sure, they want to know some of the theory, maybe a little about the technology. But what resonates with them more than anything is the background to the solutions, the journey, and where the innovators behind them got their drive and motivation. They want to resonate, to feel closer to the possibilities and potential, to see themselves in the innovator's shoes. They want to walk away with 'Well, they did it. Why can't I?'

The difference in approach boils down to one of 'mechanics vs. motivation'. The 'mechanics' world centres on business models, the quest for data, for metrics and an obsession with scale and measuring impact. Lots of tables, numbers, graphs and theories – the very things which score low on most people's motivational scale. The 'motivation' approach is built on real-world examples, inspiration and a belief that anything is possible because others have done it. That is the very reason why we chose to publish a book of case studies and not a deep functional analysis of what makes 'social entrepreneurship work'. After all, the 'a-ha' moment innovators-to-be hear about is rarely the discovery of a new metric, or a new business model, or a new way of presenting or collecting data. It's the realization that a problem can be solved, and solved in a new way. These answers often come by doing and experiencing, being out in the field, and there are almost always stories behind why the person was there, sometimes how they got there, and what they suddenly saw which gave them their big idea. You'll find those stories in this book.

FIGURE 0.7   Sharing inspiring stories of change with students, with Archbishop Desmond Tutu and Tori Hogan

PHOTO: Evan Swinehart/Unreasonable at Sea

The power of passion

Innovation and entrepreneurship start with passion, so we ought to focus more on that. We can help by speaking about our own interests, passions and stories – which most of us have – and less on the mechanical stuff (some of which, incidentally, includes the actual technology we've invented). This is why, I think, people tend to resonate more with individuals who succeed, rather than bigger organizations. The year I became a Tech Award Laureate a dozen people – not companies – were rewarded for their efforts to make the world a better place. The celebration of their achievements would have been less remarkable if they'd all been housed in resource-rich corporate environments. Innovation by everyday people, often out of scarcity, against the odds, is what seems to really excite people. Perhaps the fact they can relate to them helps a little, too.

Al Gore spoke at that Tech Awards gala. After a 30-minute speech not a single person could doubt his passion and commitment to the climate change cause, whether or not they agreed with him. There was hardly any mention of the intricacies of the science. This was a motivational speech if ever there was one. Somehow, if he'd focused on the mechanics I doubt he'd have had half the impact. Al Gore has taken a complex subject and made it accessible, and that has to be one of his major achievements.

We need to do the same with entrepreneurship, social entrepreneurship, technology and innovation. These subjects need to be demystified, and this series of case studies is our contribution towards making the discipline more relevant and approachable to students and concerned citizens alike.

About this book

Of course, there is no shortage of books on social entrepreneurship. Authors regularly place social entrepreneurs under their expert spotlight – sometimes, but not always, even interviewing them – before attempting to unpick and dissect their work. Analysis is offered on what experts consider worked, and failed, and the various theories applied give their commentary a sense of academic credibility. Surprisingly, most often missing are the voices of the innovators themselves, with the occasional quote considered reasonable exposure to the person doing the actual work. While expert analysis can be helpful, so too can the voice and story of the social entrepreneur, in their own words. This book represents an attempt to address that balance.

TABLE 0.1   Matrix of case studies

Case study	Country of origin	Region of operation	Sector	Solution
We Care Solar	USA	Africa/Global	Health	Technology
Centre for Digital Inclusion	Brazil	South America/Global	Connectivity	Technology/ human networks
I-MAK	India	India	Law/patents	Legal
Visualizing Impact	Palestine	Middle East	Advocacy	Data visualization
Magpi	USA	Global	Health	Technology
FoodCycle	UK	United Kingdom	Food poverty	Human networks
Ushahidi	Kenya	Global	Activism	Technology
Qigong Massage for Autism	USA	United States	Health	Massage
Refugees United	Denmark	Global	Humanitarian	Technology/ human networks
PlanetRead	India	India	Education	Film subtitling
Dream in Tunisia	Tunisia	Middle East	Environment	Human networks
Genetic Alliance	USA	United States	Health	Genetics
GovRight	Morocco	Global	Activism	Technology/ human networks

The 13 case studies you'll find here cover a wide range of problem areas with a wide geographical spread. The founders of each social innovation share their own stories – their background, how and where they grew up, and how they believe it helped qualify them to do their later work. They share the facts – and own analysis – of the problem they encountered, and why their solution works and why it matters. You'll get to read about their response to finding the problem – or the problem finding them – and how they went about developing a solution and then an organization to support it. You'll hear their thoughts on key decisions they had to make – funding, sustainability and organizational structure among them – and how they determine the impact of what they do. They share the highs, and the lows, of life as a social entrepreneur – what worked for them, and what failed. Theirs is no glossy account of instant success and fame, rather the often untold messy and frustrating side of social entrepreneurship. They end with reflections on lessons learnt throughout their journey, and questions you might want to consider asking yourself as you unpick their work, and offer your own expert analysis.

You may notice that these case studies are not grouped together by topic or geography, something many other books might have done. Rather, the stories are presented in a way which provides better opportunity for discovery. Too much of the social innovation sector works in silos, with health innovators hanging out with other health innovators, and political activists hanging out with other political activists. As a result, opportunities for cross-fertilization of ideas and solutions are often limited, despite it being quite possible that health professionals might learn from activists, and vice versa, if they ever found themselves in the same room. Tim Smit, founder of the Eden Project, once told me that you should attend at least one conference every year which is totally outside of your usual areas of work and interest.

It is our hope that you will discover case studies in this book that you might otherwise not have naturally gravitated towards. Regardless of your own particular focus or interest area, there's no reason why you shouldn't be able to learn something from case studies in a totally different field – in data visualization in Palestine, for example, or the development of solar technologies for maternity wards in Nigeria, or massage for autism in the United States. Remain open to solutions, wherever they come from.

Some advice for innovators-to-be

Despite the considerable amount of focus, funding and bets placed on social entrepreneurs and their ideas, many mistakes tend to be repeated over and over again, often reflecting negatively on any potential impact. Interestingly, the same problems apply in international development, where I've focused much of my time over the past 20 years. Unlocking the potential of what many people believe to be an underperforming sector is something I am often asked about, and it has become something of a mission for me of late.

Those efforts recently culminated in the launch of a Donors Charter. I decided to focus on donors because, in my view, most of the more common mistakes made by social innovators are made before they've even started their project. Raising awareness of this among donors, I felt, might mean that funding could be held back until projects had been properly thought through and planned.

Why is something like a Donors Charter needed? Well, with few checks and balances in place, what we've ended up with today is a social sector full of replication, small-scale failed pilots, secrecy and near-zero levels of collaboration. This negatively impacts not only on other poorly planned initiatives, but it also complicates things for the better ones. On top of that, it confuses the end user who is expected, for example, to make sense of all 100 or so mobile data collection tools that end up on offer. The policy of funding many in the hope that the odd one shines through – the so-called 'let a thousand flowers bloom' scenario – belongs to an earlier era. Today, we know enough about what works and what doesn't to be far more targeted in what is funded and supported.

If you have an idea for a project or initiative, I'd encourage you to ask yourself the following 12 questions (which form the basis of my Donors Charter) before going any further. These are the questions you should expect to be asked and, if your idea is properly thought out, you should be able to answer them.

Preliminary questions

1 Do you understand the problem you are trying to solve? Have you seen, experienced or witnessed the problem? Why are *you* the one fixing it?

2 Does anything else exist that might solve the problem? Have you searched for existing solutions?

3 Could anything that you found be adapted to solve the problem?

4 Have you spoken to anyone working on the same problem? Is collaboration possible? If not, why not?

5 Is your solution economically, technically and culturally appropriate?

Implementation questions

6 Have you carried out base research to understand the scale of the problem before you start? Do you have 'before' numbers so you are able to measure how well your project has done?

7 Will you be working with locally-based people and organizations to carry out your implementation? If not, why not?

8 Are you making full use of the skills and experience of these local partners? How?

Evaluation and post-implementation questions

9 How do you plan to measure your impact? How will you know if your project was a success or not?

10 Do you plan to scale up or scale out that impact? If not, why not? If yes, how?

11 What is your business/sustainability model?

Transparency questions

12 Are you willing to have your summary project proposal, and any future summary progress reports, posted online for the benefit of transparency and more open sharing?

It is my belief that if you plan to go out and make an impact on people's lives – and use up valuable funds in the process – then it's not unreasonable to expect you to have properly thought through what you're going to do first. Not only could you save a community somewhere a lot of pain and disappointment, but you might end up helping donors target their money better, and save yourself a huge amount of failed time and effort – time and effort you could instead use on something that becomes ultimately more impactful.

More broadly, I usually offer the following additional advice to people wanting to help make the world a better place:

1 *Don't be competitive.* There's plenty of poverty to go round.

2 *Don't be in a hurry.* Grow your idea or project on your own terms.

3 *Don't assume you need money to grow.* Do what you can before you reach out to funders. Prove your idea first.

4 *Volunteers and interns may not be the silver bullet to your human resource issues.* Finding people with your passion and commitment willing to work for free can be time consuming and challenging.

5 *Be relentless.* Pursue and maximize every opportunity to promote your work.

6 *Suppress your ego.* Stay humble. Remain curious.

7 *Remember that your website, for most people, is the primary window to you and your idea.*

8 *Learn when to say 'no'.* Manage expectations. Don't overstretch.

9 *Avoid being dragged down by the politics of the industry you're in.* Save your energy for more important things.

10 *Learn to do what you can't afford to pay other people to do.*

11 *Be open about the values that drive you.* People will respect you for it.

12 *Collaborate if it's in the best interests of solving your problem, even if it's not in* your *best interests.*

13 *Make full use of your networks,* and remember that the benefits of being in them may not always be immediate.

14 *Remember the bigger picture,* and that whatever you're trying to solve is bigger than any one person or organization.

15 *Don't beat yourself up searching for your passion.* You'll find it in the most unlikely of places, and if you don't it could very well find you.

16 *Write down your values, and a quote that inspires you, on a large sheet of paper and stick it on your wall.* Look at it every morning. Remind yourself why you're doing what you're doing.

17 *Finally, strive to be a good person, a role model for others.* And if you do succeed, remember the importance of giving back. We all started at the beginning once.

Discussion questions

1 How important is passion in social entrepreneurship?

2 What is your definition of a social entrepreneur? Does it matter that there's not universal agreement?

3 What do you think of the questions in Donors Charter? Do they make you think more about any projects you're thinking of starting? Are any questions missing?

4 What do you think is the role of empathy in social entrepreneurship? Is it an absolute necessity, or a nice-to-have?

5 What do you think of Ken's decision to stand down? Can you think of any other examples of founders of social enterprises stepping away? Was it the right thing for them to do?

6 Do you agree that many social innovators operate in silos? If so, in what ways might we encourage them to reach out and learn from other disciplines?

7 What do you think is the role of business in social entrepreneurship?

Further reading

You can find more material to do with this chapter at www.koganpage.com/socialentrepreneurship

Websites and articles

Ashoka Empathy – empathy.ashoka.org [accessed 10 December 2015]
Donors Charter – donorscharter.org [accessed 10 December 2015]
Ken Banks' website – kiwanja.net [accessed 10 December 2015]
Ken Banks' National Geographic profile – nationalgeographic.com/explorers/bios/ken-banks/ [accessed 10 December 2015]
Article on Ken's stepping back – clearlyso.com/a-lesson-from-rock-aristocracy/ [accessed 10 December 2015]
General anthropology resource – discoveranthropology.org.uk/ [accessed 10 December 2015]
Social innovation incubator – scu-social-entrepreneurship.org/gsbi [accessed 10 December 2015]
The Unreasonable Institute – unreasonable.is [accessed 10 December 2015]

Videos

video.nationalgeographic.com/video/news/ken-banks-es
currystonedesignprize.com/winners/frontline-sms/
Tech Awards – youtube.com/watch?v=XrtN7rtJrfM

Founders Forum for Good – youtube.com/watch?v=aLM5tHouOcg
poptech.org/popcasts/josh_nesbit_mobile_healthcare
ted.com/talks/jessica_jackley_poverty_money_and_love

Books

Doing Good Better: Effective Altruism and How You Can Make a Difference
   – William MacAskill
The Top Five Regrets of the Dying – Bronnie Ware
More Human: Designing a World Where People Come First – Steve Hilton
The Myths of Innovation – Scott Berkun
Poor Economics: A Radical Rethinking of the Way to Fight Global Poverty –
   Abhijit Banerjee and Esther Duflo

01
Wonders of the Solar System

WE CARE SOLAR – LAURA STACHEL

ABSTRACT

The two weeks obstetrician Laura Stachel spent in a Nigerian state hospital made her life's mission clear. She was looking at why maternal mortality was so high in Nigeria – 1 in 23 women died in their reproductive years from pregnancy-related complications – and was stunned by what she witnessed. Most expectant mothers arrived at the hospital with severe complications. But the hospital's sporadic power supply meant deliveries were conducted in near-darkness, hospital messengers couldn't locate doctors, haemorrhaging women couldn't receive blood transfusions, and emergency surgeries were postponed or cancelled. Women and infants were dying from conditions routinely treated in the United States.

To Laura, it was unacceptable that women and children were dying in hospitals simply because of a lack of electricity. Together with her husband, solar educator Hal Aronson, she launched We Care Solar – Women's Emergency Communication and Reliable Electricity. Their initial goal was to improve conditions in one hospital. But when surrounding clinics requested solar power for their labour rooms, We Care Solar needed a scalable solution.

Laura returned to Nigeria with portable solar electric kits tucked in her suitcase: efficient LED lights, walkie-talkies, and robust electronics powering medical lighting and mobile communication. Media attention spurred international requests for these Solar Suitcases.

Laura and Hal initially assembled Solar Suitcases with volunteers and financed the deployments with small donations. To meet growing demand, Laura built a core team and a broad network of partnerships to tackle regional deployments of Solar Suitcases. Today, We Care Solar delivers 'Solar Suitcases' to 'first' mile health centres to increase survival prospects for expectant mothers and their newborns. They have distributed more than 1,500 Solar Suitcases and spearheaded large projects in several countries in Africa and Asia, driven by their conviction that no woman should die giving life.

Why me?

In my obstetrical practice in the United States, I loved being a part of the birth process, and considered it a privilege to be included in the intimacy of childbirth. It was my duty to support and empower the women I cared for. During labour, I often imagined an ancestral line of women who had given birth, each bearing the next generation, leading to this moment in time.

It wasn't until I spent time in the darkened maternity unit of a Nigerian hospital that I began to struggle deeply with the complexity of what is medically known as maternal mortality – women dying in childbirth. For most pregnant women, the idea is an anachronism. But in the developing world, particularly in sub-Saharan Africa, death from 'complications of childbirth' happens hundreds of times a day.

As an obstetrician, I am trained to solve problems in pregnancy and labour. I analyse what I see and chart a course of action. But the problems I confronted on my first trip to Africa – the erratic electricity, surgical delays because of poor lighting and lack of mobile communication, the scarcity of medical instruments, the inadequate staffing and limited training – were symptoms of a systemic failure. Maternal care was in dire straits for reasons far beyond any medical techniques I could offer. Poverty, lack of infrastructure, gender inequity, illiteracy and politics all conspired against the health and survival of pregnant women. Within the hospital, lack of reliable electricity stood out as a major obstacle to providing effective maternal care.

I never expected to be a social innovator in the developing world, let alone an advocate for solar energy for maternal health care. But as I witnessed women struggling to survive childbirth in Nigeria, and health workers trying their best to provide care in darkened maternity wards, I knew I couldn't turn my back on this problem.

My background

My first passion in life was music and dance. At the age of 17, I entered Oberlin Conservatory and College to study for a career as a concert pianist and modern dancer. I devoted myself to practice, spending eight hours a day in the music conservatory and dance studio.

In my sophomore year, my doctor discovered an irregularity with my ovaries. Without surgery, he couldn't discern whether this was cancerous or not. As I was wheeled into the operating room for diagnostic surgery, my doctor informed me, 'If it is cancer, you'll wake up with a big bandage and all your reproductive organs will have been removed. If it is benign, you'll only have a small bandage.'

In the recovery room, I reached for my abdomen before opening my eyes. A small bandage. I hadn't lost my ovaries. But the surgery prompted a lot of questions. So many, in fact, that my gynaecologist quipped, 'If you have so many questions, why don't you become a doctor?'

It was a thought that had never occurred to me, but the idea resonated. Medicine would allow me to blend traits from my father (a scientist) and my mother (a clinical social worker). In my junior year, I left the familiarity of music and dance studios and enrolled in my first science classes. Medicine was a far cry from piano and dance, but the discipline I had developed in my artistic pursuits proved to be helpful in my classes. I studied alongside pre-med students who understood formulas and concepts that were absolutely foreign to me. It was a struggle, but I persisted.

My interest in medicine and healthcare deepened. I took an active role in women's health issues on the Oberlin campus. I became a volunteer peer counsellor at the college 'Sexual Information Center', co-taught a course on the 'History and Politics of Women's Health Care', organized campus-wide health education events, and worked with the Oberlin College Health Plan Board to expand student access to reproductive health services. These initial activities in health policy and education were immensely formative. An idea took shape in my mind – to become a physician who would have the power to make changes within the health care system.

After finishing up my pre-med requirements in the summer following college graduation, I spent a year in a research lab at the University of Chicago. I applied to medical schools all over the United States and was thrilled to be accepted at the University of California, San Francisco. As I moved through clinical rotations with my classmates, I found myself drawn to psychiatry – why people behave the way they do – and women's reproductive health, especially obstetrics. I also loved surgery, and believe that my years as a pianist endowed me with a manual dexterity that was an asset in the operating room.

At San Francisco General Hospital I had the privilege of conducting deliveries under the tutelage of seasoned midwives, and learned about natural childbirth, as well as the complications that could threaten the health of mother and baby. I was honoured to witness and participate in the miracle of childbirth. When the time came to select a speciality, I chose obstetrics and gynaecology, which allowed me to be part of the birth process, as well as to practise surgery. The field also satisfied my desire to connect deeply with my patients at such an important and vulnerable time in their lives.

I stayed at the University of California, San Francisco for my obstetric residency – four years of non-stop training that occupied up to 130 hours each week. At the time it was believed that arduous working hours, including 36-hour shifts, were necessary to prepare young obstetricians to handle any situation. The hours were intended to expose us to a wide range of complicated cases. As an intern, I remember being so tired on one occasion that I tried to decline my supervisor's request to assist with a caesarean section. I was told that if I refused, I would be denied future opportunities to gain valuable experience in surgical skills.

My first full-time job was at a progressive holistic women's practice in Oakland, California, where I worked in tandem with midwives and nurse practitioners. From the start of my clinical practice I subscribed to the midwifery model – pregnancy as a state of health – rather than the traditional Western medical model – pregnancy as a time of risk, fraught with peril. This outlook would make it all the more jarring, years later, when I encountered women dying from complications of pregnancy and birth that I knew need not be fatal events.

As my career unfolded I had three children of my own, gaining first-hand experience of pregnancy and motherhood. It was quite a juggling act. My children recognized that their mother could be abruptly summoned out of the house to attend to a woman in labour. Family time together was often interrupted by an emergency call prompting me to bolt out of the door. My practice was extremely busy, and the thousands of patients who identified me as their doctor knew that there could be a six-week wait for a routine appointment. I gained a reputation as a caring physician who loved to talk with her patients and include family members in the process of birth, often encouraging them to help with the delivery. In my practice, complications of pregnancy were unusual and tragic outcomes were rare. Joy and happiness infused my work every day.

In 2002 I was plagued by persistent back pain that eventually radiated to my neck and arms, sometimes delivering an electric-shock feeling to my hands. During one particularly arduous delivery, a searing pain tore down my back, and I knew something was very wrong. An MRI revealed the cause – severe degenerating disc disease in my cervical spine, compressing the nerves to my right arm. I was told I had to stop doing deliveries, and later, to stop my practice altogether.

My hectic life as a physician came to a halt. No more piles of charts with messages needing my attention, emergency rooms calling for consultations, phone calls in the dark of night alerting me to impending deliveries. I was the patient, and my job was to get better.

A year after I had taken leave from my practice it became obvious that I needed a vocation that would be less physically stressful. What I initially viewed as a devastating setback, I now consider the beginning of the most fulfilling chapter of my life.

I had a long-held interest in population health, and enrolled in the School of Public Health at University of California, Berkeley. Sitting up for classes wasn't easy, but I loved being a student again, and was excited to be introduced to new fields of study. Through weekly physical therapy my physical endurance improved. Four years later, when an opportunity came to consult on a maternal health research project, I jumped at the chance. At that time, half a million women died each year in childbirth, 99 per cent of them in developing countries.

Maternal mortality in the developing world

Today, maternal mortality worldwide accounts for more than 303,000 deaths a year, with 99 per cent of these occurring in underdeveloped countries. At the time I first began learning about this problem, the statistics were even more sobering – 500,000 maternal deaths each year. The majority of deaths occur in Africa and Asia, most often in regions without reliable electricity. Maternal mortality rates in Nigeria are among the highest in the world. Nigeria has 2.4 per cent of the world's population and accounts for 19 per cent of the world's maternal deaths.

Major causes of maternal death include obstetric haemorrhage, obstructive labour, eclampsia and sepsis. These emergencies cannot always be predicted, nor are they always preventable. But with prompt, appropriate and reliable medical care, they need not result in death.

Rural and impoverished women are most at risk. They are often illiterate and unable to access prenatal care or skilled birth attendants. When these women encounter complications at home, the risks are enormous. They need immediate care from skilled providers at medical facilities equipped to handle emergencies.

The erratic supply of electricity to hospitals and other health centres impairs the function of surgical wards, delivery wards, essential hospital equipment and hospital communications. This compromises the ability of health workers to provide safe, appropriate and timely medical care. Labour and delivery nurses cannot quickly notify on-call physicians of emergencies. Midwives and physicians often make treatment decisions without the benefit of necessary diagnostic tests or equipment. Obstetric procedures and emergency surgeries are conducted under grossly suboptimal conditions, and can have tragic consequences.

Driven to action

In 2008, I obtained a research fellowship from the Bixby Center for Population, Health and Sustainability to work with doctors at the Ahmadu Bello University Hospital in northern Nigeria. Daniel Perlman, a medical anthropologist from UC Berkeley, was spearheading the Nigerian research efforts, and he shared with me the 'verbal autopsies' conducted by local research fellows – interviews with family members about the sequence of events leading to maternal death. Reading these transcripts introduced me to the depth of the challenges facing these pregnant women in need of emergency care. The obstacles they listed are known as the 'three delays', an extremely helpful framework for understanding the high rates of maternal mortality.

The first delay begins at home. Impoverished, far from a medical facility, and typically without decision-making authority, rural women often are reluctant to ask for help until labour is seriously compromised. Culturally, the male head of the household is the one to make the decision to seek medical care, a move that is likely to involve spending a significant sum of money on clinic fees and transportation costs. Much time is lost as the family weighs these factors.

Transportation is the second delay, as more time is lost trying to find public transportation, a car or a motorcycle to transport the woman. It was the third delay, though, that troubled me the most.

According to the field notes from Nigeria, many women who sought medical care for severe complications of labour were turned away from health facilities – as many as four or five health centres – in their quest to get care. Some of those who were finally admitted to an appropriate facility were so critically ill that little could be done to save them. But the reports suggested that sometimes the health facilities failed to provide timely care.

Daniel Perlman was looking to conduct research *inside* the hospitals to understand more about hospital delays. Being an obstetrician in a public health school made me uniquely qualified to help. I was invited to meet with the Nigerian team and conduct participant observation at a Nigerian hospital.

In March 2008 I boarded a plane to Abuja, Nigeria. It was my first time in West Africa and I was eager to utilize my obstetric knowledge in some way. I knew little about what to expect. As an anthropologist, Daniel suggested I keep an open mind and avoid excessive literature review in advance of my visit. My job was to observe obstetric care, and to report on what I learned.

We drove four hours from Abuja to Zaria, a predominantly Muslim city in the Nigerian state of Kaduna. Daniel introduced me to the principal members of the research team – the Population Reproductive Health Partnership – obstetricians and family health physicians who were committed to improving maternal health research and outcomes. Soon he planted me in Kofan Gayan State Hospital, a large state hospital on the border of Zaria's 'Old City'.

Inside the metal gates I took note of the layout of the hospital. Each medical ward had its own building. Most of the divisions – maternity, gynaecology, male medical and surgical, female medical and surgical, and paediatric – were familiar to me as an American doctor. What wasn't familiar was the 'VVF' ward, occupied by women suffering from vesico-vaginal fistula – a dreaded complication of prolonged obstructed labour.

For my research, I was drawn to the maternity ward – a single storey building containing the labour and delivery room, the maternity room and the eclampsia room. The maternity room had 12 patient beds in two rows and a nurse's station at the other. Newborn babies shared their mothers' beds. I learned that 150 deliveries occurred in this hospital each month, with significant loss of life.

I was immediately struck by the grim conditions. The labour room had four bare metal delivery tables, a limited collection of obstetric instruments, a newborn incubator that hadn't worked in years, a broken lamp, two newborn scales in poor condition, and little else. There were no mattresses, sheets, bright lights or electronic monitors characteristic of an American hospital. Most striking were the frequent power outages that left the hospital in darkness, creating an immense barrier to care.

I learned that electricity was rationed in Nigeria, that the public utility grid in Kaduna operated only a portion of each day – at most, 12 hours. When the hospital had power, it could use its lights, refrigerator, surgical suction and other energy-dependent devices. When the power was down, the hospital was incapacitated.

FIGURE 1.1   Maternity ward in Nigeria with a nurse working in near-darkness

Courtesy Laura Stachel

A diesel-fuel generator tried to compensate during evening hours, but fuel was expensive, and the generator was used sparingly.

I had not predicted the challenges facing my Nigerian colleagues. At night, I observed maternity care, watching helplessly as doctors and midwives struggled to treat critically ill pregnant women in near-total darkness. The dim glow of kerosene lanterns often provided the only illumination. Without electricity, doctors had to postpone Caesarean sections and other life-saving procedures. When the maternity ward was in darkness, midwives were unable to provide emergency care and, on occasion, would turn patients away from the labour room door, despite their critical need for care.

The most upsetting example of this was when a woman in labour was brought to the hospital door late at night, bleeding heavily. She had a critically low blood pressure. The presumed diagnosis was uterine rupture – a life-threatening condition requiring immediate surgery. The hospital was in darkness, unable to conduct surgery or provide the immediate blood transfusion necessary to save the woman's life. The midwife advised the family to go elsewhere to get care, and the family was sent back into the darkness. It was hard to imagine she would survive.

One night, I witnessed an emergency that set me on the path to where I am today. The labour room was in near darkness, and I settled at the foot of the bed of a seriously ill pregnant woman with eclampsia. Brought to the hospital unconscious, she had suffered several seizures at home in labour, according to the family members who hovered at her bedside. Although she had been given a single dose of anti-seizure medication at the hospital, the woman had another convulsion; her family attempted to hold her body down. When the seizure was over, she lay still, her breathing abated, and I thought she had died. Tears welled in my eyes.

Anyone would have found this woman's suffering disturbing, but as an obstetrician, I found it intolerable. Eclampsia, although serious, was an eminently treatable complication of pregnancy. I stood by the bed, feeling helpless. The woman stirred. Still alive.

I thought about all the women like her, suffering in obscurity, unable to access life-saving care that I had always considered routine. I vowed to change this.

I described the desperate hospital conditions in an e-mail to my husband, Hal Aronson, who had taught solar energy technology in California for more than 10 years. Hal immediately focused on solar power as a way to provide electricity to the hospital.

The birth of a solar innovator

When I returned home to Berkeley, Hal sketched a design for a solar electric system to help the Nigerian hospital. He recommended installing four stand-alone solar electric systems targeting areas of the hospital important to maternal survival: the maternity ward, the labour room, the operating room and the laboratory, where we would install a solar blood bank refrigerator. In each system, solar panels would generate electricity that would be stored in a sealed lead-acid battery for night-time use. Each system had a charge controller to regulate electricity going into and out of the battery, as well as a load centre to power appliances. Included were 12V DC lights, a charging station for walkie-talkies, and power for other devices, such as surgical suction in the operating room and a blood bank refrigerator in the laboratory. With these systems, labouring women – and their care providers – would no longer have to be in darkness.

The project was compelling, but we needed funds. A campus-wide competition at UC Berkeley advertised a $12,500 grand prize for a technology offering a social good. The deadline for a proposal was 11 days after my return from Nigeria, and provided great incentive to draft a paper and engage the talents of two other Berkeley graduate students: Melissa Ho, from the IT department, and Christian Casillas, from Energy Resources Group. I submitted a 'white paper' on our project and crossed my fingers. A few weeks later, we learned that our project was one of 12 finalists. All of us joined forces to prepare a poster for the competition finals. Melissa and I, along with my seven-year-old daughter, Rachel, dressed in African fashion at the event as we displayed a solar panel, two-way radios, and photos of scenes I had observed at the Nigerian hospital. Our efforts yielded an honourable mention, which carried a $1,000 award, but it wasn't enough to fund my dream.

I came home from the competition, dejected, and called Nigeria to speak to Dr Muazu, the head of Kofan Gayan Hospital. 'We didn't win enough money to do the project', I apologized. Dr Muazu was unfazed. 'Don't worry, Laura', he assured me. 'You planted a seed, and from this a great tree will grow.'

A few hours later, I received a call from Thomas Kalil, a campus official who had been at the competition. 'You should have won', he told me. 'How much do you need for your project?' I knew that our true budget exceeded the competition prize, and hastily doubled the amount originally offered as grand prize. Within three weeks, Kalil had found us funding through the Blum Center for Developing Economies.

We could start. The project that would later become We Care Solar had begun.

We set to work mapping out the details of our installation. Our plan was to hire a Nigerian solar company to install solar equipment using Hal's design. We conducted research over the internet, contacted seven companies, interviewed key representatives by phone, and arranged to meet with one promising solar installer in Nigeria.

I wanted to include my Nigerian hospital colleagues in our planning. Would they like to use walkie-talkies for mobile communication to reduce delays in assembling a surgical team? Would the LED lights we found be bright enough for surgery? Would doctors and nurses find our headlamps (powered with rechargeable batteries) acceptable for clinical care? Their responses would guide our design.

As I planned a return trip to Nigeria I wanted something tangible to show my colleagues – something compact enough to fit in my suitcase. I didn't want the hassle (or potential danger) of explaining our project to customs officials at the Abuja airport. I needed this to be discreet.

Hal's solution was a demonstration solar kit to take on my next journey. He packed my suitcase with compact solar panels, a solar electric control board, a sealed battery, high-efficiency LED lights, headlamps and walkie-talkies. And he invited me to take a workshop on solar energy that he was teaching to educators.

When I returned to Nigeria, I unpacked the case in front of the surgical staff and hospital administrator. I attached the wires and plugged in the battery as Hal had taught me. A doctor flipped the switch and the lights turned on, bringing wide smiles to the hospital staff. The light was indeed bright enough for an operating room. The rechargeable walkie-talkies meant that a surgical team could be assembled in minutes instead of hours, avoiding lengthy searches for doctors and surgical technicians on the hospital grounds. The headlamps with rechargeable batteries were immediately put to use.

FIGURE 1.2　Unpacking the first Solar Suitcase in a Nigerian Hospital

Courtesy We Care Solar

I met with the Nigerian solar installer whom Hal and I had interviewed by phone, and together we surveyed the hospital, measuring the power requirements for various medical devices. Dr Muazu approved of our plans for a larger installation in six months. But one operating room technician, Aminu Abdullahi, had another idea. 'You must leave your suitcase here', he insisted. 'This will help us save lives now.' Aminu convinced me that he would care for Hal's equipment in my absence. Indeed, Aminu took charge of the solar devices, dutifully setting the solar panel outside each morning, taking it in at night, and using the system to keep batteries charged for headlamps and two-way radios. The first We Care Solar Suitcase had found a home.

Six months later, I returned to conduct the larger hospital installation, including procurement of a blood bank refrigerator for the laboratory. The hospital was immediately transformed. Midwives could perform obstetric procedures throughout the night, surgical teams were assembled in minutes rather than hours, Caesarean sections were conducted regardless of time of day, and patients were no longer turned away for lack of power. We celebrated the solar installation with a community event, including a ribbon-cutting ceremony from the Kaduna State Minister of Health. Though the hospital staff were clearly pleased with their facility upgrade, staff at one nearby medical clinic felt left out.

'We conduct deliveries in the dark as well,' the clinic manager lamented. 'Why are you only helping the hospital?'

I was initially a bit defensive, explaining that we only had funds for the hospital. However, it soon occurred to me that the suitcase-size system Hal had made for the hospital demonstration could be transplanted to the clinic. We brought the cobbled-together system to the clinic, much to the delight of midwives who no longer needed to rely on candles and kerosene at night.

I continued to conduct research at Kofan Gayan hospital, returning every few months to observe care. It wasn't long before additional local clinics asked for the 'solar doctor' and the suitcase that would light up maternity care. Hal was glad to accommodate these requests, and started assembling small solar kits for each clinic. On each trip to Nigeria, I would include a Solar Suitcase or two in my luggage.

FIGURE 1.3   Bringing an early Solar Suitcase prototype to a Nigerian clinic

Courtesy We Care Solar

Word continued to spread, and I was invited to talk about our experience at several US conferences. At one of these meetings, *New York Times* writer Nicholas Kristof gave a stirring keynote address. After his talk, I told him how his own articles had inspired our work in Africa. The next day, Kristof wrote about our mission in his online blog, and requests for We Care Solar Suitcases arrived from around the world. The need for reliable electricity for maternal health care extended far beyond Nigeria.

Each time I returned to Nigeria I visited the clinics using our solar equipment, making note of any failures as well as the successes. Incorporating feedback from our field installations, the design of our Solar Suitcases became increasingly refined. The suitcase components became more rugged and easier to use. Bare wires needing screwdrivers for installation were replaced with plug-and-play connectors. Safety fuses were replaced with breaker switches. Our simple wooden board was swapped for a plastic panel. And seeing how dirty our equipment became after months of use prompted us to enclose our components in a plastic protective case.

Hal enlisted local volunteers to help with assembly in our backyard. Soon, our Solar Suitcases were travelling to midwives in Burma, clinics in Tibet and doctors in Tanzania. Solar Suitcases would reach their destination by volunteer couriers who would arrive at our home for training, and then personally transport a Solar Suitcase to a remote clinic or hospital.

When the devastating Haiti earthquake struck in 2010, we had no choice but to get Solar Suitcases into the field as quickly as possible. Medical relief groups made numerous requests for our portable solar power stations, and many small donations poured in as well. In four days, Hal had assembled a team of volunteers to assemble the Solar Suitcases, which we promptly dispatched to several medical groups.

FIGURE 1.4   Hal Aronson leading the backyard assembly of Solar Suitcases for Haiti

Courtesy Laura Stachel

As the Solar Suitcase was introduced to new countries, we worked to adapt the suitcase configuration to meet local requirements. Sometimes we learned the hard way. We discovered, for example, that an initial design short-cut – using an American AC-style outlet for our DC lights in Nigeria – was confusing in Haiti, where AC wall outlets accepted (and overpowered) our 12V DC lamps. We redesigned the outlets, and I flew to Haiti with a volunteer engineer, Brent Moellenberg, to retrofit our Solar Suitcases with the new design.

After our experience in Haiti it became clear to us that our programme was gaining traction. Hal and I dived into the project, converting our home into a Solar Suitcase assembly line. Equipment was strewn all over the house and the living room became our shipping and packing line. We juggled a steady stream of part-time volunteers, including many who were quite talented, but none who could sustain a hefty long-term commitment without remuneration.

Eager to gain increased exposure and support, we entered several competitions, enlisting the support of a talented UC Berkeley MBA student, Abhay Nihalani, and a recent MBA graduate from Duke, Michael MacHarg. In 2010 we applied for (and won) 10 competitions and fellowships, including the Global Social Benefit Competition at UC Berkeley, the Ashoka Changemaker's *Healthy Mothers, Strong World Award*, the Global Social Benefit Incubator at Santa Clara University, and a Pop!Tech Fellowship.

This whirlwind year brought me into contact with other social entrepreneurs and mentors, and helped me gain perspective about ways to extend our reach. As I shared our limited experience in Nigeria and Haiti with social entrepreneur groups, we were asked to scale up our operations.

Hal and I had no experience in this realm. Hal had been a solar educator for years, initially creating hands-on solar electricity projects for students, and later, developing a curriculum for educators. My career in medicine demanded clinical and surgical acumen, not project management skills. We needed a thoughtful approach to scale up.

Some advisers suggested the best approach would be mass production of a simplified prototype. They encouraged us to immediately strip down some of the more costly features of our early design, and to manufacture a cheaper, less ambitious version of our product. 'Fewer bells and whistles', we were told.

We were worried about this approach. The design of the Solar Suitcase had evolved to meet the needs of health workers working in unfathomable conditions. We didn't want to downgrade the functionality of our product, and we weren't ready to commit to one particular design without more field research.

Our dream was to create an optimized version of the suitcase incorporating existing feedback from our field installations, and to conduct further research on this model in a limited number of health facilities. Since our formative experience began in northern Nigeria, we thought this would be a good testing site. But we knew this would require staff, time and money.

Structure, sustainability and scale

We decided to incorporate as a non-profit organization in order to ensure that under-resourced health centres would have access to reliable electricity. We recognized there was not a functional market for solar electricity in public health facilities in the countries most in need of our product. Our beneficiaries were government health workers and the impoverished mothers they served. We would need to seek funding from third parties that were eager to support our mission.

The World Health Organization invited us to pilot a small Solar Suitcase programme in Liberia, funded by UBS Optimus Foundation. Around the same time, The MacArthur Foundation funded us specifically to bring our innovation to scale. In awarding us a coveted grant, the foundation recognized the potential for our Solar Suitcases to 'bring light' to an area of maternal health care that had previously been largely ignored. Our grant targeted four areas – technology design, educational programming, field research and scale-up of operations. We received additional support from the Blum Center for Developing Economies. We were on our way.

Our learning curve was steep. We had never run a non-profit organization, managed international programmes, or interacted with contract manufacturers or government officials. We asked for help wherever we could find it, thankful to receive mentorship from business consultants, lawyers, industrial engineers, designers, social entrepreneurs and academicians. We are fortunate to be based in the San Francisco Bay Area, which enabled us to collaborate with a diverse talent pool: students and professors from UC Berkeley and Stanford, scientists from Lawrence Berkeley National Laboratory, other technology-oriented non-profits, and advisers from Silicon Valley.

Hal and I devoted ourselves full time to We Care Solar. We hired consultants to help lead operations and provide financial oversight. Brent Moellenberg, the engineer who had led our technical activities in Haiti, was brought on board full-time. As our organizational capacity expanded, we developed systems for accounting, data management and inventory. Hal and Brent met with lighting designers, solar manufacturers and contract manufacturers. Our aim was to 'design for manufactur-ability,' which meant making user-friendly, rugged Solar Suitcases in a factory rather than our house! We found that our mission – to use solar light and power to improve maternal health – attracted generous in-kind support. So we were able to accomplish a great deal with a limited budget.

FIGURE 1.5   Brent Moellenberg, Hal Aronson and Christian Casillas preparing version 2.0 of the Solar Suitcase

Courtesy Laura Stachel

We realized that the technology alone was not sustainable without proper usage and long-term maintenance. In addition to developing photo-rich user manuals, we printed bright laminated posters, recognizing from our site visits that in rural clinics, posters were the most common form of written information. We created educational programmes for health workers, and a basic curriculum on solar energy and optimal use of the Solar Suitcase. We prepared more advanced materials on installation and maintenance for technicians. And we piloted this programme in Liberia with 60 health providers before extending our capacity-building workshops to Nigeria, Sierra Leone, Uganda and Malawi.

FIGURE 1.6   Training Nigerian health workers to use the Solar Suitcase

Courtesy We Care Solar

As we travelled from country to country, we conducted facility assessments at diverse health centres which exposed us to variations of health facility layout, construction materials and energy needs. As a result of our research, we expanded the capacity of the Solar Suitcase, and included hardware and tools to facilitate installation. Our newer version could accommodate larger solar panels and batteries, included a fetal heart rate monitor, and had the option for additional lights that could be plugged into a 'satellite' receptacle.

FIGURE 1.7   Poster of the first manufactured Solar Suitcase

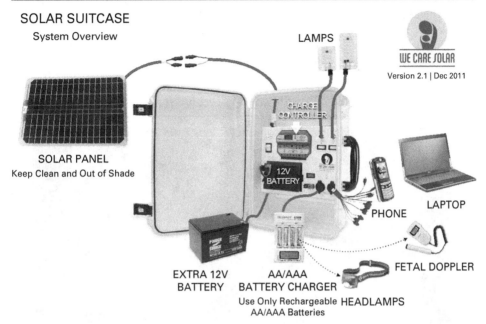

Courtesy We Care Solar

Meeting demand and measuring impact

We responded to inquiries from a range of countries. Sometimes the requests were for programmes with dozens of health centres, leading to partnerships with international NGOs and UN agencies. Other times the requests were from individuals who wanted to hand-carry a Solar Suitcase to individual clinics.

To date, we have deployed more than 1,500 Solar Suitcases across 27 countries. We have conducted programmes with 20 agencies and trained more than 5,000 health workers in our technology. Our partners have included UNICEF, the World Health Organization, Pathfinder International, AMREF, and Save the Children. We estimate that more than 600,000 mothers and babies have been served by health centres using our Solar Suitcases. And our technology has promoted environmental health as well as safe deliveries; by displacing kerosene lanterns and diesel fuel generators, our Solar Suitcases have averted 12,000 tons of CO_2.

A seal of approval from healthcare workers

Solar Suitcases enable health workers to perform procedures throughout the night. Specifically, midwives explained that it was easier to conduct routine and complicated deliveries, treat bleeding mothers, administer medication at night, keep phones charged for emergency referrals and resuscitate newborn babies. Many clinics stayed open longer hours, and patients were more likely to seek skilled care in a facility that they knew had light. We heard again and again that reliable lighting and phone charging improved health worker morale and reduced the fear that used to go hand-in-hand with working in a darkened health centre.

FIGURE 1.8   Liberian health workers receiving a Solar Suitcase at night

Courtesy Laura Stachel

We were surprised to receive requests for Solar Suitcases from large maternity wards and hospital operating theatres in need of reliable power. Even though we explain that our Solar Suitcases have a limited light supply not intended for larger rooms, hospital administrators insist that our Solar Suitcase lighting is vastly superior to the candles and kerosene lanterns that are the only source of lighting when the power grid is down. The Solar Suitcase is seen as an essential back-up source of power to the utility grid.

Indeed, when we visited eastern Uganda in the summer of 2012 to evaluate the impact of the Solar Suitcase, I was privy to a night-time Caesarean section during which the main power stopped functioning. With a Solar Suitcase light above the operating table, the surgery continued without interruption. The doctors told us the Solar Suitcase lights were better for surgery than their usual lights, and there was no longer the need to send patients to distant hospitals when night falls.

Each small success has been celebrated, but we have so much more work to do. The biggest challenge has been in designing programmes to scale up distribution and maintenance in countries with poor physical and political infrastructure. As our programmes have expanded in size, the logistical demands have increased. We partner with larger agencies that have the capacity to manage programmes serving as many as 150 health centres in a region. Their collaboration enables us to import our equipment, select appropriate health centres, schedule and conduct formal training programmes,

FIGURE 1.9　A Ugandan surgeon uses a Solar Suitcase light to conduct an emergency c-section

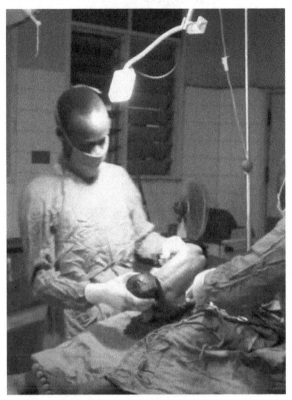

Courtesy Jacqueline Cutts

engage health technicians from local ministries to install Solar Suitcases and train midwives, and monitor our programmes. We developed a Women's Solar Ambassador programme to help lead our international training programmes. These teach our local partners how to install Solar Suitcases, teach health workers and maintain our equipment. And we are now looking at hiring local staff members to oversee our programmes, service our Solar Suitcases and promote sustainability.

The power of stories

Sometimes the pressure feels overwhelming. We have a limited staff and we are tackling an enormous problem. As we approach our breaking point, we often receive an inspiring story of how the Solar Suitcase is helping a health provider, or a clinic, or saving a life.

One such story came from Dr Jacques Sebisaho, a New York-trained doctor who operates a clinic on the island of Idjwi in the Democratic Republic of the Congo. The village had no power and at night-time it was impossible to provide adequate medical care. Dr Sebisaho returned to his village clinic armed with a Solar Suitcase, and it was quickly put to use to illuminate a twin delivery.

However, Dr Sebisaho's arrival coincided with the onset of a cholera epidemic. The clinic was flooded with patients needing intravenous fluids, antibiotics and constant monitoring. The clinic could not house all the patients in need of care, and mats were placed outside on the ground, creating a makeshift open-air infirmary. The Solar Suitcase lighting was carried from patient to patient, and enabled the team to provide constant monitoring.

Although Dr Sebisaho feared many lives could be lost, he and his team achieved something they considered a near-miracle. All the patients treated that month survived – not a single man, woman or child was lost despite the severity of many of the cases. He had expected 50 per cent of the patients to die, and said that 80 per cent of deaths occur at night.

In the case of Dr Sebisaho, the Solar Suitcase was a lifesaver, boosting the morale of health workers and inspiring the entire community:

> I believe the light was the force behind everything. I have no words to describe how confident we all were, knowing we could do anything anytime (day or night). This sounds obvious to a person here (in the USA), but the light meant the world there.
>
> We are witnessing what light can do in a community and how it can save lives in regions where night means death if (you are) sick or in need of emergency care after the sun goes down.

FIGURE 1.10   Dr Jacques Sebisaho (wearing glasses) on Idjwi Island introducing the Solar Suitcase

Courtesy Jacques Sebisaho

The stories of Dr Sebisaho, and hundreds of midwives, nurses and doctors who are grateful for the light they need to do their work, infuse us with the energy we need to continue our journey. So despite the sacrifices, the endless challenges, and the constant stream of work ahead, we continue to move forward.

We realize that the problem of reliable electrification of health facilities extends to hundreds of thousands of health facilities, and a broad range of solutions are needed. We have actively worked to put sustainable electricity on the global health agenda, and have used our success to engender broader policy initiatives. The UN began promoting its Sustainable Energy for All (SE4A) initiative in 2011. I was fortunate to play an early leadership role in the UN Foundation's Energy Practitioner's Working Groups as part of SE4A, co-chairing the group on health and energy. Through associations that were made in the working group, we were able to convene a workshop in 2012 in Washington DC on Renewable Energy for Healthcare. We invited colleagues from the World Health Organization (WHO) as well as a diverse group of stakeholders from engineering, global health and development. The meeting helped to forge a partnership between WHO and the UN Foundation, and helped to foster a platform for the United Nations called the 'High Impact Opportunity' on Energy for Women and Children's Health, bringing together the UN Foundation, WHO, UN Energy, UN Women as well as members of Civil Society, like We Care Solar. One of the most satisfying achievements was participating in the launch of this initiative both at the World Bank and later at the United Nations.

UN Secretary-General Ban Ki-Moon commended our work at Rio+20, and WHO Director-General Margaret Chan called We Care Solar 'Sunshine saving lives'. And perhaps most exciting was when UN DESA (the UN Department of Economic and Social Affairs) awarded us their inaugural 'Powering the Future We Want' award in September 2015. Speaking at the United Nations as I accepted this award on behalf of childbearing mothers and health workers around the world, I was overwhelmed with the knowledge that our mission to light up health care was receiving international recognition and support.

Just as I could not have predicted how my life would unfold at 17 when I was a dancer and pianist, nor at 40 when I could no longer continue my beloved medical practice, so too I cannot predict the journey that lies ahead for We Care Solar. What I do know is that every day women and their infants are struggling in childbirth in the dark, in remote (and not so remote) corners of the world. It is within our reach to bring them light and power for essential medical services – through our Solar Suitcases and through advocacy for reliable energy as vital for improving health.

When no mother has to give birth alone in the dark, we will have fulfilled our mission.

Lessons learnt

1 *Be open to discovering the unexpected.* I purposely did *not* read a lot about the topic of Nigerian maternal hospital care before my first trip. By becoming a participant observer, I was able to share the experience of my Nigerian colleagues and see things from a new vantage point.

2 *Failure is an important teacher.* There is so much to learn from making mistakes. The first Solar Suitcases needed many improvements. Seeing what parts of the Solar Suitcase failed in the field helped us to design a better Solar Suitcase.

3 *Perfect is the enemy of good.* Although I am by nature a perfectionist, Hal's drive to get Solar Suitcases into the field – even if they didn't look pretty or have the best user interface – gave us valuable experience. If we had waited for the perfect Solar Suitcase to be designed, I am not sure whether we would have ever conducted a field trial. By having health workers in Africa and Haiti use our early prototypes, we obtained important feedback that was incorporated into our final design.

4 *Don't travel solo. Surround yourself with the best team you possibly can.* We have learned so much from other social entrepreneurs, from mentors, and from partnerships we created around the world. There is so much to learn from other people and other organizations. Recognize your strengths and weaknesses and find talented people to complement your skills.

5 *Non-profits face many of the same challenges as for-profits.* We Care Solar was born into a very similar environment to many start-ups. We had to ask the same kinds of questions: How do we scale and continue to serve customers? Who are our competitors? How do we communicate our message effectively to attract investors (donors)? We were also faced with a highly dysfunctional market. The clinicians we visit don't have even the funds for medications. They are our beneficiaries but *not* our target customers. In our case, our customers are the governments, UN Agencies, international NGOs and foundations that support the work of these underserved health centres.

6 *Choose something that ignites your passion, because the work is really hard.* Trying to do business in Africa and Southeast Asia is hard. The infrastructure that we come to rely on in the United States or the United Kingdom is not there. You can't guarantee you will find roads, or the internet, or phone service, or even proper tools. The logistical challenges we face would give anyone nightmares. We are placing the Solar Suitcases in health centres with no practice of maintaining medical equipment – so coming up with a plan for sustainability is even harder. But the people we meet are wonderful, appreciative and eager to learn. And solving these challenges is deeply fulfilling.

7 *Start small.* If you are passionate about a problem that needs solving, you don't need to map out an entire master plan at the beginning. Take small steps. Each time you cross a threshold, you'll get some results and the opportunity to make new decisions and new choices. By making a series of small steps, your path may become clearer. Small things can lead to big things. They did for us.

8 *Don't underestimate the power of a good story.* Much of our support we received over the years was the result of learning to effectively communicate our mission. Forget about traditional slide decks filled with long narrative and multiple bullet points. Tell stories accompanied by photos that illustrate your mission and emotionally connect your audience. Let your users speak for you.

9   *One size does not fit all. Our approach in one country may not be easily replicated in another.* Even though we may now understand how to do things in Uganda, this doesn't mean we understand the market in the Philippines. Each country has specific cultural issues, regulations and internal systems. To achieve success in different locales, we need to conduct research in each country and adapt our processes to the local context.

10 *Not everything can be strategically planned, especially for an early stage company.* It was great to have some idea about the direction we were heading, but much of our success was dictated by unexpected events and opportunities, chance encounters, and our ability to pivot midstream. Being a small enterprise allowing us to be nimble has been one of the most fun parts of this work, and recognizing when nimbleness turns to chaos one of the most challenging.

Discussion questions

1   Can you identify ways in which We Care Solar did not follow traditional rules of business?

2   What were the risks and benefits of introducing a range of early Solar Suitcase prototypes into the field?

3   What do you think might be the total energy needs of health centres? In that light, what are the benefits and limitations of the Solar Suitcase?

4   Several investors encouraged We Care Solar to incorporate as a for-profit business rather than a non-profit business. How would that have influenced their trajectory?

5   What would be the most effective ways for We Care Solar to replicate its model in new countries? What might be some of the challenges?

6   The Solar Suitcase provides health workers with medical lights, phone charging and fetal monitors. What other interventions are needed to improve obstetric care for mothers and babies in rural health centres? Should the Solar Suitcase be placed in health centres that lack these other interventions?

7   The UN adopted the Sustainable Development Goals in 2015 and aims to lower maternal mortality worldwide to less than 70 deaths per 100,000 live births. What are effective strategies to lower maternal mortality worldwide?

Further reading

You can find more material to do with this chapter at www.koganpage.com/socialentrepreneurship

www.wecaresolar.org
PBS Newshour: www.pbs.org/newshour/bb/globalhealth-jan-june12-solarsuitcase_04-04/ [accessed 10 December 2015]

KQED: www.youtube.com/watch?v=3h_Quso1QyM

CNN: www.cnn.com/SPECIALS/cnn.heroes/2013.heroes/laura.stachel.html
[accessed 10 December 2015]

www.cnn.com/2013/03/01/world/cnnheroes-solar-suitcase/index.html [accessed 10
December 2015]

TED WOMEN: www.youtube.com/watch?v=bz8V-qUs_2w

UN DESA Acceptance Speech: www.youtube.com/watch?v=eEjvtg0f2B4&feature=
youtu.be

World Health Organization (2015) *Access to Modern Energy Services for Health
Facilities in Resource-Constrained Settings* http://apps.who.int/iris/bitstream/
10665/156847/1/9789241507646_eng.pdf

World Health Organization (2015) *Trends in Maternal Mortality*
http://apps.who.int/iris/bitstream/10665/194254/1/9789241565141_eng.pdf

UNFPA (2014) *Setting standards for emergency obstetric and newborn care*
http://www.unfpa.org/resources/setting-standards-emergency-obstetric-and-
newborn-care

Acknowledgements

My life partner, Hal Aronson, was the driving force behind the Solar Suitcase. From the moment I shared my observations of the effects of energy poverty in a Nigerian hospital, Hal dedicated himself to developing a solution for this problem. In addition to being the true innovator of the Solar Suitcase and the co-founder of We Care Solar, Hal provided technical expertise, engaged countless volunteers, offered constant emotional support, and became the primary caretaker for our family during each of my trips abroad. Hal's endless devotion to creating solar solutions to serve last-mile health centres is a major reason for our success.

02
Closing Latin America's 'digital divide'

CDI – RODRIGO BAGGIO

ABSTRACT

Imagine a world where you could use technology to build a fairer and better society. This is our aim at CDI (Centre for Digital Inclusion), a pioneering social organization focusing on digital empowerment in Latin America. Founded in 1995, CDI uses technology to empower communities and encourage entrepreneurship, education and citizenship. CDI is the result of a dream – literally. In 1993, I dreamt of young people from a poor community, a favela, using technology and transforming their lives in a positive way. When I woke up, I clung to the idea that we could transform lives and strengthen low-income communities by empowering people with information and communication technology skills.

At the time there was a kind of digital apartheid, a youth deprived of technology because of their economic conditions, and I felt driven to find a solution to this problem. Almost immediately, I began to collect outdated but serviceable computers and printers and create 'computer schools'. It was the embryo of what would become CDI: today a global non-profit network headquartered in Rio de Janeiro, with operations in 15 countries helping almost 2 million people. CDI has become a leader in digital inclusion and one of the most recognized organizations in the non-profit world, having received more than 70 awards and prizes from renowned national and international institutions including the UN, UNESCO, UNICEF, the World Economic Forum, TIME, CNN, the Tech Museum, and, more recently, the Clinton Global Initiative. We also won the Entrepreneur for the World Award in 2014 from the World Entrepreneurship Forum – recognition for years of devotion to social entrepreneurship.

When I first started CDI I couldn't imagine scaling it up, and I had never dreamed of becoming a social entrepreneur, talking about social change at an international level. Today I live in Washington DC where I lead the global governance of CDI and a global project for developing the social entrepreneurship field as Senior Vice President of Ashoka. But more than being proud about my journey, I feel fulfilled. For me, this is not work, but a passion, a way in which I can contribute to rebooting the system and creating a better world.

A faltering start

I was born and raised in Rio de Janeiro, Brazil. I had my first breakthrough experience when I was six years old. It took place at school, where I proved to be very clever, but struggled to read and write. The situation was extremely unpleasant as the other children used to make jokes about my problem, saying that I would never get things right. At the same time, I was not able to stay seated in the classroom all day; I had a hard time with concentration. I was bursting with energy with an urgent need to stand, walk and move. My teachers and classmates thought of me as undisciplined. One month I was sent to the Educational Guidance System in order to find out what was wrong with me. They advised my parents to hire a speech therapist.

My parents accepted the school's advice and took me for an appointment with a speech therapist, Ana Pracownik, who diagnosed my dyslexia and hyperactivity. She also discovered a way to keep my attention so I could learn how to read and write. As soon as she knew I liked to see pictures in comic books, she created a method in which she linked images to words. Thanks to Ana and her method, I finally learnt how to read and write. This breakthrough was extremely important in my life, as I learned early on how to overcome the difficulties that came up on a daily basis at that time.

Learning how to read further amplified my passion for comic books, and I became a voracious reader. Over time, I ended up with a large number of these comic books at home and, of course, my mother became more and more irritated at seeing my bedroom filled with them. So I decided to sell some in a street nearby, but I would always buy even more comic books with the money. My great collection was far from finished. However, besides selling my things and earning my own money, I also interacted with passers-by, talked to them, and that was fascinating. In a sense, I consider this activity as my first experience as an entrepreneur.

Two passions

When I was 12 years old, I went to a lecture at school about a person who, together with the Archdiocese of Rio de Janeiro and the Brazilian Navy, had founded the first project to work with street children in the city. Whenever I rode past in my father's car, I saw kids by the traffic lights asking for money and I wished I could do something to help them. Watching this lecture, I discovered one way. The next day I went to the Archdiocese to work as a volunteer. It was not easy though. People looked at me and said, 'Go back to school, boy' or 'Go have some fun with your friends', as if that kind of work were not for me. But I did not give up; I was firm in my goal. So I saw a priest and I went to talk about the situation. Actually, I begged him to persuade the Archdiocese's employees that I was able to work as a volunteer. He talked to them, so in the end they accepted me.

The experience was absolutely wonderful. I started as a sports supervisor with the street kids. My job was to organize the football and volleyball matches. Being the referee was not easy during the more intense football matches, in which any sharp move could lead to a fight between the children, usually involving pocketknives.

These were even more frightening than a regular fight with punches and kicks. But the experience worked out well and was important. I helped in the process of dealing with the boys. I also experienced challenging situations, such as when there were conflicts between rival groups and I was needed to calm people down and negotiate for peace between both sides. They were kids; we were the same age, but they trusted me. Similar situations taught me lessons as valuable as those taught at school. From that time forward my passion for social work was born. I could contribute to providing a better life to those children! It was fantastic! I went through my teenage years doing social, student and environmental work.

Also at 12 years of age, there was another occurrence that had a definitive impact in my life: my father gave me one of the first personal computers that arrived in Brazil. At that time he was a computer technology director and provided maintenance services for large computers in DPCs (Data Processing Centres). Once in a while, he would take me to work with him and I loved the captivating environment. He noticed my curiosity about that world and he gave me a TK82. Younger generations may not have heard of it: it was a computer without an operating system from the early days of computer science, a time when even Windows didn't exist. In order to use this computer I had to program it in the BASIC language. There was no floppy disk. People used cassette tapes inside a recorder. For the screen we used a black-and-white TV. Even though it was a primitive machine, it was the best present I had ever received because it made me interested in learning more about it. I devoured my TK82 manual up to the point of understanding all its functions. Shortly afterwards, I started to create games and teach my friends how to operate it. It was an amazing experience, which led me to discovering my second passion in life: technology.

My confirmation came in a dream

As an adult, I went to work for companies such as Accenture and IBM and, later on, resigned so I could create my own company, Baggio Information Technology (BIT). We created software for other companies and I got great clients, such as Globo Television Network, the largest TV network in Brazil. In 1993, I was 23 and already a successful IT businessman. My friends still lived with their parents but I had my own flat, car and even a boat. But in spite of my quick professional and financial success, I did not feel fulfilled in life. I wondered about my next 10 years at 33 years old and I saw a rich man, but not with a sense of accomplishment. I saw myself with money, but not happier.

I was driven by an intense desire to develop a social project, something that would help to improve people's lives. I wished I could do something similar to what I had done when I was 12 with those street kids. I wanted to change my life, I had this powerful drive, but I did not know what I should do. I spent the year of 1993 trying to find something. I meditated, thought it over, and met with people, all in hopes of finding an answer.

At the end of that year, surprisingly, the answer to my unease came at night, literally in a dream. The dream was vivid, dominated by a theme of technology helping empower a poor favela community with knowledge and information. When I woke up, I realized I had an idea and, more than that, a mission; to transform people's lives by means of technology. I was full of energy, with all the strength and heart required to turn my dream into reality.

The first step was to create a computer network, a Bulletin Board System (BBS). It was not like it is today, when everyone has the internet at the palm of their hands. Access was restricted to universities. The only means of communication between computers was through a modem, by establishing a network which enabled people to exchange messages. I visited Charles Miranda, owner of Hot Line, the biggest BBS of Rio de Janeiro, and I invited him to participate in the project. He loved the idea and agreed to be part of it. I gave it the name 'Jovem Link' ('Young Link' in English) and the goal was to make it available for young people of all classes, the rich and the poor. The idea was that through our chat rooms children of all ages and classes would be able to connect, discuss and debate things that mattered to them. This first initiative, launched in March 1994, was a great success and many articles were published about it in the press.

I was a computer science teacher at schools and I connected my pupils and colleagues to Jovem Link. I was very happy for having created this network, as a large number of people were connected to it. However, after some research about the users' profiles at the Jovem Link, I found out that 100 per cent of the users had come from the upper classes. They were my students from the upper class school. To my great disappointment, the young people from the lower classes were not able to access this service, that I had struggled to offer. I wondered why and it did not take long to find the answer. They did not access the BBS because they did not have computers. It was one of those a-ha moments – when the penny dropped about their real need. The very technology that I had hoped would help connect youth was, for those with no access, marginalizing them even more. We needed to find a solution to this problem and it was urgent! It could not wait any longer.

Therefore, still in 1994, Jovem Link created a campaign aiming at collecting second-hand computers called 'Computer Science for All'. This leading action was known as the first campaign for technology recycling in Latin America. I obtained the valuable help of 70 volunteers who wanted to join in the work. Many donations of company and personal computers were given. I received a call from a businessman in Niteroi, a city in the state of Rio de Janeiro, who had loads of computers to donate. According to him, there were so many that I should take them in a lorry. I did not have a lorry, but this little problem was not going to stop me. I borrowed one and, with a volunteer, I went to get the computers. We spent the day carrying these machines; we were exhausted, but we came back to Jovem Link very happy. The great surprise was when we turned on the computers: not one of them worked. They were old machines, real technological garbage. So what now? What should we do?

The solution appeared on the same day. Jovem Link was located really close to Morro Dona Marta favela, today's Santa Marta, and we decided to invite some young residents to learn how to fix computers. They accepted and started doing maintenance services, rendering these computers ready for use, which later on would be given to community organizations in the favelas. I saw the eyes of these disadvantaged people shining in front of the computers. They said they had never imagined touching a computer and yet they were doing even more than that; they were fixing and setting up computers.

But there was another problem to be solved: the computers were given, but they had not been used to their full potential. It was necessary to create a computer science culture to teach people how to use technology to transform their lives. And that was when the idea of creating an Informatics and Citizenship School for residents of impoverished communities emerged.

A dream comes true

I had been filled with great enthusiasm with the possibility of putting this new project into practice. I talked about the school with family, friends, businessmen, journalists, anyone willing to hear about it. But I noticed that most people did not understand my goal and, worst of all, they despised it. They said, 'Rodrigo, you are crazy. The poor have a poor mind: they will never learn how to use a computer.'

But I did not agree with this kind of thinking. There is a pop song by Titãs, a famous rock band from Brazil in the 1980s and 90s, which goes, 'We don't want just food. We want food, fun and art.' I remembered these lyrics and I thought, 'The poor don't want just food. The poor want food, fun, art, and... technology.'

I persisted in my goal, even though I confronted incredulity from many people – even from my family, who understandably were worried about my future. They believed I should return to IBM, a stable job with good professional opportunities. Every day I would meet with businessmen to share my idea of informatics teaching as a social project. It was not an easy mission. Until that time social work was re- garded as giving food to the poor. I showed them a pioneering proposal, but without any examples, so it was hard for them to understand the importance of my project and even harder to convince them to contribute. However, my persistence and ability to communicate – which dated back to my childhood, when I sold my comic books – impacted them in a positive way. A large store decided to support the project, C&A Modas. Working in the clothing sector, the company was a pioneer in corporate volunteer programmes in Brazil, and they understood and supported the project, donating five computers (but not just any old computers – these were the very latest model at the time). When we received these machines, I still needed to find a place for the school.

For the location of the first Informatics School and Citizenship (EIC, in Portuguese), we chose the Morro Dona Marta favela, from where the first volunteers came to do maintenance service. We worked together with a church and a local NGO and I went up to the favela. At that time, it was an extremely dangerous community in Rio. It was controlled by Comando Vermelho, a criminal organization involved in drug dealing – one of the largest of its kind, which still controls some communities in the city. Drug dealers were regarded as idols by the youth. Every boy dreamed about being like them: with money, power and women. In this complex situation, I went up to the slum three times a week to teach 10 youngsters to be teachers of informatics and citizenship. These young people would be multipliers. In other words, they would learn and then share what they learned with other people.

March 1995: the first informatics school and citizenship (EIC)

For the occasion, the community leaders of Dona Marta were invited, in addition to people from other places in town. For media coverage we had journalists from 11 newspapers, seven broadcast companies, three radios and two magazines. They were so excited with what they had seen that people started to call me a young visionary, which made me think, 'From a crazy man to a young visionary in just 24 hours! Awesome!'

I was deeply moved by one person who acknowledged the importance of the work we did: the sociologist Herbert de Souza ('Betinho') because I was a true admirer of his. In 1993 he created the committee 'Action of Citizenship against Hunger, Misery, and for Life Campaign', a mobilization with great support from the middle class to fight against hunger in Rio. I remembered well the day when he saw me in the storage room in the EIC, sweaty, together with the volunteers, carrying the donated computers like a worker hauling bricks one a construction site. He was surprised by the scene, and asked what we were doing. After I explained about the donation, he started helping me in every possible way.

In the schools I taught, I established what I called holistic computer science. Holism is a concept aiming at understanding a phenomenon in its total and overall aspect. In other words, through computer science, we showed the students the Solar System, the Earth, and the human body. When I initiated the first school in the favela, I updated what I had been practising in order to use technology as an instrument of deliverance for the youth from impoverished places.

This very pedagogical method takes its inspiration from Paulo Freire – a Brazilian educator and philosopher, globally known in the field – who created a brilliant method for literacy to be put into practice along with the students in their daily routine and social condition. To a certain extent, something similar to what my speech therapist Ana had done with me by using comic books to teach me how to read. Based on Paulo Freire's method, we made use of the five steps and adapted them for digital empowerment, which includes:

1 read the world, where students are encouraged to analyse their own reality;
2 research the facts, when they arrive at a conclusion for a problem common to all;
3 plan a social campaign, where they must propose a way to solve the problem;
4 act and create impact, which involves community mobilization for action;
5 evaluate success, closing a cycle and beginning a new stage.

Our teachers were trained in this methodology, in which the technology becomes a means not an end. Our biggest aim was to develop awareness about citizenship with a view that the students could transform their surroundings into something better and greater.

As we continued to work at EIC, Globo Television Network – who had become very excited about the project – started to broadcast an advertisement about the school. Every day starting around five in the morning I would receive calls from people who wanted to be volunteers. Curiously, the number that appeared on the advertisement was for my house, which I had given without realizing.

As a means to take hold of these people who called, I decided to set up a meeting with them. On the day scheduled, no fewer than 80 people showed up. The number was infinitely more than what was expected to keep one EIC working. However, I could not dismiss those people; it would have been such a waste to give up on so many people who had a strong desire and willingness to help.

On the opening day of the EIC, among the guests there were community leaders of other places in Rio de Janeiro. In admiration, these leaders claimed schools for their neighbourhoods. Another good idea came up: why don't we use these 80 volunteers to spread EIC throughout other regions?

The committee

The second EIC was inaugurated in the Rocinha favela and, at the same time, another in Morro dos Macacos favela, in the north of Rio. Inspired by the committees which Betinho had created to fight against hunger, I decided to organize my own – the Centre for Digital Inclusion (CDI), with the aim of mobilizing people and transforming communities through technology. We fulfilled our mission by creating CDI Communities, as we called them, which were self-sustainable and self-run social ventures with the objective of training agents of transformation. With volunteers, in 1995, we set up more EICs and proceeded with the 'Computer Science for All' campaign, which made the number of computers rise. CDI improved schools, replacing the equipment.

FIGURE 2.1   Rodrigo Baggio at the first Informatics School and Citizenship at Morro Dona Marta

Image Courtesy of CDI

On the first day at our schools, the students went to the community and immersed themselves in that reality. They took pictures, recorded the surroundings, talked to the residents, sought awareness of their problems. Subsequently, they returned to the CDI school and shared the images and discussed their experiences.

To give an example, I remember when the students saw that the main problem in a community was the proliferation of rats and went to research the subject on the internet. They figured out that the existence of these animals was caused by the improper disposal of garbage. They realized that the rats were a result of the problem, rather than the cause. And the cause was exactly what needed to be combated. Using text tools, they created leaflets and banners to mobilize the community by means of lectures on waste collection. They also sent videos recording the problem to the local cleaning company. As a result, 100 per cent of the residents started properly disposing of their garbage, with the support of the cleaning company. The final result was that the rats disappeared entirely from the community.

Innovations have always caught the attention of the media. In the press there were so many articles about us that our project became known by people from other states, like Minas Gerais, São Paulo and Bahia, who called us and were willing to start CDI in these places. Regional CDI units and EICs were then inaugurated. In this process, we arranged a partnership with the Fenasoft – a national software exhibition – to establish collection points where computers could be donated to Computer Science for All. Max Gonçalves, then president of the company, offered us a stand free of charge for e-waste recycling. The idea was spreading through the country.

Social franchising

In order to implement its mission, CDI started forming partnerships with community associations to create, collaboratively, informal education centres. In the partnership selection process, CDI sought to identify the most bona fide, well-established and respected organizations that were already installed on site. Partner institutions had to offer a space in which the school could function, with all the infrastructure needed for computer installation, and support the school management. Following the CDI model, the centres of digital inclusion needed to be self-sustainable and managed by the community members themselves. Even the educators were chosen by the partner institution and were also local residents, to create identification amongst the students and facilitate the replication of knowledge. Both the CDI centres' educators and coordinators received not only technical training, but also training in essential concepts and practices for the full exercise of citizenship. This was the basis of the quantitative and qualitative expansion of the model.

The model had multiplied beyond the borders of Rio de Janeiro, and the need to formalize what has come to be defined as a 'social franchise' was urgent. All the essential aspects for the operation of the franchise were defined: the pedagogical proposal, standardized methods for quality control, and a legal contract that would regulate the relationship between CDI and the regional franchisees. The model has been successful and has evolved into the concept of network – 'the CDI network' – formed by regional and international CDIs whose activities are autonomous, but accompanied by CDI. This network is constantly expanding, and today has offices in 16 Brazilian states and 15 countries, all with administrative autonomy, replicating the experience and the educational methodology of CDI.

1996: discovering Ashoka

One year later, I encountered Ashoka, the largest network of social entrepreneurs in the world, present in 85 countries with about 3,000 members, the so-called Ashoka Fellows. Bill Drayton, its president and founder, is regarded as the father of social entrepreneurship. Moved by their work, I applied for membership as an Ashoka Fellow. Once a member, I travelled to Washington DC for a month. In the process, I did my first roadshow for the purpose of fundraising in the United States. This step was my initial contact with the American culture of philanthropy with foundations. In Seattle, I met an Ashoka member, the Global Partnerships Foundation whose co-founder and president was Bill Clapp. Bill decided to invest in CDI, and that was our first investment in order to strengthen our professionalization. The sum of US$100,000 was invested, which allowed us to set up a team of contributors.

During my second visit to Seattle, then in association with Global Partnerships, I was invited to a lecture where Bill Clapp introduced me to Bill Gates Senior, one of the board members of Global Partnerships. The experience was amazing, because in addition to meeting him I met people who took part in the foundation of Microsoft, had quit their jobs, became millionaires, and started their social projects. Thanks to this meeting, I made many connections with Microsoft in Brazil. The president of the Brazilian company headquarters had already received many calls from Seattle about the CDI. When I returned the calls, I was invited to a meeting, so he could meet me. As a result, a partnership was started in 1997. Today, CDI is the largest partner of Microsoft in Latin America.

1997: informatics as a dream of freedom

With all the success, we started to spread the CDI model into other environments. We began to work in mental health hospitals, penitentiaries, detention centres for minors, river-bank communities, African communities and even indigenous villages. In 1997, I visited Lemos Brito, a high-security prison. The inmates had read an article about CDI, and the institution asked me to install an EIC there. As soon as I arrived, I was moved by what I saw; the relationship between the policemen and the inmates reminded me of the one between masters and slaves. We began working and soon the inmates were enabled to teach computer science to others. After a while, seeing how the inmates understood the subject and multiplied the knowledge among their companions, the prison guards began to claim their right to learn too. Therefore, the inmates started teaching informatics and citizenship to the guards, and that meant a great change in their relationship. Furthermore, the inmates created income with digital inclusion projects. Consequently, Lemos Brito has become the penitentiary with the lowest level of riots in Rio de Janeiro.

Also in this prison, I met a man named Ronaldo Monteiro, who was serving his 36-year sentence for extortion and kidnapping. He was credited with planning the first kidnapping in the country, a real teacher of crime who also taught guerrilla tactics to his peers. When I met him, he had been in prison for 14 years. But with the CDI school, he has been through a radical change in life, a true transformation. He has become one of our coordinators and teachers. In 2006, when he left the prison for good behaviour, he founded a Social and Cultural Integration Centre (CISC, in Portuguese) in his hometown, which presently offers classes to the residents, among them the CDI classes.

But Ronaldo realized that those who had left prison often turned again to a life of crime due to lack of work. What did he do? He invited these guys to learn computer science, citizenship, and entrepreneurship, and how to become multipliers. Nowadays Ronaldo has 195 microbusinesses, created by the 195 former prisoners. For his excellent work as a social entrepreneur, I recommended him to be an Ashoka Fellow. But they never answered. One day when I was in Oxford, England, I met Bill Drayton and I asked about it. He said, 'Rodrigo, whoever you recommend we accepted, but this time you have suggested a criminal, a kidnapper, a drug dealer.' I told Bill Ronaldo's story. In the end he applauded, deeply touched by that great breakthrough and man's strength to transform. And Ronaldo was finally called: becoming the first former prisoner to be named an Ashoka Fellow.

1999: including indigenous communities

FIGURE 2.2   Indigenous tribe Ashaninka in Acre, participating in the project 'People of the Forest Network'

Image Courtesy of CDI

Our first contact with an indigenous community was in 1999, when a school in the Sapucaí village of Guarani Indians was opened in Angra dos Reis, a town 93 miles from Rio. The experience was wonderful. It was a chance to teach informatics and citizenship to the Brazilian natives. In the beginning, we faced a problem: there was no electricity in the Sapucaí village. In order to turn on the first computer, I needed to use solar power. Computers in the village helped people preserve their indigenous folklore and traditions by allowing it to be recorded and documented before it disappeared, in addition to being an important tool for literacy. One day the chief called me saying that they did not want to call the computer a 'computer'. I suggested that they should make up a word for it in their own language, Guarani. They said 'ayúrirúrive', which means 'box to collect the language'. In the Amazon Forest, we established a 'computer science and *florestania* school' (*florestania* is a relatively new term which, in very simple terms, translates as 'citizen of the forest' as opposed to a city or urban area).

The work generated many results so that, in 2003, in conjunction with one of the biggest Indian leaders in Brazil, Aílton Krenac, we created the People of the Forest Network. The first community was the Ashaninka, whose village was in the Acre State, just four miles from the Peruvian border. Benki Pianko Ashaninka, the chief's son, has opened his eyes to computer science and its possibilities, asking us to set up a centre in the village. The tour to this new school was actually an adventure. I took a flight to Sao Paulo, then to Brasilia and another to Rio Branco, the capital of Acre, where I had a short flight to Cruzeiro do Sul. There I entered in a single-engine plane to Marechal Thaumaturgo and said to the pilot, 'Captain, the seat belt is not working'. He answered, 'It has never worked'. After two hours in that aircraft flying over the forest – which, from above, looked like a vast green ocean – we still had to travel by canoe for an additional 10 hours. Finally arriving at the village, I thought the trip was worthwhile, despite all the effort, as my eyes witnessed a real paradise. However, I showed up in a troubled moment. The Ashaninka were in crisis. The indigenous area has been overrun by clandestine woodsmen from Peru who use it to transport drugs and steal wood. Some Indians were killed and women were raped by these criminals. At night, during a meeting around the fire, the Ashaninka decided to wage war with the Peruvians, who walked around fully armed while the Indians had only their bows and arrows. An Indian came up with an alternative idea. He said, 'We have a powerful weapon, the internet'.

They wrote an e-mail to the President of Brazil at that time, Luiz Inácio Lula da Silva, about the problem saying they would fight the Peruvian drug traffickers to defend the country's sovereignty, because the Brazilian army was not there. The e-mail was read by the Presidency and forwarded to the Federal Police and the Army. Helicopters were sent to the place and the intruders were imprisoned. From that time, to prevent new invasions, the Army and the Federal Police started patrolling the area. The Ashaninka people won a war because they used the internet as a tool for liberation.

April 1999: international expansion

Perhaps because of my religious upbringing, I have always felt that I am on an apostolic mission. I go to places feeling excited, enthusiastic, with eyes sparkling and totally connected to the things I love. Many people from different places wanted to have a CDI unit or to create their own NGOs. We went to the Inter-American Development Bank events in Latin America. In our lecture, we were the only ones there talking about digital inclusion, using technology to solve social problems. Surprisingly, we were able to influence governments and the structuring of the field.

I can recall, when we were still creating the culture of computer donations in April 1999, I was invited by the JCA-NET – a Japanese provider which helped non-profit institutions to publicize their work on the internet – to give a lecture in Tokyo. Walking in the city streets, I was shocked at seeing good computers thrown in the garbage, just because they were out of date. I wished I could have taken them all as they would have been so useful for the poor.

After my talk, we established a committee within the CDI which, supported by volunteers, organized a donation campaign in association with Peace Boat, an NGO that took Japanese people to travel the world to raise awareness about the effects of Japanese imperialism in other countries. They travelled by a transatlantic vessel whose cargo compartment was always empty. It enabled worldwide transportation and distribution of the computers collected. UNESCO received these computers in the countries where the Peace Boat had passed. Latin America, Uruguay, Colombia, and Chile received the benefits. In 2001, in partnership with YMCA, we opened CDIs in Honduras, Guatemala and South Africa.

2008: CDI international

CDI expanded internationally and set up offices for fundraising in London and New York. We did it for two reasons: first, Brazilian law does not allow international organizations based in Brazil to receive funds or to allocate financial resources to other offices; secondly, we could manage our expanding network globally. We had one office and one employee in each country and were able to form an inspiring board of individuals who also supported us in networking.

2008: the reinvention of CDI and the first social business

The charitable sector was being dramatically impacted by the US financial crisis. Our sources of American and Brazilian funding started decreasing. As a result we began to evaluate new opportunities. After I had the great good fortune to meet Muhammad

Yunus, the Nobel Peace Prize winner 2006 and the father of microcredit and social business, I had the inspiration to think that this would be the way in which CDI could develop the logic of financial and social self-sustainability, connected with his mission. Thus, two initiatives arose: CDI LAN and CDI Consulting.

FIGURE 2.3   Rodrigo Baggio receiving from Muhammad Yunus the Vision Award – Berlin 2008

Image Courtesy of CDI

The CDI LAN, co-founded by Marcel Fukayama, former CEO of CDI Global, was a network of 6,500 LAN house affiliates to distribute products and services in education and financial inclusion. This was instrumental in creating a development model for new ways of doing business and impacting on the planet. Its main investor was Vox Capital, one of the pioneering managers of business impact investments in the world, which identified the real impact of the business. The project helped us to create a mental model of development for new ways of doing business and generate impact on the planet. That was the beginning of a CDI journey in social business. We learned how to customize products and co-create this type of business still unknown in the country at that time and, because of the 'market' demand, we began to act as social business consultants. So we launched CDI Consulting, a consulting service offering to large companies solutions in products and services for the most socially and economically marginalized (often known as 'those at the base of the pyramid'). With this social enterprise, we helped private companies to enhance their social business products. The initiatives we worked on included the Energy Efficiency Program of Light, Coca-Cola Collective, new Epson printer models for emerging markets, micro-insurance for Generali and further projects with companies including Accenture, Casas Bahia and Microsoft. All of the revenue from these activities was directed back to the CDI NGOs.

2009: Middle East expansion

In 2009, with the support of James Wolfensohn, the former president of the World Bank, we incorporated the NGO Shabakat in Jordan, which worked with digital inclusion, to become another CDI. Currently, we have 120 informatics and citizenship schools throughout Jordan.

2010: the creation of CDI apps for good

After we had set up our fundraising office in London, CDI England actually received more proposals to initiate CDIs there than offers to make donations to Latin America. We decided to adapt our methodology for the situation in England, which is how Apps for Good was created. Apps for Good is an open-source technology education movement that partners with educators in schools and learning centres to deliver our course to young people (between 10 and 18 years of age). CDI provides the course content, training and connections to our expert volunteers; then we let local teachers inspire and guide the young people. In the course, the students work together in teams to find real issues they care about and learn to build a mobile, web or social app to solve them. Like professional entrepreneurs, students go through all the key aspects of new product development, from idea generation, technical feasibility and programming, to product design, business models and marketing.

We started the project in a neighbourhood that had the highest number of homicides in England. Young African immigrants learned how to use Android mobiles to improve a local issue. By applying the CDI methodology, the biggest challenge that these young people pinpointed was Stop and Search. They created an app called Stop and Search, which informed people about their rights and duties when it came to the police. By accessing Google Maps, it was possible to know where and how each person experienced being frisked. Citizens could send information to the authorities about the conduct of police officers during their stop and search. This was also a positive step for British police stations, as it helped to improve relationships with young citizens through improved communication and trust. Other apps have since been created and CDI was able to provide a new paradigm in England. We won awards, were portrayed in a BBC series and appeared in articles from *The Guardian* and *The Independent*. We set up the Apps for Good culture in the country and today we have more than 500 schools in Britain and throughout the rest of Europe.

2012: B Corps

The impact of CDI LAN allowed us to be one of the first B Corps in South America. B Corps represent an emerging group of companies that are using the power of business to create a positive impact on the world and generate a shared and durable prosperity for all. Currently, we are already a global movement with more than 1,400 companies in more than 42 countries. However, in 2012 this ecosystem was still weak, especially in Brazil, and we saw the opportunity to be a catalyst in this new field. Thus, the alliance among B Lab, B system in Chile and CDI was born, and in February 2013, we created the B System in Brazil, still led by our organization.

2013: NegóciosSociais.com

Still intending to create and strengthen the impact of the social business ecosystem, we realized that there were no investors, case studies, public policy or culture of social business in Brazil. So we launched an initiative, the NegóciosSociais.com (SocialBusinesses.com). It was a great mobilization of over 50 business impact companies in Brazil for a year in a process of formation and selection that reached 15 finalists. During the 2013 Social Enterprise World Forum in Rio de Janeiro, the CDI awarded the three best companies with US$10,000 to strengthen the development of their business.

2014: entrepreneurship synapses

In 2010, I had an encounter that was very remarkable for me. I met Peter Senge, one of the biggest leaders in the management world. He is American and author of 'The Fifth Discipline' and the concept of the learning organization. Senge invited me to join him in workshops in Vermont and Boston. The experience was incredible. We went to Santiago, Chile, to participate in a meeting with Humberto Maturana, philosopher and biologist, in his Matristic school. Maturana was one of the authors of the autopoiesis theory, which refers to the capacity of living beings to reproduce, along with many other theories which created a foundation not only for biology, but also for philosophy and other sciences. We and other advisers of Humberto and Peter spent three days in deep meditation about the purpose of life. There were two inspiring personalities: Peter Senge, writer and mentor for big companies' boards, and Maturana, an 82-year-old man, averse to technology, who did not have a mobile phone or a computer. Making him understand my life purpose, a mission of somebody who since he was 12 years old has considered technology as a meaningful part of life, was not an easy task. Up to the point that, after a while in silence, in an a-ha moment, he said, 'Hormigas'.

He meant, 'ants'. So Maturana talked about these tiny creatures, the most successful on the planet. According to him, ants are the real architects, builders of wonderful projects. They are living beings, yet they have no intelligence, no reasoning. He outlined the vision of the future, fulfilling the CDI mission in the preservation of humans as ethical, loving and entrepreneurial beings. Making this analogy with the ants – as well as honey bees – which self-manage their colonies, Maturana outlined a vision of humans as having the same organization as the ants. But, the greatest difference was the use of intelligence; in this case, the technology used as a tool for ethical, loving and entrepreneurial beings, that would lead humanity to a whole new level, constructing a new self-ruling, global society. Those were the words from one of the most respectable biologists on the planet, after three days of introspection with Peter

Senge and me. From there on, we established the concept of 'e-topia', through which we imagine a world where people use technology for the purposes of a fairer and better society.

Bringing this concept to the reality of social entrepreneurship in the world, we detected more than 200 small and medium-sized NGOs in more than 75 countries working in much the same way. There is great potential for them to become a network in order to carry out social transformation, our 'e-topia'. Together we can be much stronger than we would be working separately, with each having to publicize its own organization. This is related to what the Ashoka thinks about social entrepreneurship, the Entrepreneurship Synapse, which means neurons gathering information, reconnecting themselves and redesigning new connections. The vision we want to develop for this new CDI network is to have a network of digital inclusion NGOs and digital entrepreneurs to build a new level of technological entrepreneurship and digital empowerment. So, I invited the NGOs of digital empowerment of the world to be united with a conduct code to raise a new movement. This is a vision of a smart network. The possibility of strengthening ties toward a new level of digital empowerment is absolutely inspiring.

2015: rescuing the essence

CDI celebrates its 20-year anniversary and in order to face the current needs of society, assumer the evolution of the organization's mission. As a result, we launched a digital empowerment movement: Recode. This was an invitation to young people to reprogram the current system, and build a brand new one.

The challenge of marketing, measuring impact, and sustainability

For over 10 years, the CDI fundraising model was used by partnerships, which were responsible for ensuring sponsorship and essential support for multiple demands. We had very different kinds of support from companies and organizations (everything from *pro-bono* services, volunteer staff placements and free equipment) enabling us to start the CDI projects. This had been our business model until mid-2000. We needed to reinvent, as the global financial crisis of 2008 meant that companies started cutting their investment in social business. Non-profit foundations also began to shift focus, many concentrating more on impact. As a result, The Skoll Foundation, The Bill and Melinda Gates Foundation and others started to invest more in social business, and this suffocated the Third Sector.

As CDI had already been close to the social business model, we worked on alternatives for the organization; we had not been caught off guard. We reacted with many initiatives in the management area. The fundraising model used by most of the

Third Sector is quite perverse, being based on mostly short-term project-based grants with little thought of sustainability. As a result, it avoids long-term partnerships, imposes the creation of a specific structure for each project, does not pay the institutional development and, therefore, creates a distance between the organization and its mission. We then realized that we needed to see CDI as a product. We initiated a long process of change management, restructuring the organizational culture and the CDI identity. Part of this process involved us establishing relationships based on a more results-orientated culture and improving transparency with partners. It also meant that we were more likely to decline on some projects if they were not closely aligned to our core business. We redesigned our work process to improve efficiency and improved our human resources management: incorporating strategies for talent acquisition and employee retention, as well as allowing our teams to have greater involvement in decisions and planning.

In this new path, CDI created experiences to motivate social entrepreneurship. Two great events were born, the Startup Weekend Rio Favela (2014) and the Startup Weekend Changemakers (2015); the latter occurring in 11 cities in the world simultaneously. The main proposal of these initiatives was to build and connect strong communities of leaders and social entrepreneurs in order to create solutions for social problems and, thus, inspire and share the knowledge that everyone could be a change agent, reprogrammers of the current system and programmers of new solutions for their lives and for society.

As a result of three years of deep transformation, we redefined the purpose of the organization, present in the 'Recode Movement'. Three products were developed for contemporary needs regarding the use of technology:

1 Recode Programmes: for companies who want to invest in schools, public libraries and community centres, teaching young people how to use informatics and communication technologies (TIC, in Portuguese), problem solving and skills for the 21st century;

2 volunteering: for companies who want to involve their employees with the cause, in a way that can offer knowledge in communication, technology and CDI education management;

3 revenue generation: for we understand that the main value young people see in joining CDI is the opportunity to reposition themselves in the labour market, generate income and improve employability and entrepreneurship.

Assessing, measuring and understanding our impact

More important than the awards or my personal journey is seeing that the dream I had that night in 1993 is now spreading throughout the world. Today there are 842 CDI communities in 15 countries. More than 1.64 million people have already been positively affected by CDI.

FIGURE 2.4 CDI Impact Infographic

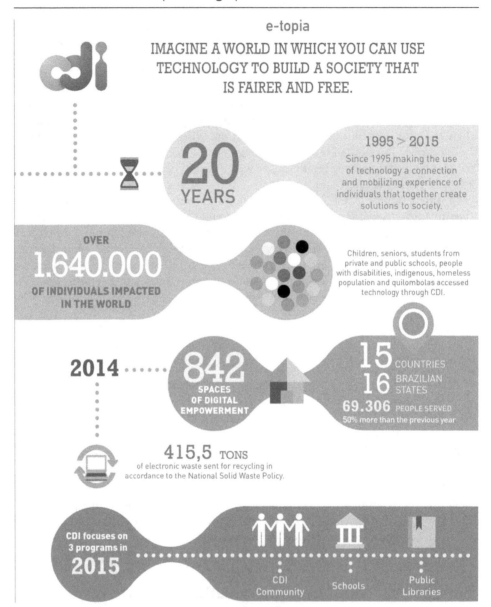

e-topia

IMAGINE A WORLD IN WHICH YOU CAN USE TECHNOLOGY TO BUILD A SOCIETY THAT IS FAIRER AND FREE.

20 YEARS

1995 > 2015
Since 1995 making the use of technology a connection and mobilizing experience of individuals that together create solutions to society.

OVER
1.640.000
OF INDIVIDUALS IMPACTED IN THE WORLD

Children, seniors, students from private and public schools, people with disabilities, indigenous, homeless population and quilombolas accessed technology through CDI.

2014

842
SPACES OF DIGITAL EMPOWERMENT

15 COUNTRIES
16 BRAZILIAN STATES
69.306 PEOPLE SERVED
50% more than the previous year

415,5 TONS
of electronic waste sent for recycling in accordance to the National Solid Waste Policy.

CDI focuses on 3 programs in **2015**

CDI Community Schools Public Libraries

Image Courtesy of CDI

Reprogramming the world

In 2015, when CDI had its 20-year anniversary, CDI launched a global movement: the 'Recode'. As a result of the evolution of the NGO's mission, CDI wants to enable people to reprogram their lives through the technology. We invite people to reprogram the current system, and build a brand new one. It happens when we see a new enlightenment in the academy, through quantum physics, molecular biology, the reinvention of science, and spiritual consciousness that prompts seeking a new quality of life. When we see people who want to reinvent democracy, like the Occupy demonstrations, outraged by the way political parties and corporate groups criminally acquire power in our countries, it represents what is to come in society.

The 'Recode' is a digital empowerment movement to reprogram the world, allowing young people to 'recode' the current system and, becoming connected, to propose new solutions for global problems. In schools, communities, and libraries, our goal is to form autonomic and connected individuals who use technology to promote a positive shift in their society. A continuous and customized learning method can enable a person, from 14 to 29 years old, to support programmes for entrepreneurship and to enter the labour market. The youth will be 'reprogrammers' of life and members of a global network that will connect them to innovative experiences worldwide.

We want to form autonomous and connected individuals who, from a new perspective, use technology as a tool to cause a positive impact on their surroundings. We need to know our time challenges, be aware of the transformational power of technology, and use it so we can create better solutions in life.

My future as a social entrepreneur

I currently live in Washington DC, where I lead the global governance of CDI and a global project for developing the social entrepreneurship field as VP Senior of Ashoka, beside Bill Drayton. Twenty years ago, when I was in Santa Marta, I could not even imagine a future for myself. I feel that I have fulfilled my pursuit of success and happiness. Different from what I used to think 20 years ago, there is no place called happiness. This place exists in the present and it is here where it flows. We need to build this place day by day. I feel fulfilled in this task. For me, the present prevails, because the past is over, and the experiences are the way to reinvention, to evolution, and to improving ourselves. But the future is being built now in the present. And, of course, in the Ashoka, CDI and in our networks, we're working to build this future.

Lessons learnt

1 *Identify opportunities in difficult situations.* In 1993 Brazil was taking the first steps in digital inclusion. This was restricted to the elite: large companies were computerizing, private schools were creating their first laboratories. Our goal at that time was already to bring technology to low-income people, and fortunately for us this made us stand out from many of the other initiatives springing up at the time. We could never have competed at any other level. The lesson is that there is always opportunity, always a gap, even in the most unlikely situations.

2 *Understand and respect diversity.* To globally expand sustainably we must understand and respect diversity. When the CDI began to expand, we had adopted the model of social franchising, to ensure expansion with quality. Our challenge from then on was to ensure alignment between different people. We needed to create a network of culture in CDI, which embraced cultural diversity among our different partners.

3 *Connect to grow.* Once a CDI organization was formed, it was necessary to create a network of people connected by purpose and passion. This view had to be suitable to our proposal , after all everyone was from different backgrounds, united in a network with a digital empowerment culture. It was a great job of co-creation.

4 *Sustainable growth is key to success.* We develop strategies to motivate and ensure the growth of our organization and the growth of leaders. We use performance evaluation tools such as impact measurement. We also propose several changes to create a development environment continue in the social sector.

Discussion questions

1 I had two great triggers that pushed me into working for social change. The first happened when, as a teenager, I had the chance to mediate in conflicts between homeless children. The other was a dream I had in which I took computers to the underserved in the slums of Rio. In your personal experience what has inspired you to become a change maker?

2 CDI's methodology encompasses the use of technology to solve social problems. What are the greatest challenges in your community and what business opportunities could you derive from them?

3 Social media and the internet are becoming increasingly important tools for activists and socially-focused organizations. Is there a danger that we might focus too much on what happens online, and forget that it is actions offline, in the real world, that often facilitate the most change?

4 The majority of people who have access to the web use technology tools for personal reasons and only a very small minority are empowered to create social change through the available tools. What could you do to help empower people to create solutions for social problems using technology?

5 Martin Luther King had a dream and engaged people in civil rights. Dreams have the power to show you an image of what you can do to improve your and others' lives. What is your dream to improve your life, your world and the world?

Further reading

You can find more material to do with this chapter at www.koganpage.com/socialentrepreneurship

The Innovators – Walter Isaacson
The Fifth Discipline – Peter M Senge
Bold – Peter Diamonds and Steven Kotler
How to Change the World – Social entrepreneurs and the power of new ideas
The Kingdom of God is Within You – Leo Tolstoy
Anna Karenina – Leo Tolstoy
Origem do Paraíso – Francis of Assisi
Quem se Importa – Documentary by Mara Mourão
I Ching – O Livro das Mutações – Richard Wilhelm
Negócios com impacto social no Brasil – Marcel Fukayama
Banker to the Poor: Micro-lending and the battle against world poverty –
    Muhammad Yunus
Creating a World without Poverty: Social business and the future of capitalism
    – Muhammad Yunus
*Building Social Business: The new kind of capitalism that serves humanity's most
    pressing needs* – Muhammad Yunus
The Fortune at the Bottom of the Pyramid – CK Prahalad and Stuart Hart
Cannibals with Forks: The triple bottom line of 21st century business – John
    Elkington
The Singularity is Near: When humans transcend biology – Ray Kurzweil

03
Patent wars: fighting big pharma to enable access to drugs for all

I-MAK – PRITI RADHAKRISHNAN

ABSTRACT

A stranger's heartbreak can be unforgettable. As I prepared for a client meeting with Rahim – his name is changed here for confidentiality reasons – I had no clue my life was about to change. An attorney by training, I was working in India as the project manager of a legal aid organization that represented and advocated for indigent HIV-positive clients. Through this work, I frequently encountered clients who could not afford anti-retroviral therapy or medications for opportunistic infection.

Rahim stood out, though. At 17 he was so severely malnourished that he looked no more than seven. He was sweet, articulate and desperately fighting to continue his education, despite his illness. The recipient of a negligent blood transfusion at a government hospital in Tamil Nadu, India, HIV had ravaged his delicate frame. As I prepared to file his petition in court to seek damages and free medication, I realized something had changed within me. After five years as an attorney, I was no longer satisfied only to advocate at the local level for impoverished patients and communities. I needed to change the systems that were standing in the way of getting treatment to all patients. I needed to bring together experts that could take on a market that was failing communities – communities whose immunologic failure could be reversed. With the right team of lawyers and scientists – those who had spent decades at law firms or pharmaceutical companies, and were committed to solving this problem – we could change the system that allowed companies to price lifesaving drugs out of reach of patients.

That is how my journey to build I-MAK – a team of lawyers and scientists committed to increasing access to affordable medicines to everyone – began.

Activism in the family

In truth, my journey began when I was seven. My Delhi-based grandfather gave me a dictionary, and these words from the Pakistani poet Faiz: 'I shall place a tongue in every link of chain that fetters me'. My grandfather was a pioneer of the working journalists' movement and a freedom fighter in Gandhi's struggle for independence. He explained to me that while he was imprisoned in Alipuram Jail, he started an underground newspaper written on slates, dreaming of a better tomorrow for the dispossessed. In that moment, my grandfather gave me a precious gift. He showed me that words are a weapon, to be used with skill and for peace.

He altered the course of my life with that gift – along with the rest of our family. I grew up thinking that it was normal to have a family for whom the ability to hold, house and uplift an entire community was not a righteous aspiration, but a calling.

I am born from this blood.

I needed to go back to the place where they did their *seva*, or service, to understand the communities that made up my family's country. I now realize that my family is anything but normal: a collective of organizers, scientists, teachers and journalists in which fierce political discussions around the dinner table were the norm. I needed to go back so I could learn how to do my own *seva*, with more depth and precision and understanding, and not from a comfortable law office in Los Angeles, or from a prestigious office desk in Geneva.

I needed to sit with communities day in and day out, year after year, to know first-hand the struggles they endured, without prescription or any assumption that I could possibly understand what needed to be done. And after sitting quietly for some time, perhaps I could begin to roll up my sleeves and take on the tasks they felt needed to be done.

I walked into a travel agent and bought a one-way ticket to Delhi.

Life-saving drugs, denied

The biggest fight loomed ahead. India, which supplied affordable medicines to most of the developing world, had reached a crossroads. It had committed to introducing a patent law that would provide ownership rights to pharmaceutical companies, a new and troubling direction for the country.

This was an ominous policy reversal. India had a long history of progressive action on affordable medicines. After ousting the British in 1947, India realized it had some of the highest medicine prices in the world, and set up a committee to investigate whether this hangover of colonial rule – the patent law – was meeting its society's needs. After finding that most patent holders were foreign companies, India made a courageous move. In 1972, the country decided to abolish its patent law, allowing for the emergence of a domestic industry that could supply its citizenry.

Over the next 25 years, India became a self-sufficient country. Without foreign companies holding monopoly rights on medicines, India was able to grow its own drug industry, and provide its citizens with more affordable drugs. Importantly, India's drug industry started supplying the developing world. It became the world's 'pharmacy for the poor'. India went from having the highest prices to the lowest prices – all by removing its patent law and promoting its own drug industry.

And in 2001, in a move that would shape the course of my own life, India broke the dominant paradigm. At a moment when Western pharmaceutical companies claimed they could not bring annual HIV drug prices below $10,000 per patient, the Indian generic industry said it would provide the medicines for less than a tenth of that cost. From that moment, India became the supplier of low-cost HIV medicines to the Global South.

But then India joined the World Trade Organization (WTO), setting in motion a series of events that led to the weakening of its own industry by providing ownership rights to pharmaceutical companies. With a new WTO-backed patent law on the way – likely to destroy the domestic generic industry – the need for action was urgent. In neighbouring countries, drug prices had surged as high as 700 per cent. And in India, drug prices began to rise after the government signalled its willingness to become a part of the international trading system.

Everyone at the Lawyers Collective got to work. For two years I visited villages across rural and urban India, working with my team to organize, educate and advocate with community members. The subject matter – patent law – was complex, but community activists who lived with HIV and cancer were able to make the issues clear to everyday people. From garment workers to sex workers, from farmers to day labourers, people realized the severity of what was happening. Together these groups mobilized, organized and came together in conjunction with treatment activists around the world. Protests took place from Delhi to Nairobi, from Bangkok to Rio, to New York and Johannesburg.

An activist re-born

In 2003, I joined the relentless human rights non-profit organization, the Lawyers Collective, which advocated for communities affected by HIV, pushing the Indian government to introduce a free programme for HIV-positive patients. I helped coordinate these efforts nationally. India expanded its free treatment programme, and patients such as Rahim underwent dramatic transformations in their health. Through this journey, I witnessed first-hand the power and direct effects of advocacy on behalf of those who cannot give voice to their lack of access to health services and treatment.

Sleepless nights: the passage of the Indian Patent(s) Act, 2005

After months of organizing, the moment came when we least expected it.

In March of 2005, the Lawyers Collective convened a meeting in Mumbai with people living with HIV and leading treatment activists from all over the Global South – Brazil, China, Sri Lanka, South Africa, Thailand and more. Our plan was to spend three days envisioning the road ahead for the global movement.

But that conversation never happened. By sheer coincidence, on the very day the leading voices of the treatment activist movement landed in Mumbai, the Indian

Parliament began debating the Patent Bill which was set to provide unfettered owner-ship rights to the multinational pharmaceutical industry. In other words, there were insufficient public health safeguards in the Bill to ensure access to affordable medicines. I have never been a big believer in destiny, but there are no other words to describe this moment.

Our coalition jumped to action to stop the Bill from passing without public health safeguards. We organized a press conference featuring activists from around the world who had spent years fighting for access to medicines. The South Africans led by writing a song that railed against HIV scepticism. The Indians led us in protest chants from the Indian labour and independence movement. The head of the Indian Cancer Patients Aid Association spoke with a trembling voice about the plight of low-income cancer patients unable to access life-saving medication.

The next morning we flew from Mumbai to Delhi, where we worked day and night for nearly a week to lobby Parliament to reject a patent law that did not include public health protections. I will never forget sitting in an office crammed with activists from all over the world, calling up Indian Members of Parliament – usually older family men – at 2 am to demand that they listen to our communities and stop the Bill that was set to pass at sunrise. We chased down parliamentarians at their homes, did media interviews and wrote article after article.

Hours later we heard that the Bill had passed, with public health safeguards. Communities alone could not have won this battle, and the generic companies alone could not have prevailed. This victory spoke to the power of the treatment activist movement from around the world, which mobilized to ensure that access could be a reality.

India took a tremendous step as a leader in the developing world to ensure that the new patent system would not override the public health of their citizens or decimate the domestic generic drug industry. The law created an open and democratic system that allows for a 'citizen review' in which anyone can register opposition to a patent. And it required pharmaceutical companies that were re-tweaking older compounds to show actual therapeutic benefit for patients. This was an unprecedented move by India, the first of any country to make a patient-centred demand of pharmaceutical companies. The global trade balances had tilted in favour of the voiceless.

Our first patent case

The thing that still surprises me even after all these years is that we won the battle and got health safeguards into the patent law. We won. Any activist will tell you that victories such as this are few and far between. When they come, we savour them. Often, we use that victory as fuel for years, to remind us that we are not simply fighting in the face of futility.

Shortly after the patent law passed, while still working at the Lawyers Collective, I created a unit to engage in citizen review of patents using the newly enacted health safeguard. Our intention was to ensure that unlawful patents would not be granted, particularly those that could block access to affordable medicines. In that capacity, our team filed the first citizen intervention using the newly enacted patent law in

India. Remarkably, we moved from protests on the street to technocratic fights at the patent office.

Our first case was filed on behalf of an organization providing life-saving drugs to low-income cancer patients at little or no cost. The case was against the Swiss company Novartis, who had obtained an exclusive right in India to an important leukaemia drug. The price of Gleevec, a drug for chronic myeloid leukaemia, had skyrocketed to $2,600 a month from $200. In a country where the majority of citizens live on less than $2 a day, where there is no comprehensive insurance system nor any broad social safety net, these cancer patients could not afford this drug even if their lives depended on it, which they did.

Over the next year we followed our case against Novartis with advocacy, using the legal system in an unprecedented way and registering our resistance to a new global trade regime that threatened the rights of low-income patients. To support the opposition, my team met with communities in a series of town hall meetings across India, explaining the legal nuances and organizing media briefings. And in fighting the case, we helped create a new movement of political resistance against unfettered private rights across the developing world. Our victory in shaping the patent law was giving birth to a whole new wave of activism.

My work on the Gleevec case had helped me understand that I could no longer serve as a community organizer and advocate. India's new patent law created a need for lawyers to take on the multinational pharmaceutical industry and the systems that propped the industry up – on their own turf. And the work had to be done not only in India, which served as the supplier to most other developing countries, but also in those recipient countries. Unless we removed patents in low- and middle-income countries as a parallel effort to our Indian opposition, access would be obstructed. There was a need for a global public interest group with top-notch intellectual property and pharmaceutical sciences expertise to represent the interests of low-income patients around the world.

Managing this group would mean that I could no longer do the work that, quite simply, made me come alive – working with people living with diseases within their communities, addressing their immediate legal and advocacy needs. But I was needed elsewhere – to help create the team of highly skilled and nimble lawyers and scientists, who could help stop the seemingly unstoppable pharmaceutical industry, that would be I-MAK.

However, I still shuddered at the thought of managerial responsibility and administrative work, of leaving my communities in India to work globally. The thought of focusing exclusively on patents instead of working comprehensively on access issues terrified me. In fact, I could not think of anything less interesting than working on patent issues from a desk in New York rather than engaging daily with the Indian institutions and individuals obstructing access for my clients, and taking action locally. If anyone was ever reluctant, it was me.

And yet, that is where my life was headed.

At the time I didn't pause to stop and think about the decision. The long road to becoming a human rights lawyer and community organizer gave me a profound understanding of the commitment that I was about to make in starting down a new path – one that would be longer and more intensive than anything I had ever experienced. I was prepared for those challenges. For me this was no longer a choice. I was compelled by my experiences to make this commitment to the communities I had worked and fought alongside. And, with a generous offer made by seed funders who wanted to launch I-MAK, I had the ability to make that commitment a reality.

The early days

My initial drive and enthusiasm to take the opportunity took me away from my work at the Lawyers Collective in a direction which would lead to the creation of what was needed – a new global, tightly focused, nimble organization. Out of this, I-MAK was born. We hit the ground running. Myself and the other co-founders, interns and consultants huddled around my dining table working on cases late into the night. We hopped on planes and filed cases in the patent offices of Kolkata, Chennai, Mumbai and Delhi, building relationships with patent examiners and learning the system from the inside out.

Those were lonely days. Other NGOs shunned us as they felt that our intervention could have been built into one of their existing organizations. We felt they did not understand the necessity for a new organization, one that could be nimble and responsive, that would not face bureaucratic hurdles and bottlenecks. Where they saw insult, we saw opportunity, and it took many years for us to repair the relationships that grew strained during that time.

But we plodded on, confident in our vision. We filed case after case, built our team of lawyers and scientists, raised money, built our board, and put up a website. Step by step, I-MAK came into its own. I can recall taking 60 flights a year in those early years, speaking publicly, attending conferences, visiting patent offices and communities without access across the developing world. I was on the road to building a lasting organization, but I was also walking down a path to burnout. I just didn't know it yet.

Political and personal struggles

My story is incomplete without details of the political context of this period, and my personal struggles as a consequence.

In July 2006, with I-MAK still in its infancy, my soon-to-be-husband and activist partner was a target of racial profiling. As a Muslim of Pakistani-British descent, he had the misfortune of flying from Mumbai to London the week of the Mumbai bomb blasts of 11 July, 2006. He had finished giving a talk for generic companies, and stepped onto the plane, thinking of nothing but work, visiting his ageing parents in London and coming back to India to be with me. However, he never made it: at the consulate of India in the United Kingdom, he was denied a visa back to India without explanation. I will never forget the moment when the police arrived at my Bangalore apartment to investigate him, when they tapped his Indian mobile phone, or when I opened his closet, and, painstakingly and with an ache in my heart, packed his clothes into suitcases.

One injustice compounded another. For a year we lived apart, yet continued our work to ensure access to medicines, and took care of our relationship by meeting in Brazil, South Africa and numerous parts of the United States and the United Kingdom. But the political fallout against Muslims in the post-9/11 world had changed everything.

In our visits to the United States and United Kingdom, I sat waiting as my partner was taken away for 'secondary inspection' or selected for a 'random security check', often spending uncertain hours in anguish wondering whether I would see him again, or whether we would be allowed to enter the country. We wanted, badly, to be angry and hurt. Instead, we learned to practise compassion and forgiveness.

This, I thought, was the true test.

In late 2006, I received an e-mail in Delhi that altered my life forever. My 'little brother', Vinay, had leukaemia. Without hesitation I packed up my belongings and moved to Boston. My entire life shifted in focus, both to the United States and to a new role. I became his caregiver: nurturing, sustaining, healing. Vinay needed a bone-marrow transplant and there weren't enough minority donors for him – or other patients – to find a match. So I started a bone marrow donor campaign. We beat every record: 25,000 minority donors in eight weeks. Sheltered by our community's strength, we cared for thousands.

Against the backdrop of these challenges, my work had to continue. I worked from Vinay's room at the Dana-Farber Cancer Institute, and was blessed to have guardian angels such as Jim Kim, who ensured I had a space to work at the Harvard School of Public Health. At every critical step of the journey, I had benefactors who helped me and ensured that the work could continue. From these rooms in Boston, I-MAK filed one of our most important patent challenges, against a company called Abbott Laboratories, to increase affordable access to the HIV drug Kaletra.

In early 2008, my childhood best friend, Priya, died of a sudden neurological complication. We sang to Priya's body as she slipped away. Then, Vinay succumbed to the leukaemia. Organizing two funerals two months apart, and reciting prayers for parents saying goodbye to their children, are fates I wouldn't wish upon anyone.

'Om purnamadah purnamidam … when fullness is taken away, fullness still remains.'

In the months that followed, I allowed myself to completely absorb the loss. The years of working 100-hour weeks in India, of constant travel to rural villages and visits across the urban centres of many countries in the Global South, had caught up with me. In my deepest grief I recognized that losing my dearest friends was compounded by years of working with people living with serious diseases. I watched children being taken away to orphanages and ashrams as their parents succumbed to opportunistic infection, and parents holding their dying children because HIV treatment was unavailable. Seeing these moments year after year had broken my spirit. To lose friends I had known longer than any others made life feel unbearable. At 30, I turned away from my work, feeling a visceral rejection of any mention of access to medicines from the open wound inside of me.

Healing

During the following year – 2009 – I made a daily choice not to yield to the traumatic stress that threatened to engulf me. I went inward and I went deep. I danced, cooked, practised yoga, cried, knit, laughed, planted and taught pilates. Pilates, an approach to mind-body movement, would ground me in the years to come. I learned to nurture myself with the same intensity and gentle touch I gave to others. This descendant of a Gandhian family had to learn that *seva*, or service, must be practised through non-duality: there is no difference between you and others. Loving-kindness must be imparted to all, equally. Even in the face of tragedy. Even to your own self.

And through this journey, I learned to let go of my work. No longer did I have the desire or the drive to bulldoze through my caseload, stay up through sleepless nights or fight with gentle ferocity to make changes within a system that imposed seemingly endless structural resistance. With a heavy heart, and a significant amount of guilt, I let go, gently, of my work. I slowed down significantly, only taking on what I could accomplish without my heart. It made me feel less alive, but looking back, it gave me the space I needed to heal and move forward. It is one of the hardest lessons I have learned and it needed me to completely crumple in order for it to happen.

Another loss

On this new path of *seva*, I learned to meditate through the layers of dizzying loss, and sit with my *satya*, or truth. Loss changes you: it goes to the very integrity of the structures that comprise you and it erodes and remakes them. My husband and I – we were different now.

Forgiving myself for changing was the hardest step of my journey. It taught me how to move halfway into my *asana*, upside down and in between, how to breathe into the unknown. It compelled me to just be, to accept what is real. And once self-forgiveness came, the rest fell into place. With grace, love and honesty, I said goodbye to the man who had danced in my heart for nearly a decade. There is an agony and a joy that unfolds when we tap into the courage we never knew lived within us, a wholeness that emerges when we are strong enough to listen to the voice that resides in the shadows of that temple within.

The voice says, 'fly.'
I'm soaring now ...

Finding my way back

After nearly three years tending to the work of my soul, I acknowledged that my relationship to my work was now different. I accepted my detachment from the subject matter, although I continued to feel wistful about the impact that my loss of passion would have on communities I worked with. I viewed the shift within me with the finality that young people do when they don't know any better, when they don't know that life keeps changing and that, with it, you will, too. I looked at my days as a fiery treatment activist as a relic of the past, with a mixture of bittersweet relief and guilt. But then, as they do, things changed again.

Sometimes it doesn't take a life-altering moment to bring you back. After walking on a very dark road for a very long time with nothing to illuminate the path, I had learned to just place one foot in front of the other, find steady ground, and to keep on moving. And then one day, just like that, I walked myself into the light. I just stepped into my old-new self and found an energy. I'll never understand how it happened, but maybe I don't need to. What matters is that I never formally left I-MAK during those years. My organization, my co-founder, my board and everyone around me were supportive of re-designing my role to meet my reality during those difficult days. For this I will be eternally grateful.

After I found my way back to my work, I discovered a new energy to advocate on issues of access to treatment. As I-MAK expanded to new countries, to new diseases, I found myself engaged and inspired by my partners in middle-income countries, and delighted to discover my old skills of excavating information and strategically intervening to support communities in their quest to increase access to medicines.

The truth, for me, is that burnout happened in part because in my line of work I am never going to meet the vast majority of people I have helped. There was no energy coming back my way to help restore and fuel me for the next round. On top of that, in the private sector, compensation or revenue help determine an individual or institution's worth. In the NGO sector, particularly in health, most of the value is derived from public profile. It is why even the best NGOs are drawn into the ego game, and it is why the lack of recognition or profile can start to affect people with the most noble of intentions. It took me years to recognize these realities and even longer to design a life that could nourish me and enable me to work effectively.

In the last year, I have finally dissolved the guilt that I carried for lessening my role in I-MAK. To others it sounds crazy that I would carry guilt when I cared for a cancer patient, ran a bone marrow campaign to help save a life, and recovered from the unexpected loss of my two best friends. But my commitment to treatment activism was so unwavering that I did not understand what to do next. We do a disservice to the work, and to the communities that we serve, when we give 300 per cent of ourselves to it. That's a sure-fire recipe for burnout. It decides for us that we will not last over time. It depletes us long before it should.

Today, I work differently. I take pride in the fact that I have been a treatment activist for a decade, and that I-MAK is now in its seventh year of operation. But as I board a flight to Pakistan or South Africa or Argentina, I stop to buy a neck pillow. I mark off days in my calendar to recoup when I get back. I teach mindful movement three days a week in New York City, ensuring I have a practice that grounds me, that helps me remember the mind–body connection, and that balances my activism.

And this summer, when we were dealt a severe blow with the unanticipated death of a staff member, I paused to absorb the loss. Not only was he the driving force behind I-MAK's scientific work, he was a friend and a mentor as well. After years of dealing with loss, I felt unprepared for yet another goodbye. But this time was different, because I instinctively gave myself the space to absorb the shock, to grieve, to express the pain, to send love to his family, and months later to begin to rebuild our team. This time there was no guilt around the process and no self-forgiveness needed. I had finally learned that when life happens, resistance is futile.

Reflections on impact and our journey so far

When thinking about real impact and how to design for it, I realized that, for an activist, the ultimate expression of love is real, measurable change. As taught by impact expert, Kevin Starr, there are two questions that matter the most: what are we trying to do, and do we know that it is working? I started to apply rigorous tools for impact measurement as a vital component of advocacy. I brought evidence-based insights into the field of access to treatment to show which strategies were and were not working and how they could be improved. As Gandhi famously said, 'Be the change that you wish to see in the world'. Learning to understand and measure our impact, while organizing with love, allowed us to be that change.

And so we worked tirelessly to show that it was possible for a small group of individuals to combat injustice. In doing so, we sought to 'lead from behind' by providing niche technical expertise to affected communities and serve as the front line of defence against corporations, shaping the global agenda around unjustified patents, which were being ignored at the cost of human life. I-MAK has filed or technically supported patent challenges in multiple jurisdictions around the world, including Argentina, Brazil, China, Egypt, Europe, India, Morocco, Russia, Thailand, the United States and Ukraine (a total of 42 countries). We have landscaped or filed patent challenges related to eight different diseases (including HIV, HCV, HPV, pneumococcal, rotavirus, tuberculosis, leukaemia and diabetes) and 15 related therapies. To date, I-MAK is the only global legal entity focused exclusively on drug patent challenges, pharmaceutical patent informatics and market intelligence, and social justice.

As a result of this work, I-MAK has been able to elevate the under-the-radar issue of unjustified patents and their impact on people across the world. Over the last 10 years, we won more than 90 per cent of the patent cases that we filed, selectively targeting only unjustified patents that have blocked the possibility of low-cost generic versions from entering the market. The work challenging patents in India, a global supplier country, on just three HIV drugs alone has enabled half a billion dollars in cost savings over the last five years.

These victories only drove us to want to do more. The exploding hepatitis C epidemic kills 700,000 people every year, and community members reached out to us to file or support cases on key hepatitis C patents to remove barriers for six key countries – Argentina, Brazil, China, India, Russia and Ukraine, which can potentially result in more than $270 *billion* in cost savings. We are already seeing results: we won the case in China, the first civil-society case of its kind filed against the pharmaceutical industry in that country. After this victory, Gilead Sciences (self-described as 'a research-based biopharmaceutical company focused on the discovery, development, and commercialization of innovative medicines') sat down at the negotiating table for the first time with the Chinese government. And initial cases in India and Ukraine, where we partnered and supported local HIV-positive networks, have been successful: the patent offices decided to reject key patent applications, which garnered hundreds of articles in the global, mainstream press. At the time of this writing, we are focused on ensuring that people living in low- and middle-income countries are not denied life-saving treatment as a result of unjustified hepatitis C patents.

Defining our structure, strategy and approach

In 2013–14, I-MAK's revenue increased by more than $100,000. Our general and administrative costs remain low as we intentionally run a lean organization, directing 83 per cent of funds to programmes and services and leveraging a pool of consultants on targeted interventions to operate cost effectively.

Looking back, however, starting a non-profit organization was a stroke of luck. In 2006, I was living with a close friend and her husband in Bangalore. They were a married couple from California, and one night over dinner after I returned home from a town hall meeting we stayed up late into the night talking. I was irate about the price of the Novartis leukaemia drug in India, and distressed at how low-income patients could access the drug until the case was resolved, if an injunction against generics was issued. My friends asked if I had thought about starting my own organization to address this problem on a global scale. I said I hadn't, and they asked what it would cost to get it off the ground. When I responded that I had no idea, they told me they wanted to write me a check for $200,000 to see what I could get done.

In retrospect, I marvel at my luck. It is the dream of most entrepreneurs to have such friends, and such a moment. We did not know it at the time, but a year later, my friend's husband would be diagnosed with cancer. He would go on to beat it back home in California. And his and their generosity would ensure that other patients without access to medicines would have an opportunity to do the same.

Nearly 10 years have passed since that moment. And in those 10 years, I-MAK's mission became increasingly visible, thanks to the incredible support of organizations like Doctors without Borders/Médecins Sans Frontières. Our work flourished in large part because of the relationships we built along the way, growing the team and the resources we needed to file and win cases, and to use this evidence to change the public conversation and offer new solutions to the access problem.

Today, I-MAK has become something of a go-to organization on the issue of drug patents and pricing, for media, policymakers and other key stakeholders. This growth has taken time, and is the result of our unwillingness to compromise on our vision and our principles. We were careful and deliberate in growing our business, because, at the end of the day, a non-profit organization is a business like any other. We guarded our mission with gentle tenacity, and remained steadfast in our belief that over time we would receive the opportunity to change seemingly entrenched systems dominated by well funded and powerful opposition.

Reflections on a journey not yet complete

In one of the critical turning points in my journey as an activist, I began to integrate a principle that my friend and activist Ai-Jen Poo taught me – to 'organize with love'. Most of us activists run on the fuel of passion, adrenaline or even anger at injustice. When you organize with love – engaging governments, companies and international institutions as partners instead of advocacy targets – a shift takes place. I found that I was no longer depleting myself of critical energy reserves. And that internal shift also reflected itself externally. This new approach drove collaborative responses and moved debates that were previously entrenched in disagreement.

Victory

After all of this learning and evolving, I had completely let go of any expectation of winning. Being a treatment activist means you learn how to fight against structural resistance month after month, year after year, with little expectation of conquering the system. I had survived on passion and adrenaline years ago when I filed important cases that I hoped might open the door to affordable medicines for the Global South. And, now, I had learned to work through the phases when my passion felt extinguished. But I rarely, if ever, wondered how the story would end.

In 2011, we won the case against Abbott Labs for an HIV drug, the one we first filed sitting in that hospital room in Boston. I remember the moment I heard the news. I was incredulous, filled with disbelief. It had taken four years for the decision to come down. That a few lawyers and scientists sitting on their laptops could take on a behemoth company with an army of lawyers and unlimited funds was improbable. Yet the Indian law itself gave us the opening, since it allowed for 'citizen review' of patents at little or no cost. All it took was a team of experts who cared enough to commit to the cause. On our first three cases alone, we estimated that more than 700,000 lives would be affected in the first five years. Margaret Mead's quote, which I had always believed to be true, came alive for me at this moment:

> Never doubt that a small group of thoughtful, committed citizens can change the world. Indeed, it's the only thing that ever has.

In 2013, those words rang true again. Eight years after the first case against Novartis was filed, eight years of work by lawyers, activists and patients around the world, the Indian Supreme Court decided in favour of patients, the access to medicines movement and of India to preserve its right to enact health safeguards in the context of trade. The victory was groundbreaking, and I sat in stunned silence for nearly a day and absorbed what it meant to win with this leukaemia drug. The next day, the *New York Times* called to ask what I-MAK thought of the decision. Our response was swift and decisive: the ripple effects of this decision would be felt across the globe, and other low- and middle-income countries would follow India's lead. Beyond increased access to affordable versions of this leukaemia drug, other countries including Argentina have now moved to protect public health within their patent regimes.

In the end, this victory took eight years to come to fruition. Eight long, lonely, tiring years of my own life, years where I wondered if our movement would ever make a dent in the uncompromising machinery of the pharmaceutical industry, or the systems that protect profits at the expense of human life. Eight agonizing years of watching children say goodbye to their parents, and parents say goodbye far too early to their children. If this decade has taught me anything, it is that great change takes time, and patience is the cornerstone of *seva*.

And today my understanding of that *seva* is different. It is no longer a perception of giving wholly of oneself, of service at the expense of the self. I ensure that work–life balance exists, and I serve as a mentor to younger activists and entrepreneurs to help them shape their lives to best serve themselves, and to best serve the work. In the end, the lesson I learned on duality at a meditation retreat is the one I continually come back to, remembering I am not different or disconnected from the communities I seek to serve, or the world, which I believe are interconnected. So today, *seva* to myself is an integral part of my larger service.

Integration

As I sit here today, writing these words, it amazes me how much has happened in the last decade. I think about my grandfather seeing me now, sitting at this small wood table, typing furiously, feeling proud because I am flourishing. The drive he instilled in me, the drive he possessed every working day of his life to give voice to marginalized communities, still propels me forward. His values of living simply, as a senior-level journalist until the end of his days without a car or a telephone, are ones I share and constantly strive to emulate. I believe that if he could see I-MAK, now working across the world with communities in many countries, working on more diseases, with a growing team, I think he would be over the moon.

I look back on the last decade of my life and sometimes think that I wouldn't wish it on anyone. But the truth is, my hardships gave me new life. This great and sometimes overwhelming grief showed me parts of life that I may have been too caught up in to otherwise notice. In the end it was my very suffering that 'compelled me to reach'. And that's my (simple, complex, boundless) truth.

Lessons learnt

1 *Never underestimate the power of giving voice to the voiceless.* Throughout my journey, I witnessed first-hand the power and direct effects of advocacy and, despite the enormous scale of the challenge, we threw ourselves at it and gave it our all.

2 *Victories can come in surprising, and unexpected places.* Even though you may think it's unlikely you'll win, that should never stop you from trying. The tougher the challenge, the bigger the reward.

3 *It takes a village or, in our case, a community.* Sometimes even the most unlikely of alliances can come together if they share a common purpose and goal. With I-MAK, our victories would not have been possible without a wide group of global companies and activists.

4 *Turn your anger into something positive.* When you come across an injustice in the world, channel your energies into finding a solution. Show compassion and understanding, even if you don't agree with the other's viewpoint.

5 *Remember to look after yourself, and be aware of burnout.* We do a disservice to the work, and to the communities that we serve, when we give 300 per cent of ourselves to it.

Discussion questions

1 Like Priti's grandfather, is there anyone in your life that has directly influenced the course of your life? Who, and how?

2 How do you feel about people's lack of access to life-saving drugs? Should it be a basic human right to have access to treatment if it exists, and is available?

3 How important is it that highly skilled and professional people, such as lawyers, turn their backs on lucrative business careers and take on issues, such as drug patents, that few other people could tackle?

4 'Companies who spend vast amounts of money on research and development should be entitled to sell the end product at whatever price they like, even if that does mean some of the poorest and most vulnerable people in society can't afford them.' Discuss.

5 Priti's story talks about unexpected tragedy and an unforeseen stroke of luck that led her on her path. Does anything about this resonate in your own life? What do you think it would take for you to live with purpose, and be the change you wish to see in the world?

Further reading

You can find more material to do with this chapter at www.koganpage.com/socialentrepreneurship

Dying for Drugs (film): www.cultureunplugged.com/play/5080/Dying-For-Drugs [accessed 10 December 2015]

Fire in the Blood (film): http://fireintheblood.com [accessed 10 December 2015]

Angell, M (2005) *The Truth About the Drug Companies: How they deceive us and what to do about It*, Random House

http://www.i-mak.org [accessed 10 December 2015]

http://poptech.org/popcasts/priti_radhakrishnan_health_access [accessed 10 December 2015]

Challenges to India's Pharmaceutical Patent Laws, Science Policy Forum, 29 July 2012

04

Data science, technology and design for social justice

VISUALIZING IMPACT – JESSICA ANDERSON AND JOUMANA AL JABRI

ABSTRACT

When was the last time you came across a spreadsheet that made you laugh, cry, or spring to action? Our human brains are narratively and visually wired. Even highly trained statisticians understand, remember, and act on visualized information more effectively than tabulated raw data (Nate Silver, 2014). This is because well-executed visuals have the power to reveal hidden connections and mute numeric noise, placing insights at the forefront. This makes data journalism a powerful tool for advocacy. The goals and strategies of the advocacy community, meanwhile, can link knowledge to concrete human struggles.

Visualizing Impact (VI) applies data science, technology, and design to communicate critical social issues. The experiences of co-founders Ramzi Jaber and Joumana al Jabri provide context for its emergence amidst social, political, and economic unrest in the Middle East and North Africa (MENA) region. Their first collaboration on TEDxRamallah brought them close to the problems that sit at the heart of VI: access to information; the impact of power asymmetries on knowledge dissemination; and the 'infoxication', or feeling of disorientation resulting from information overload, created by modern trends in communication.

The chapter's chronological exploration of VI focuses on the initiation of its pilot project, Visualizing Palestine (VP), and its transition toward an expanded mandate. VI's work now covers topics such as censorship in post-revolution Egypt, MENA youth unemployment and digital rights. It has been used globally to support advocacy and education in 79 cities across 29 countries. Here we offer a glimpse into the mechanics, impact model, and mindset of a team operating remotely across a fractured physical landscape and constantly changing digital landscape.

Monday afternoons in Beirut

Weekly team meetings at Visualizing Impact make an interesting scene. The largest part of the Visualizing Impact team gathers in the garden of a Beirut co-working space. The setting feels almost embryonic, offering a rare pocket of tranquillity in a vibrant but chaotic city with less than one square metre of green space per capita. At the centre of the table, a laptop connects the Beirut team to colleagues in Amman, Dubai, Ramallah, Cairo, Milan and Toronto. They exchange a repeated chorus of 'hello' and 'can-you-hear-me?', in multiple languages. At 4 pm Beirut time, co-founder Ramzi Jaber, based in Toronto, is still on his first coffee of the day. The VI tech team is a full day ahead of the rest of the team in their work week, operating on Amman, Ramallah and Cairo's Sunday to Thursday schedule. Remote options have become commonplace in the modern workforce, but dealing with disconnections – from distance to power outages to sub-par wi-fi access – is essential to maintaining cohesion in the fractured Middle East and North Africa (MENA) region.

FIGURE 4.1   Part of the VI team gathers in Beirut, Lebanon.
From left: Shorouq Ghneim, Chris Fiorello, Jessica Anderson, Joumana al Jabri, Ramzi Jaber, Livia Bergmeijer, Ahmad Barclay, Fadi Shayya

For as long as Visualizing Impact has been operating, journalists in Beirut, Lebanon, one of its main bases, have predicted that this tiny country could be pulled into the devastating Syrian conflict next door. In many ways, Beirut is a city deeply strained by conflict, both past and present. In July 2015, the government halted waste removal services, leaving 20,000 tonnes of refuse to pile up in the streets and triggering the formation of a large protest movement focused on government corruption (Aljazeera, 2015). Just a week after the start of the garbage crisis, one of the major power plants serving Beirut suddenly shut down, leaving the already energy-challenged capital mostly in the dark for a full week (Mohammad Zaatari, 2015). And as the international media heavily covered Europe's refugee crisis, Lebanon was hosting more refugees per capita than any country in the world, including a conservative count of 1.2 million Syrian refugees alongside a national population of 4.3 million. Yet if these conditions represent Beirut through one eye, the other eye will find the city's thriving creative culture, artistic hubs, and growing entrepreneurship ecosystem.

Joumana al Jabri

In 2004, a few years into her professional life as an architect, Joumana al Jabri joined two partners in co-founding an architecture firm in Beirut. A year into their work, they were in the process of securing a first investment for a norm-breaking residential project. On 14 February 2005, a Monday, a large explosion went off a few hundred metres away from their office location, shattering the glass of their rooftop office. The explosion targeted and killed Lebanese Prime Minister Rafik Hariri and 22 others. Within 24 hours, the investors pulled out and the project went with them. The assassination set in motion the withdrawal of the nearly three decade-old Syrian military presence in Lebanon which, combined with the absence of Hariri, deeply shifted the country's political landscape.

Over a year later, the firm's partners were set to begin construction on a project they had been conceptualizing with six other creative companies for several months. They would be turning a warehouse at the fringes of Beirut into a space to house those creative companies and provide public programming, a model rarely found in the region at the time. The partner companies on the project had processed an advance payment for the first six months of rent. On 12 July 2006, as Joumana was preparing documents for contractors, she received word that the Israeli military had struck the Beirut International Airport, freezing major economic activity. During the 34-day war that followed, the partners scattered and the project halted. The firm closed completely a few months later.

From political to economic instability

A few days into the war, Joumana left Beirut, joining a friend and colleague, Hani Asfour, on a visionary project in Dubai. The project sponsors wanted to disrupt the real-estate devoured city, building its knowledge economy. When the world economic crisis set in, over half of all construction projects in Dubai were put on hold or cancelled. In her third case of *force majeure*, Joumana's entire team was laid off in 2009.

The word 'dissatisfaction' comes to mind when Joumana reflects on the circumstances surrounding her work at the time, and the energy she spent with no output. Her experiences inspired her to explore whether it might be possible to achieve long-term impact through smaller, short-term outputs. Such an approach could advance incrementally while withstanding likely disruptions. She also developed a much stronger awareness of her desire to connect her professional path to a larger exploration of personal and collective purpose and potential. One of these explorations included the initiation and co-organization of the Palestine Children's Relief Fund's participation in the 2010 Dubai Marathon, where Ramzi Jaber registered as the first full-length runner.

Ramzi Jaber

At the time of registering for the marathon, Ramzi was in the early years of his career in Dubai as a structural engineer. Like Joumana, he was working in the shadow of the economic crisis, but only one of the projects he was working on, the Dubai Pearl, was affected. His drive to explore different approaches was not about external disruption, but about a recently discovered passion for behavioural science. He was particularly fascinated by studies on the power of networks, and how ideas, norms, and behaviours spread. For example, having obese friends in your first degree network raises your risk of obesity by 45 per cent. If your friends' friends are obese, your risk is still 25 per cent higher. Even if your friends' friends' friends – people you've never met – are obese, your risk is 10 per cent higher (Nicholas Christakis, 2010). As he read up on human psychology and economics, Ramzi found himself relating such insights to social problems close to his experience. The combination consistently triggered his creative energy, and a vision began to take shape.

In the midst of mapping out his next step, Ramzi started reached out to TED organizers. Although applications for the upcoming TEDIndia conference were closed, his consistent efforts to connect resulted in an exception. He was invited to attend the event, organized around the theme 'the Future Beckons'. There, he had space to engage with a group of people who had taken risks and weathered failures to bring innovative perspectives to their fields. During the event, TED organizers from New York saw 'Palestine' on Ramzi's name tag and suggested that he should organize a TEDx event – an independent conference in the style of TED. By the time he left, the momentum around the idea led him to apply for a licence for TEDxRamallah under the theme 'inspiring stories of Palestine'.

TEDxRamallah

From the start, TEDxRamallah was a uniquely difficult event to organize, especially from the perspective of inclusiveness. It had to mirror the complex geographical, political, and social realities of the community it highlighted; who were under siege in Gaza, under occupation in the West Bank, and barred from returning in the diaspora. While accounting for these conditions, TEDxRamallah also aspired to move beyond them, bringing forward human truths. A passionate team of people joined Ramzi to take up this challenge. Joumana came on board in what would be their first formal collaboration. From London, future Visualizing Impact information architect

Ahmad Barclay set up a live-streaming programme. Hani Asfour, founding partner of Polypod, an award winning Beirut-based multidisciplinary studio, offered to do TEDxRamallah's branding. Polypod later became a core partner and creative force within Visualizing Impact. When it went live, TEDxRamallah hosted its 28 talks in three cities in the Middle East and live-streamed them to 20 cities around the world. The speakers were diverse, from Pulitzer Prize winning poet Alice Walker to Palestinian hip hop collective DAM to comedians, filmmakers, architects, engineers, entrepreneurs, and human rights professionals.

From stories to action

While organizing TEDxRamallah in the midst of the Arab Spring, Ramzi began to hear stories of content disappearing from social media platforms with no explanation. In 2010, digital rights activist Jillian C York wrote a post about the discovery that Facebook had blocked users from creating new pages featuring the word 'Palestinian', an issue they later resolved (Jillian C York, 2010). Meanwhile, the Egyptian activists behind the now-famous 'We Are All Khaled Said' Facebook page struggled with account closures because, in the context of revolutionary struggle against an authoritarian regime, they refused to use their real names to administer the page (Anver Emon *et al*, 2011). Particularly in countries where freedom of expression is threatened, Ramzi saw such reports as emblematic of the vulnerability of free speech in digital spaces. As a Stanford University 'Ripples to Waves' social entrepreneur in residence, he experimented with technology and the idea of setting up a platform to gather data on how social media platforms control user content. Rebecca MacKinnon, an internet freedom advocate, co-founder of Global Voices and director of Ranking Digital Rights, partnered with Ramzi for the first iteration of the project. Later York, Director of International Freedom of Expression with the Electronic Frontier Foundation (EFF), joined as co-founder of Onlinecensorship.org. In 2014, the site won the Knight New Challenge on 'strengthening the Internet for freedom of expression and innovation'.

As he developed Onlinecensorship.org, Ramzi continued to reflect on his own story and identity. 'Even as a Palestinian who grew up immersed in certain narratives about justice', he notes, 'I was inundated with information and data about my own community that I didn't know'. How, then, could he expect those with a less direct connection to the history and experiences of Palestinians to show interest or concern? He started pairing the data and statistics with true human stories. One such story was of his dating a woman who held a different coloured ID from him, affording them different rights. Though they were both Palestinian, she carried an East Jerusalem ID and he a West Bank ID. According to Human Rights Watch, over 640,000 Palestinians are at risk of forced separation from a direct family member (spouse, sibling, parent) due to Israel's ID policy (Human Rights Watch, 2012). They lived only a few miles apart, but had to travel to and from their meetings in different vehicles using different roads. In the West Bank, 79 kilometres of roadway are reserved exclusively for use by vehicles with yellow Israeli licence plates. An additional 155 kilometres are subject to restricted use by Palestinians.

Visualizing Palestine

Ramzi had a need to better communicate social justice narratives. Joumana needed continuously to explore her dissatisfaction with current ways of working. They found alignment on the relevance of data science, technology, and design to these needs, and in 2012, Visualizing Palestine became Visualizing Impact (VI)'s pilot and flagship project. Each of the team members who joined VP, which would later become VI, had their own personal drivers, contributing to a collective with diverse skills and backgrounds, but a common belief in challenging the status quo. A strong tenet of their collaboration is a willingness to repeatedly engage with what is dissatisfying and to test alternative approaches.

The access to knowledge movement

Imagine for a moment that someone created a useful map of a complex city. Perhaps you are visiting that city for the first time, or perhaps you have lived there your entire life. The developers of the map are experts, and they make sure that the results of their cutting-edge work are free and available online. With the way we often treat knowledge today, celebrating its production rather than analysing its reception, the map's story might end there. But to the person lost on the ground, no navigation tool matters unless it is in their hands. To the lifelong resident of the city, the map might not make sense at all if it doesn't resonate with the language and cultural symbols they use as a basis for understanding the space. Numerous other factors could prevent the map from serving as a resource to someone in this hypothetical scenario, and addressing those limitations is as important as creating the map itself.

In 2003, a conference in Berlin produced an ambitious vision for the dissemination of knowledge. 'The Internet has fundamentally changed the practical and economic realities of distributing scientific knowledge and cultural heritage', the Berlin Declaration on Open Access to Knowledge begins. 'For the first time ever, the Internet now offers the chance to constitute a global and interactive representation of human knowledge, including cultural heritage and *the guarantee of worldwide access*' (emphasis added) (2003). By 2013, over 450 organizations signed the declaration, which was a major milestone in the mobilization of the Access to Knowledge (A2K) movement.

One of the movement's great successes has been its ability to define certain types of knowledge as a public good. This mentality is now evident within many of the largest and most well-funded development organizations, as well as entrepreneurial spaces, where Creative Commons and open technology licensing has become symbolic of socially innovative approaches.

Today, the United Nations has a task force dedicated to the role of science, technology and innovation in advancing the Millennium Development Goals (and the new Social Development Goals), describing itself as 'at the forefront in the drive to establish open access to information and technology' (Calestous and Yee-Cheong, 2015). In 2012, the World Bank spent $690 million on core knowledge services

(World Bank, 2013), much of which is freely available online via its Open Knowledge Repository. But as investment in and commitment to A2K rises, it is important to reflect on challenges that limit the concept of access.

Analysing openness

In 2014, the World Bank released a study assessing the effectiveness of the policy reports it shared on its Open Knowledge Repository. Unsurprisingly, the study found that 31 per cent of the reports had never been downloaded, while 87 per cent had never been cited in any other relevant work (Doerte Doemeland, 2014), despite the reports' explicit aim to shape and influence debates on development policy. Far from a condemnation of open access, the study is a reminder that even open knowledge cannot influence closed minds or closed spaces. It is an invitation for the broader field of knowledge creators, from academics to policy makers to alternative media groups to human rights advocates, to think about the tools they use and the choices they make to communicate. On a personal level, the study mirrored VI team members' own struggles to bring new information into spaces where decisions and opinions on social issues take shape and are made.

If knowledge on social issues is a public good – something worthy of worldwide access – how can we ensure that it is legible to more people, particularly those who are typically marginalized from the production and dissemination of this knowledge? Ultimately, the question is: is our content *really* accessible? To whom? Knowledge creators make choices about which audiences to target. These choices influence the issues we prioritize as well as the language, tone, and medium of communication. Habits audiences have developed about where and how to seek trustworthy information also influence the absorption of data on social issues. Finally, the fast paced and demanding environment surrounding media consumption leads to fatigue and ever-shortening attention spans.

Communicating on power and justice

Power asymmetries in our communities deeply influence the production and dissemination of information. While organizing TEDxRamallah, Ramzi was heavily exposed to the specific power imbalances that influence communication on Israel and Palestine. Because of this, Palestine became the initial context for Visualizing Impact as it explored problems of access and communication up close.

Israel is indisputably the stronger player in terms of both hard power (military, security) and soft power (diplomacy, public relations). In April 2008, Israel established a National Information Directorate, which centralized core messages related to its goals and perspective. The Israeli Ministry of Foreign Affairs has spent tens of millions of dollars disseminating these messages through its 'Brand Israel' campaign (Sarah Shulman, 2011). The American Israel Public Affairs Committee (AIPAC), the largest pro-Israel lobbying organization, has an annual budget of over $60 million to influence

US policy and public opinion (Robert Dreyfuss, 2009). The centralized power provided by these and other factors serves to obscure narratives focused on human rights and social justice.

For years, certain topics relevant to the Palestinian context were taboo in mainstream media, such as the non-violent Boycott, Divestment, and Sanctions movement. After Operation Protective Edge (OPE) in 2014, *New York Times* public editor Margaret Sullivan wrote a letter that addressed some specific persisting issues related to the objectivity of *Times* reporters (Margaret Sullivan, 2014). She highlights specific issues related to the objectivity of *Times* reporters:

- They were based in West Jerusalem rather than in Palestinian areas.
- Several *Times* reporters had children in the Israeli Defence Forces.
- None covering the conflict were native Arabic speakers.

Sullivan defended the *Times'* coverage, but also issued several intriguing recommendations about how it could be improved, including by adding more historical context and to 'stop straining for symmetry'. Organizations such as the Institute for Middle East Understanding (IMEU) are supporting these efforts by working to compile links and resources for journalists reporting on Palestine and Palestinians. Alternative media such as Electronic Intifada, Jadaliyya, and Mondoweiss are also contributing to sharing more diverse narratives focused on human rights and social justice. Joseph Kahn, the *Times'* International News Editor, speculated that visual approaches could complement more traditional media, communicating through a fresh lens.

The Middle East Peace Process (MEPP) is one of the most high-profile spaces for knowledge creation on Israel and Palestine, but it suffers from a severe lack of legitimacy among key stakeholders. During six cycles of negotiation since the Oslo Accords in 1993, Israel has continued to lengthen the West Bank separation wall, which is currently 437 kilometres long, while building 50,000 new Israeli settler homes beyond the wall in the occupied Palestinian West Bank.

Since 2010, Israel has spent US $6.3 billion expanding the settlements across the green line. As a result, the West Bank is divided into 167 small enclaves, pushing the possibility of establishing a viable Palestinian state farther out of reach with every passing year.

In its work on Palestine, VI made an explicit choice to operate within the normative framework of the human rights field, where organizations produce an immense amount of data annually. Over the last 67 years, reputable international, Israeli and Palestinian organizations have collectively produced a wealth of information to illustrate dynamics of power that perpetuate social injustices in the world. Yet much of this data never becomes part of a broader communication strategy on Palestine, whether directed at Palestinian communities themselves, whose lives it attempts to capture; the Israeli public, who often live disconnected and sheltered from the effects of the occupation; or the international community, which has a strong influence over the conflict dynamics.

FIGURE 4.2   Gaza's Untold Story. This infographic was created one year after the end of Operation Protective Edge to document how displacement preceded death for most of the 2,219 Palestinians killed. See a larger version of this visual at http://visualizingpalestine.org/visuals/gaza-refugee-deaths

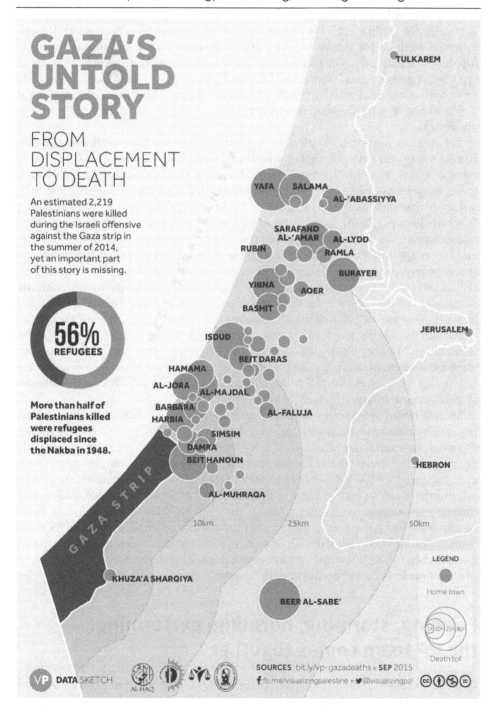

The digital double-edged sword

In recent years, there has been a substantial global shift to online media consumption. In the MENA region, this trend is accompanied by high mobile penetration and access rates, with a large number of users, particularly in at-risk communities, coming online for the first time via mobile devices. The internet has been an undeniably powerful medium for communicating inspiring recent social movements, from the toppling of dictatorships in Tunisia and Egypt to the mass digital protests surrounding US Congress's consideration of the Stop Online Piracy Act (SOPA). During the Arab Spring, regional activity online was heralded as the harbinger of a new era in which ordinary activists and citizens are a highly visible and influential source of information.

Yet it is an oversimplification to hope that simply adding technology to the equation can solve deeply rooted structural inequalities in the MENA region, or other contexts. Kentaro Toyama, former leader of the Microsoft Research Lab in India, suggests that the safest assumption when dealing with the internet and technology is that they will serve 'to amplify human forces', either positive or negative (Kentaro Toyama, 2015). In addition to creating new opportunities, the internet has also elevated risks for activists as a tool for government surveillance and censorship, and has exaggerated certain existing gaps in access. Unlike our physical cities, the spaces where we express political and social opinions online, while increasingly critical to our lives, are often not truly public, vulnerable to control by private corporations. The online space for communication is also competitive and overloaded. In 2010, a barrage of 34GB of information per day assaulted the senses of the average American *outside of work*. This includes an estimated 100,500 words (Global Information Industry Center, 2010). The vast majority of this information does not leave a lasting impression, if it is consciously absorbed at all. Visuals have an advantage in this space, as we absorb visual content more quickly than text and remember it more accurately over a longer period of time.

Sharing information with a wide audience in today's environment of 'infoxication' requires specialized training and skills which cut across multiple fields and disciplines. Organizations and independent groups representing marginalized perspectives often do not have the resources to take full advantage of the digital communication space, or to mitigate its risks. Visualizing Impact exists to address issues surrounding access to information in an independent, transparent and non-partisan space, and to continually explore new modes and forms of communication on social issues. In doing so, the team has gained deep insight into the needs and challenges faced by those communicating on social issues. Data science, technology and design are the primary tools VI currently applies to these challenges, developing independent and collaborative pilot projects that experiment with new approaches.

Forming, storming, norming, performing: the VP team comes together

July and October 2011. VI's flagship project, Visualizing Palestine, kicked off with two workshops, one in Amman and one in Dubai. Ramzi, later joined by Joumana, used the workshops to gather designers and researchers in the same space to produce infographics. Despite having access to many interesting datasets and producing a number of visually appealing concepts, the early process was untested and in its infancy. As a result, it challenged everyone involved.

October to December 2011. Ramzi and Joumana continued to work remotely with a dozen designers after the workshops, testing process and skillsets required to produce the content they envisioned. In late 2011, Ahmad Barclay produced the first complete infographic. Luma Shihabeldin created the Visualizing Palestine logo. At this point, all team involvement was on a *pro bono* basis.

January 2012. Ahmad Barclay quit his job in London as an architect and joined VP full time. He started with remote work, then moved to Amman in February. Turning Ramzi's living room into a makeshift office, the three-member unit worked for over a month to refine their process.

February 2012. Palestinian prisoner Khader Adnan entered the second month of his hunger strike in protest of administrative detention and conditions in Israeli prisons. Medical experts declared that he could die at any moment. After another long work session ending in the early hours of the morning, Ramzi noticed a hashtag trending on Twitter, #DyingtoLive. He and Ahmad began following Khader Adnan's story, and the mainstream media began to pick it up.

February 19, 2012. Joumana called designer Naji El Mir in Paris to ask if he would join the team in producing an infographic on the Khader Adnan story. As Adnan's health teetered on the brink, the team worked urgently to provide a context to his hunger strike; one which went beyond Palestine and conflict and which highlighted the universal elements of this non-violent form of action.

February 22, 2012. After 72 hours of intensive production and very little sleep, Visualizing Palestine debuted publicly with its first infographic, released bilingually in Arabic and English. The final concept drew on historical information of prominent hunger strikers, such as Nelson Mandela (seven days on strike), Mahatma Ghandi (21 days on strike), Layla Soueif (22 days on strike), and Bobby Sands (66 days on strike, eventually leading to his death in prison). Based on medical research, the infographic also portrayed what one could expect to happen to the human body during a total voluntary fast, a level of hunger that most people cannot fathom. Though they had done nothing to publicize Visualizing Palestine, and didn't yet have a website or full branding, 'Hunger Strikes' received 15,000 views in its first 24 hours.

March 2012. Hani Asfour of Polypod joined Ahmad, Ramzi, and Joumana for regular 48-hour production sprints in Amman. The team developed its first vision document, with the original vision 'to develop a factual, rights-based narrative of the Israeli-Palestinian situation for social justice'. For short they used the tagline Visual Stories for Social Justice.

March to August 2012. VP published seven additional infographics in English and Arabic with a clear brand direction. The brand emphasized credibility and openness via a page footer containing Creative Commons (CC) licensing information and detailed sources for all data included in the graphics. After several successful cycles of production, the VP team were able to document the steps involved in creating a strong infographic.

FIGURE 4.3   Process Wheel. VI uses the Process Wheel regularly to introduce new partners to the process of moving from data to story to design

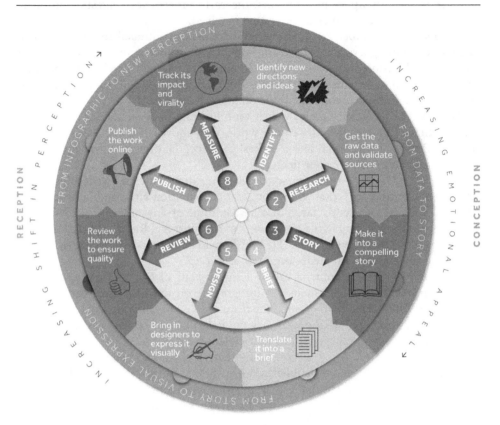

PRODUCTION

They captured these steps in a 'process wheel' which mapped the core value add of VP's approach: its ability to transform complex information into compelling insights and disseminate them broadly. A community of supporters grew organically around VP and the published visuals received coverage from both mainstream and alternative media outlets. External funding started to arrive in summer 2012 via reaching out to introduce VP. One early funder replied within 48 hours: 'Well, I was able to get a couple of friends to put together US $10,000 to contribute to this great initiative.'

September 2012 to April 2013. VP produced eight more visuals while beginning its transition from a self-funded pilot to a non-profit social enterprise. Ramzi and Joumana shifted their attention from content to mapping out a business model and operating structure. Without actively seeking clients, VP received requests from potential partners yet, despite this, procurement was not easy. As the first data visualization specialists in the MENA region, VP was engaging a frontier market that was both eager for the product and uneducated about its value.

IGURE 4.4   Checkpoint Births. This infographic is an example of data-driven orytelling. It creates a point of contrast between the average reader's story and ose of individuals living under occupation. Published January 2013. See a larger ersion at http://visualizingpalestine.org/visuals/checkpoint-births

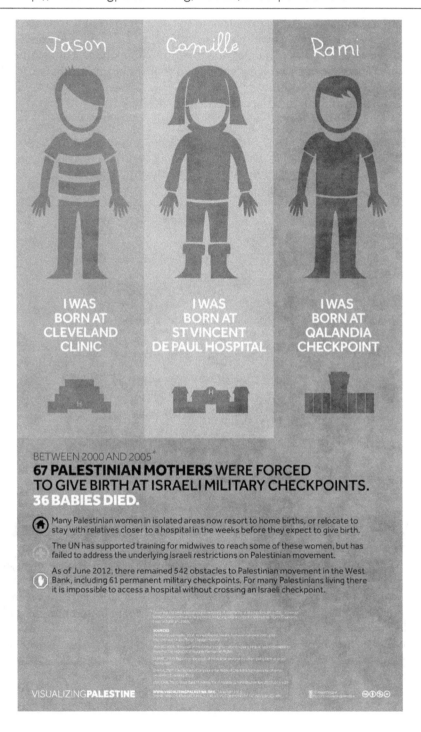

Shortly after formalizing registration as an organization in Palestine, Israeli border security denied entry to a key VP team member. Lack of freedom of movement throughout the region made it impossible to resolve this in a way that suited everyone, so VP began developing its remote operating procedures between Ramallah, Beirut and Amman.

In early 2013, Ramzi received an invitation to speak at Arabnet in Beirut, and was able to obtain a visa to enter Lebanon, a difficult feat, as Lebanon often does not issue visas to Palestinian ID holders. At the same time, Joumana and Ramzi faced limitations in finding the right designer profiles to join the team in Amman. With several creative team members already based in Beirut, it made sense to formally locate the team there and tap into the creative energy of the city.

FIGURE 4.5   Uprooted. This infographic is an example of data-driven storytelling, where the objective was to make a piece of data resonate with a US audience. Published October 2013. See the full visual at http://visualizingpalestine.org/visuals/olive-harvest

From Visualizing Palestine to Visualizing Impact

May 2013. With a promising pilot in hand as proof of concept, the team began fielding interest and requests for bodies of work on Bangladesh, India, Egypt and Syria. To open up an avenue for the growth of their vision, Joumana and Ramzi registered Visualizing Impact as a non-profit company in Lebanon in May 2013 with an expanded mandate. VI's reformulated vision positioned it as a laboratory for innovation at the intersection of data science, technology and design. Under VI, Visualizing Palestine would remain at the forefront within the broader perspective of continuously challenging communication on critical social issues.

June 2013 to December 2014. Both Ramzi and Joumana received fellowships to support the development of VI – Ramzi as an Ashoka Fellow and Joumana as a Synergos Arab World Social Innovator Fellow. Much of the initial work under Visualizing Impact was experimental. The team produced video content; devised and launched its first public ad campaign, which reached over 100,000 people; built a technology team in partnership with Ahmad Ghunaim; and developed several one-off visuals with new partners. VI's first visual beyond Visualizing Palestine, 'Politicians' Salaries and Income Inequality', developed with Lebanese alternative media group Raseef 22, went viral in Kenya.

During this period, Visualizing Impact received international recognition for its work from Prix Ars Electronica in Austria, Kantar's Information is Beautiful Awards in London, and Deutsche Welle's BOBs award for Best Social Activism.

FIGURE 4.6   Jessica Anderson receives the Deutsche Welle BOBs Award for Best Social Activism on behalf of Visualizing Palestine from Shahidul Alam at the 2014 Global Media Forum

Photo credit: DW Media Services GmbH

VI worked on maturing its revenue streams and operational structure, receiving several substantial grants; conducting what was at the time one of the highest grossing crowd-funding campaigns in the MENA region, exceeding $70,000; receiving several commissions from inter-governmental and non-governmental organizations; and launching a test batch of print products, including coasters and posters. Ramzi and Joumana elected a board of advisers to support organizational transparency and accountability.

In late 2014, VI began testing a scaling model called Visualizing X (VX), where partners could come aboard the VI platform based on a geographical or thematic expertise. 'X' could be Syria or Bangladesh, or it could be poverty, mental health or gender. Under the Visualizing X model, VI would benefit from the knowledge of its partners, while partners would benefit from the creative and technical expertise of VI, as well as its financial and operational support. Based on strength of partner interest, importance of topic and team interest, the first VX partner was Mada Masr. A collective of 22 Cairo-based independent journalists, Mada Masr, had lost their jobs in the post-coup, Sisi-era clampdown on free expression. Together, they began research for Visualizing Egypt. Meanwhile, Ramzi and Jillian York's fledgling project Onlinecensorship.org won the Knight News Challenge on strengthening the Internet for Free Expression and Innovation, formally opening up a digital rights-focused area of work. The grant allowed VI to partner with the Electronic Frontier Foundation (EFF), a prominent US-based digital rights organization.

Future goals and directions

Entering its fifth year of operation, Visualizing Impact continues to refine its model and re-evaluate its priorities. 2015 activities centred heavily on the following areas:

Strengthening operations. The team now consists of nine full-time staff, rotating interns, multiple design, creative, and content partners, and a network of professionals. The team is also more widely dispersed than ever. As a result, developing sharp operational structures and processes has been the top priority.

Refining impact measurement and communication. Previously, VI has talked about impact primarily in terms of the size of its audience. However, reach only opens the door to potential impact, rather than representing actual engagement or action in itself. In 2015, the team focused on developing impact indicators beyond audience size, and refining how it communicates its intended and actual impact.

Strengthening partnerships. Several promising new long-term partnerships emerged in 2014 and early 2015, and partnership is increasingly central to VI's business model, particularly when it comes to scaling. Learning how to engage with these partners proactively and efficiently, and to exchange knowledge with them, has been a strong focus of the team.

Enhancing the tech portfolio. Most of Visualizing Impact's work in 2015 was on tech-based outputs that maintained a strong data-driven focus, rather than static infographics.

A social business model

In April 2015, VI was a winner of the MIT Enterprise Forum's Arab Startup Competition in the Social Entrepreneurship category. In May, it was chosen as a semi-finalist by the World Bank's WE'REsilient Cities startup competition. These developments are symbolic of VI's ability to communicate a business model that is innovative, viable and socially focused.

Impact-led and experimental

Over the course of 2014, more than 75 different organizations approached VI to ask for data visualization work related to social issues, without VI doing any marketing. The first question VI asks is always 'what is your goal?' If the inquirer's response is heavily output-related (ie 'we want a clean, clear infographic') VI is happy to guide them to one of its network of partners who can provide these services. This relates to VI's first core principle: what others can do as well as VI, others should do. This allows VI to focus on experimental and boundary-pushing projects, which require significant investment of time, creative energy and resources. VI's second principle is to use impact as a primary measure of success. The team opts to work with clients that are driven by impact-related goals, such as scaling the reach of a certain message by 100,000 new viewers; engaging a previously untapped audience; or exploring an unfamiliar medium or user-experience. This is where VI moves forward to brainstorm, with data science, technology, and design as starting points.

Value proposition

Beyond VI's data visualization, technology and design expertise, its solution stands out from other offerings on the market for several reasons:

- Openness. VI works almost exclusively with Creative Commons/open licences.
- Closeness to target communities. The VI team has experience working in complex socio-political contexts in the MENA region and uses a bilingual production process.
- Partner-driven approach. Rather than working with 'clients' that impose deliverables, VI strives to work with partners where there is a strong sense of co-ownership of challenges, alignment on goals, and a willingness to explore various solutions.
- Impact focus. VI's role does not end with production. It participates in disseminating its tools and assessing their effectiveness.

Team structure

Visualizing Impact is a multi-disciplinary team of experts spanning the fields of social science, data science, communications, design and technology. It is spread across six cities in four time zones, operating on the basis of networks and partnerships in order to form teams with the right combinations of skills to address specific social issues and challenges. This model requires a high degree of agility in operations and management. This is the vision and strength that Joumana and Ramzi bring to the team as co-directors, each with distinct areas of responsibility. The external leadership includes an active board of advisers.

The team, including external partners, is horizontally structured around two roles: project-focused and area-focused. Project-based contributors to VI invest their energy in a specific body of work – a project on the Palestinian economy, or censorship in

Egypt, or youth unemployment, for example. Such team members include Ahmad Barclay, who focuses on Visualizing Palestine's multiple portfolios, and Mada Masr, who focuses exclusively on Visualizing Egypt.

Area-based contributors cover one of several areas: research, information architecture, design, technology and impact strategy. These are individuals that may work on many different bodies of work. For example, web developers Bassam Barham and Morad Taleeb work across Visualizing Palestine, Visualizing Egypt and the digital rights portfolio. Ahmad Ghunaim, a full stack web developer who has advised on the role of technology within VI since day one, mentors the technology team. As research network lead, Shireen Tawil is responsible for managing a network of area researchers, challengers and interns that VI can tap into depending on the needs of each project.

Content strategy

Currently, Visualizing Impact's content is focused primarily on Palestine, where the team tests approaches it hopes to transfer to other issues. VI has also seeded areas of work on Egypt and digital rights. Out of a nearly infinite array of topics they could have chosen, these have been developed based on strength of partnerships, importance of topics and team passion. The VI leadership revisits its content strategy annually to ensure that the *why* behind the organization remains central to the choices it makes around both content and mediums of creation.

Financial structure and sustainability

VI operates as a non-profit, while consciously differentiating itself from the NGO space, which relies heavily on funding from European and American organizations and governments. To support content objectivity and sustainability, VI aims to become financially independent, operating more like a social enterprise than an NGO. Its sustainability model draws on its key strengths – its highly engaged community of interest and its brand image of quality and innovation – to draw revenue through multiple streams. In 2015, its revenue came from:

- philanthropic grants;
- client commissions;
- donations via a network of high-value supporters;
- pro bono support by both co-founders and design partners;
- experimental or fledgling streams, including print-based products, crowdfunding, small but recurring donations and the provision of knowledge services such as workshops or consultancies.

As these revenue streams grow, the team will gradually shift reliance away from less sustainable sources. VI's expenses at present are mostly related to human resource.

Market

The primary 'market', or audience, for VI's work are the communities whose lives are affected by the absence of effective communication on the issues pertinent to them. The 'trick' is to find a way to produce work that is both effective in the above context, and maintains a market logic. We therefore find ourselves frequently 'creating' a market by proving our value and relevance as communicators for social change.

With this in mind, our market consists of individuals who 'own' the problem of communicating on social issues. These include:

TABLE 4.1   The market for Visualizing Impact's work

Owner	Perspective and pain point
Participants in the rapidly growing Access to Knowledge (A2K) movement	See knowledge as a public good that must be shared as openly and as widely as possible, but struggle to deliver/execute on this vision effectively
Knowledge investors, such as elite universities or institutions	Believe that knowledge plays an important role in social change, but often operate in a space disconnected from their intended beneficiaries
Representatives of vulnerable communities or marginalized issues	See and feel the pain of critical social issues up close, but often do not have the skills or resources to communicate them widely

VI also relies on what it calls a 'virality market', or the market for content among groups that share, use, and republish media online.

Competition, collabovation

In the corporate space, the idea that businesses need to 'adapt, evolve, compete or die' is dominant. In a world of over 7 billion people and numerous unresolved challenges, VI prefers to shift this mantra to 'adapt, evolve, collaborate or die'. While social entrepreneurs do operate in competitive spaces, there are numerous opportunities for competition to be turned into collaboration. Collaboration is not just an altruistic goal but a tactic for building community, exchanging knowledge and demonstrating relevance. VI's goal is not to survive for its own sake, but to only die at the right time for the right reasons, such as resolving the issues the team set out to address or migrating to a better model to address them.

The number of successful companies specializing in information visualization is growing globally. These firms are more specialized than other design agencies, and thus avoid competing with designers at large. There are a number of NGOs focused on the use of information in activism, such as Tactical Technology Collective, Internews and Small Media. VI is also aware of media outlets and human rights organizations setting up their own internal data visualization teams, such as the *New York Times* and Human Rights Watch.

Although these entities are potential competitors in many senses, many of them are interested in collaboration and exchange. VI has referred projects to these organizations; developed joint proposals; participated in joint fundraising and programming; joined trainings as both facilitator and trainee; and collaborated on creative work.

From reach, to engagement, to impact

How do you track decentralized networks of people sharing content across a nearly endless array of platforms? In early 2015, Jessica Anderson addressed this question as we began revising VI's impact measurement methodology, picking up threads of systems that had been started in the organization's early days, dropped because they were too intensive to maintain or didn't include the right metrics, and sometimes picked up again. There is no standard system in place that VI is aware of for measuring impact related to digital media content, so the challenge is to build a system that is meaningful, contains valid metrics and is realistic for a start-up team to maintain. There are moments when the time and energy required to find a system can feel like a drain or distraction from the core work.

So let's start with the seemingly obvious. Why measure impact at all? For VI, it is about answering broad questions such as *why does this work matter? What is our value?* It is also about gathering details that aid in decision making, helping the team to assess its strengths and weaknesses and the potential to scale its ideas. Impact is not just about proving success, but about recognizing failure and knowing when a small shift in thinking or a major pivot might be needed. Finally, a team that not only believes in its impact but has a clear understanding of its real accomplishments and limitations has a clear upper hand on the road to sustainability.

Entering its fifth year of operation, VI is still growing in its ability to understand impact. It tends to look at this from several vantage points: impact on specific communities affected by social injustice; impact on organizations and groups whose work is connected with the communities above; and impact on team members and partners looking to build social consciousness into the heart of their life work.

The process underpinning VI's approach to impact is currently based on four steps:

- Set 'SMART' goals for each new project – Specific, Measurable, Achievable, Results-focused and Time-bound.
- Monitor and evaluate progress toward these goals throughout the implementation period, and produce a final impact assessment for all closed projects.
- Cultivate a team culture where each member can speak clearly and confidently about intended and actual impact.
- Communicate impact insights clearly and regularly to the VI community.

What is VP trying to accomplish?

Visualizing Palestine aims to use under-circulated data about Israel and Palestine to deepen mainstream knowledge and awareness, particularly among US-based and Western audiences. In doing so, we are striving to shift attitudes, beliefs and norms. VP also aims to provide practical tools to a focused set of strong emerging ideas and movements for social justice within the Palestinian context, improving the capacity of organizations and collectives to pursue their missions.

Who is VP engaging?

Online

VP's largest audiences are located in the United States, the United Kingdom and Jordan, according to data drawn from analytics of the VP Facebook and Twitter accounts and the VP website. In 2014, its audience size grew by 45 per cent, and the VP Facebook page broke 20,000 followers in 2015. Since 2012, the VP team conservatively estimates that its work has reached 2.5 million viewers, with specific efforts such as our 2013 campaign on institutionalized discrimination reaching over 100,000 unique viewers. In the first half of 2015, VP's three most widely shared pieces of content collectively reached over 160,000 people.

Offline

As of March 2015, VP has been issuing short surveys to individuals downloading the visuals from its website. This was an important step toward understanding offline engagement, providing hundreds of data points on the people and organizations using VP's work, and their purposes for using it. The team regularly cleans incoming survey data to eliminate invalid or repeat cases, and codes it by use case:

- academic use;
- advocacy campaigns;
- political campaigns (lobbying);
- cultural exhibitions;
- media;
- other.

Based on this process, VP knows that its visuals have been used offline across at least 79 cities and 29 countries, with an average of 88.5 individual downloads per month. Users tend to be journalists, professors, researchers, students, activist collectives or human rights and development professionals. Through targeted efforts, VP or its partners have presented visuals to US Congress-people, UK parliamentarians and UN officials. Finally, through its partnerships, VP is directly engaging with 11 organizations working in Israel, Gaza, the West Bank, the United States and the United Kingdom.

How are these audiences engaging with VP?

Data on social media likes, shares, and comments are not central to VP's understanding of engagement, as we consider this to be limited engagement. The team must assume that a like or share on social media only means exposure to or consumption of content, not necessarily absorption or action. Examples of deeper forms of engagement might include:

- using the content to take tangible action;
- contributing to the content as a pro bono professional or donor;
- initiating collaborations and partnerships around the content.

Our use case data provides insight into these deeper, more active forms of engagement.

TABLE 4.2   Case data

Use case featuring VP	Number of uses March to June 2015
Cultural exhibitions	42 exhibitions
Public lectures	20 lectures
Academic use in a lecture, curriculum, or for research purposes	5 universities
Media references, including mainstream and alternative outlets	20 articles
Student advocacy campaigns connected to official university organizations	8 student campaigns
Advocacy campaigns (excluding student campaigns)	33 campaigns
Use by professionals in the human rights/development field to illustrate the Palestinian context	3 organizations

VP content has been republished by well-known English media outlets such as the *Guardian*, the Huffington Post, *The Washington Post* and Washington Post Data Blog, the Daily Beast, Al Jazeera English, Open Democracy, Policy Mic, Fast Company and *The Irish Times*. It has also been consistently republished by the largest alternative media voices on Palestine, such as Mondoweiss, Jadaliyya, and Electronic Intifada.

A portion of VP's audience chooses to engage via financial support. During its 2013 crowdfunding campaign, VP received donations from over 400 individuals.

Engaging the VP team

Engagement with the VP core team has been high throughout its operation, limited only by the core team's capacity to organize and supervise volunteers. Since its establishment, volunteers have worked with VP's designers to implement translations of its visuals in 10 languages beyond English and Arabic. VP has worked with at least 100 pro nobo professionals, interns or volunteers in the areas of research, design, technology, communication, event organizing and fundraising. From March to June 2015, 32 new volunteers registered to work with VP via the community section of its website, and volunteers have logged over 1,500 hours on VP projects in the same period.

VP's audience also views individual team members as thought leaders. Members of the team have delivered workshops and lectures on VP at the Harvard Graduate School of Design, the MIT Center for Civic Media, Tufts University and the Columbia University Global Center; have been present as speakers at conferences such as the UN Media Conference on Peace in the Middle East and the Women Digital News Entrepreneurs Summit; and have held fellowships with Stanford University, Ashoka, Synergos and the Ford-Mozilla Open Web programme.

Finally, Palestine-based organizations and movements continuously approach VP with ideas, data or messages they would like to disseminate more broadly and impactfully, meaning that its work organically facilitates partnerships with key target groups. VP collects testimonials from these groups to add qualitative depth to insights in the raw numbers.

Room for improvement

Visualizing Palestine examines its audience not only in terms of size and demographics, but also psychographics, including factors such as membership, state of mind, belief and behaviour. Currently, there is insufficient data available on VP audience beliefs, but it would be safe to guess that a substantial portion of VP's engaged audience includes people who have already taken a strong position on Palestine prior to exposure to VP. This 'preaching to the choir' effect plagues many socially progressive approaches. Therefore, the audience that is most critical to target includes individuals that are generally interested in social issues, but may feel distant from, neutral to, or undecided on issues about Palestine. Targeted messaging, either on- or offline, could help VP expand that audience.

Additionally, VP must continue to challenge itself to make conversions on its impact, increasing overall reach, engaging highly influential individuals, encouraging offline action, and engaging the community as volunteers, donors or partners.

Lessons learnt

1 *Prioritize trust.* One of VI's strongest assets amongst its core team members and partners is trust on two fronts: trust in vision, which is centred on

systemic long-term change; and trust in the value each team member brings to the vision. Geographic distance, economic realities and day-to-day operational and geopolitical stresses can strain the development of trust. It is therefore important to invest in face-to-face time; develop good communication practices; and seek mentors who have worked on similar models and are familiar with the challenges.

2 *Cultivate flexibility.* Working in a volatile environment can stifle innovation. Being willing to set up unconventional working arrangements, such as a remote team, can actually be an innovation in itself, as it contributes to developing models of resilience. Being willing to break down a big idea into smaller parts can also help to ensure that an unpredicted challenge does not dismantle an entire project. However, flexibility does not mean compromising on operational best practices. In fact, strengthening these practices is key to ensuring that sacrifices made on behalf of flexibility do not become sacrifices in the culture or vision of the organization.

3 *Seek the innovator in every team member.* The bar for calling oneself an 'innovator' seems high, and the field of participants overwhelmingly competitive. In reality, innovation is situational. It depends not on genius or on identity, but on establishing processes and practices to facilitate creativity, which can be learned by nearly anyone. Good leaders will look for sparks of innovation everywhere. For VP, this means not just the creative and technical team members, but all team members and the extended network.

4 *Collaborate with the competition.* Typical business thinking requires you to stake out your competitors. While it is important to know who is working in the same sphere as you and how your offering compares to theirs, one way to ensure that you remain relevant is to be an enthusiastic collaborator and to support others working in your space. In our opinion there is a shortage of collaborative energy in the social justice ecosystem, and in light of staggering need, this is a huge missed opportunity for any social business.

5 *Channel quality and integrity toward sustainability.* VI could write an entirely new chapter on its fundraising learning curve alone. When we started, the team focused on the quality of the work and the first funds followed at an extension of that. As VI expanded and professionalized, it quickly became necessary to be more deliberate about seeking funding and developing distinct revenue streams. Now more than ever, there are numerous creative ways to gain funding, but the most important piece of the equation remains this – doing high-quality work with integrity, and understanding its value.

6 *Stay open to failure.* William Faulkner once said, 'In writing, you must kill all your darlings'. As an entrepreneur, it is sometimes necessary to let go of ideas or projects you may have spent a long time building and nurturing to focus on an area that has more potential. This feeds into impact measurement as well. We are all invested in succeeding, but thinking of impact measurement as simply a way to prove success is self-defeating. At times, it is likely that you will hear yourself tell a story that is very appealing, and then look at what you have actually achieved or how your work is geared and find

a huge gap. That gap may arise from having been too open to opportunities, choosing a short-sighted way to solve financial issues, or other reasons. Be patient with impact, but willing to admit when the metrics are not up to par. Notice when you are straying from your vision. Take the time to reflect on the 'why' behind the work.

7 *Reach out.* Skilled and talented individuals today are looking for meaningful work. Mentors, employees and volunteers are available if you pay attention for opportunities and are wise with asks. That said, do not expect to receive energy without substantial input of energy. This goes for mentors, employees, volunteers, interns, partners or anyone else engaging with the work.

8 *Don't lose the passion in the details.* When rock climbers are up close against a wall mid-climb, it can be hard to see a foothold that is obvious to someone on the ground. We know the texture of the rock in front of us like no one else, but not the view from the top or the enthusiasm we had for the challenge as we stood at the base. For beginners, a 'belay' person on the ground will often point out the best course when a climber gets stuck. Social entrepreneurs tend to start their project from a place of passion. You will love the topic or be excited about how the solution fits with the challenge as you see it. The day to day can quickly overwhelm that perspective, replacing it with the minute texture of financial, legal and operational details that don't necessarily tap directly into your passion. It is easy to lose sight of footholds that keep you and your partners on course with those passions. It is important to take time to remember why you started the climb and to reach out to those 'grounded' people in your life who might be able to help you see the overall picture, or just the next key step.

9 *Mark successes.* Engrave them in your mind, hand in hand with a deep recollection of what it really took you to get there.

Discussion questions

1 Do you feel that the knowledge produced in spaces like universities, or in an organization like the World Bank, operates in isolation? Give some examples to support your answer.

2 What sites of knowledge creation do you believe are under-represented? Why?

3 Have you encountered any models of innovation operating in volatile contexts? How did they foster resilience?

4 Share an example of a media or content creation project that you find impactful. How did you personally engage? Why did the content make a mark on you?

5 Have you ever used impact metrics to support a pivot or to move away from an idea in which you were previously deeply invested?

6 What do you think about the relationship between competition and collaboration? What are some examples of potential competitors joining forces?

7 Consider a project you are working on. Does this project relate to a vision for your lifelong journey? How?

8 What is the role of technology in social change? What are some examples of technology-led approaches that have succeeded? Failed? What role did the technology *really* play?

9 Visualizing Impact has an exit strategy – to shut down when its work is complete. Why do so few organizations in the NGO sector have exit strategies? Does this imply that many only exist for their own benefit and perhaps, ironically, they need problems to persist in order to survive?

Further reading

You can find more material to do with this chapter at www.koganpage.com/socialentrepreneurship

On VI and VP:
visualizingpalestine.org [accessed 10 December 2015]
visualizingimpact.org [accessed 10 December 2015]
onlinecensorship.org [accessed 10 December 2015]

On data journalism and social impact:
Tactical Technology Collective: Visualizing Information for Advocacy, https://visualisingadvocacy.org/ [accessed 10 December 2015]
Data Journalism Handbook: http://datajournalismhandbook.org/1.0/en/ [accessed 10 December 2015]
Heath, Chip and Dan: Made to Stick

On impact measurement:
Learning for Action: Deepening Engagement for Lasting Impact, a framework for measuring media impact and results: www.learningforaction.com/wp/wp-content/uploads/2014/08/Media-Measurement-Framework_Final_08_01_14.pdf [accessed 10 December 2015]

On Palestine:
Adalah – www.adalah.org/en [accessed 10 December 2015]
Al-Haq – www.alhaq.org [accessed 10 December 2015]

The Institute for Middle East Understanding – www.imeu.org [accessed 10 December 2015]

The Boycott, Divestment, and Sanctions movement – www.bdsmovement.net [accessed 10 December 2015]
Pappe, I, *The Ethnic Cleansing of Palestine*

Key process-related words:
Biomimicry
Sharmer, Otto: Theory U
Scrum Methodology
Reed's Law

References

Silver, N (2013) *The Signal and the Noise: The art and science of prediction*, Penguin Books Ltd

'Lebanese protest against waste-disposal crisis', Aljazeera English, 26 July 2015 [accessed 19 August 2015]: http://www.aljazeera.com/news/2015/07/lebanon-beirut-trash-rubbish-crisis-150725060723178.html

Zaatari, M 'Power shortage causes massive blackouts', *The Daily Star*, 5 August 2015 [accessed 19 August 2015]: http://www.dailystar.com.lb/News/Lebanon-News/2015/Aug-05/309734-power-shortage-causes-massive-blackouts.ashx

Christakis, N 'The hidden influence of social networks', TED Talk, 2010 [accessed 19 August 2015]: http://www.ted.com/talks/nicholas_christakis_the_hidden_influence_of_social_networks/transcript?language=en

York, J 'Facebook: No Palestinian Pages', 25 July 2010 [accessed 19 August 2015]: http://jilliancyork.com/2010/07/25/facebook-no-palestinian-pages/

Emon, Anver *et al* 'We are all Khaled Said', *Boston Review*, 3 November 2011 [accessed 19 August 2015]: http://www.bostonreview.net/khaled-said-facebook-egypt-revolution-interview

'Israel: End Restrictions on Palestinian Residency', Human Rights Watch, 5 February 2012 [accessed 19 August 2015]: https://www.hrw.org/news/2012/02/05/israel-end-restrictions-palestinian-residency

Berlin Declaration on Open Access to Knowledge in the Sciences and Humanities, 22 October 2003 [accessed 19 August 2015]: http://openaccess.mpg.de/Berlin-Declaration

Juma, Calestous and Lee Yee-Cheong, Innovation: Applying Knowledge in Development, UN Millennium Project [accessed 19 August 2015]: http://www.unmillenniumproject.org/documents/Science-complete.pdf

World Bank Budget FY14, September 2013 [accessed 19 August 2015]: http://documents.worldbank.org/curated/en/2013/08/18105068/world-bank-budget-fy14

Doemeland, Doerte; Trevino, James, 2014, Which World Bank reports are widely read?, Policy Research working paper; no WPS 6851. Washington DC: World Bank Group. http://documents.worldbank.org/curated/en/2014/05/19456376/world-bank-reports-widely-read-world-bank-reports-widely-read

Shulman, S 'A documentary guide to "Brand Israel" and the art of pinkwashing', Mondoweiss, 30 November 2011 [accessed 19 August 2015]

Dreyfuss, R 'Is AIPAC Still the Chosen One?' Mother Jones, September 2009 [accessed 19 August 2015]: http://www.motherjones.com/politics/2009/09/aipac-still-chosen-one

Sullivan, M 'The Conflict and the Coverage', The *New York Times*, 22 November 2014 [accessed 19 August 2015]: http://www.nytimes.com/2014/11/23/opinion/sunday/the-conflict-and-the-coverage.html

Toyama, K Geek Heresy: Rescuing social change from the cult of technology, *PublicAffairs*: 2015

'How Much Information', Global Information Industry Center, January 2010 [accessed 19 August 2015]: http://hmi.ucsd.edu/howmuchinfo_research_report_consum.php

05
Bringing the Silicon Valley revolution in technology and business to global health

MAGPI – JOEL SELANIKIO

ABSTRACT

Global health has been suffering for decades from a data famine. Programmes designed to improve child health don't know how many children are sick. Organizations dedicated to reducing malaria today are stuck using old data on malaria prevalence collected years ago. Even basic data on populations is old, inaccurate, or missing. This data famine persists despite the astonishing penetration of information and communications tools like the mobile phone and the internet into the poorest and most rural places on Earth. Early in the digital revolution, paediatrician/epidemiologist (and former Wall Street computer consultant) Joel Selanikio was sent into the middle of sub-Saharan Africa with a brief to collect public health data. Confronted by an existing laborious and environmentally wasteful paper-based system, Selanikio intuited that new technologies – and business models – from the likes of Hotmail, Google and Skype might be just what was needed to transform global health data collection. Working to bring Silicon Valley approaches to some of the most remote locations on the planet through his data collection application, Magpi, he has successfully managed to revolutionize public health data collection – and show a new path and a new business model in the use of technology for development.

Techie turned doctor, turned tech-doctor

When I left college in the late 1980s, I had a degree in sociology but had also taken a course in computer science in those very earliest days of the personal computing revolution. I was lucky enough to get a job working as a computer consultant for Chase Manhattan Bank (now merged with JP Morgan), and I worked for that bank for a number of years, helping them figure out how to connect their mainframe-based databases with the 'personal computers' that were coming out at the time. This wasn't bad, considering that there were neither computers nor computer science classes available when I graduated high school just a few years before.

While the work paid well enough, at that young and idealistic age I was looking for a calling and not just a job, and I soon left Chase to pursue first my pre-med qualifications and then medical school. Medicine, it seemed to me, would challenge my intellect, was oriented towards serving others and, yes, would let me make a good living.

At that time I honestly thought that I was leaving behind my work with information technology – not realizing that a tsunami of IT was just picking up speed that would soon transform the world, and that my skill and understanding of IT might be useful in such a world.

In fact, though I did not realize it at the time, my computer expertise would later become a major driver of my life's path, as IT grew enormously important in all of our lives.

Lesson 1: Most of us are oblivious to the great societal and technological changes occurring around us.

Medical training is famously long and arduous, and mine was no exception. I spent one year studying the pre-medical requirements I had never taken as an undergraduate, then four years at Brown University Medical School – not the best years of my life, but among the most interesting and challenging. This was followed by three more challenging and exhausting years of paediatric residency at Emory University.

During medical school, I was able to earn money for room and board and books by doing computer programming on the side for my old colleagues at Chase, which was a huge financial help. Luckily, it also kept me thinking about technology, although I still didn't think that it would ever be applicable to a career in medicine.

As I approached my final year of paediatric residency, I was presented with a choice between two options: doing further 'sub-specialization' within paediatrics (eg becoming a paediatric nephrologist, or paediatric oncologist), or going into private practice.

While those were usually framed as being the only two options available, I also learned of a third option: doing a fellowship at CDC (the US Centers for Disease Control and Prevention) in Atlanta, Georgia.

I'm sure most paediatric residents never even know that this possibility exists, and I hardly understood what CDC was or did, but by pure luck I had done residency in Atlanta, just a mile or two from CDC, and there were many at Emory who had a current or past affiliation with the institution: the public health agency of the United States.

The CDC-connected people seemed to feel that I'd do well there. To this day, I'm not quite sure what they saw in me, or why they thought it was a match, but I was intrigued enough to apply to the Epidemic Intelligence Service (EIS), a CDC fellowship programme lasting two years, during which a fellow was expected to learn statistics, epidemiology, and – most importantly – the practical aspects of public health, from media relations to outbreak investigations.

Since the EIS was founded in 1951, partly due to US fears of Cold War bioterrorism, EIS officers have led all sorts of investigations into deaths and disease around the world. If you've seen the movie *Contagion*, you will have a sense of what the EIS does. In it, Kate Winslet plays an EIS officer investigating a raging epidemic that eventually kills her. But that movie was still years in the future, and I had visions of exotic field epidemiology in my mind (rather than death from Ebola or other infection) when I was accepted into the programme.

Over the course of my EIS fellowship, and my subsequent years at CDC, I would investigate disease outbreaks in Chicago, Borneo and Haiti; respond to hurricanes and anthrax attacks; help recover pieces of the doomed space shuttle Columbia from the Texas countryside; and work on malaria, measles and other infectious diseases still common in poorer countries.

It was this latter work, which typically involved collecting a *lot* of data, that first turned my thoughts to the possible application of information technology – and specifically the mobile technology that was beginning to emerge – to the needs of global health.

During this period of my life I thought that CDC was my career, full stop. Looking back, though, I realize that my time at Chase, at Emory and at CDC were all just three preliminary stages helping me to add three skill sets – computers, medicine and epidemiology – skill sets that I would later combine into my real life's work at Magpi (formerly DataDyne): creating technology that solves problems for global health and international development.

What we don't know can kill us

During all the various activities I was pulled into while at CDC, the single common thread was 'data', but not the kind of data to which I was accustomed while working as a paediatrician. CDC introduced me to the concepts of 'public health', as opposed to 'clinical medicine' (ie what happens in the clinic), and taught me that determining the cause of a disease in a whole population, or a group of people, involved a different set of skills and a different kind of thinking than determining the cause of disease in a single patient.

Clinical doctors are usually focused on the data from one patient at a time, and the way we present that data is typically as a chronology or 'patient history'. In my clinical practice at Georgetown University Hospital, I very rarely look at anything like a spreadsheet, and cannot ever remember performing any statistical analysis on any patient's data.

By contrast, *public health* focuses on populations rather than individual patients, and one of its most potent tools is the collection of large datasets (just picture a big spreadsheet). These kinds of data might be related to the characteristics of people in the United States who are HIV positive, or the percentage of rural Bolivians who have access to clean water. They might quantify the percentage of children eligible to be vaccinated in Zambia who actually receive their vaccinations, or the mortality rate of pregnant women in Burma from infections.

Such data allows public health professionals to establish baselines, plan activities, measure progress (or, sometimes, the lack of it) and effectively pursue many other essential and life-saving activities.

Without these datasets we are stuck with guessing and approximating and extrapolating, which are never as useful as actually knowing. Even incomplete data are much better than nothing. To quote computing pioneer Charles Babbage: 'Errors using inadequate data are much less than those using no data at all'.

The problem is that in global health – and in global development in general – we are not usually choosing between 'good data' and 'better data'. We are usually faced with minimal data, old data, or no data.

Lesson 2: We don't know what you think we know.

I find that those not working in the field of global health are often astonished to discover this. Surely our health institutions aren't spending millions, or billions, without really knowing the result? I assumed that, too, until I was dropped smack into the middle of sub-Saharan Africa to collect data and I began to realize the extent of the problem.

A friend of mine likens my reaction to that of Neo in the film *The Matrix*, when Morpheus explains to him that his most basic assumptions about the world are incorrect: I thought I lived in a world run (or at least mostly run) by data. I found out otherwise. And just as with Neo, after I realized this, the more I investigated, the worse I discovered the situation to be, and the more I became determined to change things (this is where the parallels between me and Neo end, if you were wondering).

Most people working in global health appear to take one of two approaches: they are either accustomed to operating with no data, having worked in a data desert their entire careers – or they deny that there is a problem. That is, even though they would think it strange to try to manage their finances if their bank only issued statements every five years, they think that managing child health in Bolivia works just fine with data collected every five years.

Just a few examples of the things we just don't know (ie the data we don't have):

- how many refugees there are on the planet;
- how many clinics in poor countries are currently without life-saving drugs;
- how many children were born last year in Bolivia or Bhutan;
- how many children died last year in Cambodia or Congo.

And here's the *pièce de résistance*. After years spending billions of dollars collectively on HIV/AIDS in Africa (with, it should be noted, indisputable life-saving effect), for a long time none of the organizations involved could tell us whether the prevalence of HIV/AIDS over much of the continent (ie the percentage of people in the population infected or showing symptoms) was going up or going down (in fact, things *are* starting to get a little better).

There are many reasons why we often lack even the most basic data, though the most frequently cited reason – lack of money – clearly does not apply to the HIV/AIDS in Africa issue.

Other reasons can include poor organization of health departments, inertia, lack of supervision, lack of understanding of the importance of data, fear of change, war, and other security issues.

And, of course, people and organizations (and donors) are often less than enthusiastic about collecting information that may show their activities in a bad light, something noted in a recent comment from a user of our Magpi software who is collecting data on education in sub-Saharan Africa: '[The Ministry of Education] doesn't like the data we collect, because it shows they are not doing their job.'

It would be difficult or impossible, even for a large organization or group, to deal with all of these issues. Given my background in computing plus medicine plus public health, I began to feel during my time at CDC that there was *one* part of the problem that I might be uniquely suited to tackle: the unbelievably inefficient use of paper forms to collect required data.

The paper problem

This problem, which I thought my strange journey through banking and medical school and government might have put me in a good position to address, was concerned with the *technology* of paper forms that were (and still predominantly are) used to collect all the global health data.

Paper forms have dominated data collection in health for generations, both in clinical medicine and in public health. Think of all the forms used in a single clinic: the patient registry, the drug supply books, the blood supply records, the patient medical records, consent forms, staff records, lab reports, and many more.

In poor countries, where few people ever access a clinic, public health practitioners are responsible for the health of most, through clean water campaigns, vaccination campaigns, bed net distributions, and many other activities. And without collecting data in surveys and other activities it is simply not yet possible to know very much about the population, or about your programmes and their effectiveness. If you want to know whether someone smokes, you need to ask them. And if that someone happens to live in Sierra Leone, you have to go to Sierra Leone to ask them.

Because of these factors, it is in public health, with its need for gathering and analysis of large datasets, that paper creates the greatest problems for health in poor countries (with all due respect for the current push for electronic medical records in the United States and elsewhere).

Paper is slow

Imagine a single survey to be administered to 5,000 households in a poor country, with a couple of hundred questions on 20 sheets of paper. That amounts to 100,000 sheets of paper. In many such locations, it is likely to take several months, at least, to 'do the data entry' (to type the data on those sheets of paper into a computer for analysis). Sometimes it can take considerably longer – even years – before the data can ever be put to use in saving lives or improving health, by which time it is increasingly out of date.

And, not uncommonly, the data are never actually entered into a computer at all. Think about that. All the weeks if not months of data collection, all the labour of the data collectors, all the money spent, all the benefit that could be derived from the collected data ... all comes to nothing.

When we began contemplating the use of electronic data collection, of course, we realized that all that time and effort of data entry could simply be eliminated. And there would never be a situation where the data was collected but never entered.

An environmental disaster

Frequently, hundreds of thousands or even millions of sheets of office paper are used (then, typically, warehoused or just discarded) for just one field survey. And just one single survey of 5,000 households involving 20 sheets of paper per household is roughly the equivalent of 12 trees.

With thousands and thousands of these surveys, and other data collection activities, taking place each year – this represents hundreds of thousands of trees that would be saved if the data were collected instead on mobile phones or tablets (which are in many cases going to be produced for other purposes anyway).

Wasting trees is not the only way in which paper-based data collection is an environmental nightmare. Because it is heavy, it increases fuel costs for all the vehicles that are used to carry it to the field. In the example above of a 5,000 household survey, those 100,000 sheets of paper weigh about 1,100 pounds (500 kg) – and the EPA suggests that every additional 100 pounds in a vehicle reduces its fuel economy by 2 per cent.

On top of that, the production of every sheet of paper can use as little as 1.5 cups (0.35 litre) or as much as three gallons (11.3 litres) of water, meaning that our household survey consumes as 'little' as 10,000 gallons of water (about 38,000 litres) – or possibly as much as 300,000 gallons (more than one million litres).

So, just to review, our single 5,000 household survey consumes:

- 12 trees;
- thousands of gallons of fuel;
- hundreds of thousands of gallons of water.

And that is just for one single survey. Can you imagine how many trees, how much fuel, and how much water was consumed for the US census in 2010 – which was done on paper (despite the very large number of Americans that have access to the internet)?

Data collection in global health was ripe for disruption, and that's exactly what we set out to do.

A glimmer of hope: the Palm PDA (late 1990s)

While CDC was immersing me in the data process and I was coming to realize just how little data we actually had, a device invented to help businesspeople keep track of their calendars – the Palm PDA – gave me a little hope that progress could be made.

The Palm PDA ('Personal Digital Assistant'), originally called the Palm 'Pilot', was the first really affordable handheld computer. It debuted in 1996 at a price of just $249 (the ill-fated Apple Newton, released a few years before, had cost almost three times as much). The Palm had more than enough computing power to display forms, given the right software.

For me, that software came in the form of a program called Pendragon Forms. Pendragon was the first software I knew of that allowed me to easily design mobile electronic forms. I took to it quickly, and began experimenting with using it for field data collection in poor countries.

In 1998, I worked with a group of US Army nutritionists to do a nutrition survey of Burmese refugees in a Thai refugee camp. The resulting publication, 'Mobile Computing in the Humanitarian Assistance Setting: An Introduction and Some First Steps', published in 2002, was the first to detail the use of mobile electronic data collection within international health, or within the humanitarian setting.

It was my hope at the time that our demonstration of the use of new Palm technology for humanitarian public health purposes would open the floodgates. Surely *everyone* would want to use this new technology now that we had told them about it?

But that's not what happened.

FIGURE 5.1   Pocket World Changer

PHOTO: Joel Selanikio

The floodgates didn't open (2000)

In fact, what was most remarkable in the wake of our publication was the widespread failure to use Pendragon, or any other software, to collect data with Palm or other PDAs. It wasn't that no-one was using this – or similar – technology, but I doubt that at the height of the PDA era even 1 per cent of public health data was being collected this way.

In trying to make sense of this, I managed to grasp at least one reason: it was too hard. I just stated that Pendragon 'allowed me to easily design mobile electronic forms', and it was true. For a long time I thought of Pendragon as being easy.

At a certain point, however, I realized that what was easy for me – with my computer science and programming background – was not easy for most people. Optimal use of Pendragon required some programming skills – skills that the vast majority of people simply do not have.

Imagine designing a coffeemaker that required a computer programmer to set up each morning. Could you see yourself using it – unless you were a computer programmer?

> Lesson 3: Technical people always underestimate the scarcity, and the cost, of their own expertise.

This concept made me believe that the key to increasing adoption of technology like Palm PDAs for data collection was to make it so easy that the average health worker could use it – without having to hire any technical experts.

FIGURE 5.2   Collecting Data in Thailand with Palms, circa 1998

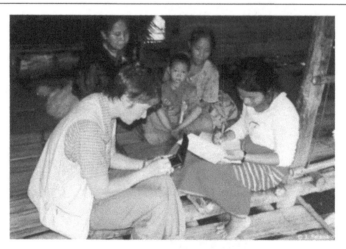

PHOTO: Joel Selanikio

EpiSurveyor phase 1: it's the technology (early 2000s)

While I was working with Palms and Pendragon at CDC, my future business partner Rose Donna was doing similar work at the American Red Cross (ARC). ARC was involved in what would become one of the most successful global vaccination campaigns in history, the Measles Initiative. A critical success factor would turn out to be the pioneering use of mobile technologies for the collection of data that help them understand when they were doing well and meeting programme goals, and when they were not meeting them.

I met Rose in 2002 while temporarily assigned to ARC, and with both of us tiring of the bureaucracy in large organizations we decided we would try to work together in the hope of moving further and faster and with fewer meetings.

In retrospect, I realize that meeting Rose was one of the most important points of my life, because:

Lesson 4: You cannot do this alone.

We were lucky enough to secure a few grants in relatively short order, from the World Bank and the ARC, which proved enough to hire a programmer. My computer skills were definitely too rusty by then. We quickly began creating what I named 'EpiSurveyor', the first do-it-yourself system for mobile electronic data collection that didn't require any technical expertise at all (the name was changed in 2013 to Magpi in part due to its increasing adoption outside of global health).

EpiSurveyor consisted of a PC-based programme that allowed the user to design forms, and a Palm PDA-based programme (what we would now call an 'app') to deploy the forms on the device in the field.

Initial use of the software was promising, but revealed that it still was just not easy enough. There were two issues in particular that proved difficult to overcome.

Easy to use, hard to install (2004)

As we developed a prototype and then a first real version of EpiSurveyor, Rose and I began to fly around the world to train health programmes that might want to use it. This was more than a little ironic, since the software was designed to be do-it-yourself.

A major problem was that the initial version of EpiSurveyor followed the model of all software at that time: the PC component had to be downloaded and installed onto a laptop or desktop, and many people had difficulty with the process. Furthermore, it required that the Palm Desktop software provided with the PDAs also needed to be installed, *and* that the Java utility software *also* needed to be installed.

Three installations on the PC, and one installation on each PDA, just to get started.

This presented a series of hurdles that tripped up many people trying the software, and we needed to engineer around this problem. Unfortunately, I didn't initially know how we might do this.

No PDAs in Africa

The second major problem, in addition to installation, that we encountered in those early days was that Palm PDAs were essentially a rich world product. It was difficult and/or expensive to buy them in African countries, where we initially focused. This led to years of wheeling rugged Pelican cases full of PDAs from country to country.

The lack of a locally available technology for data collection was an enormous hurdle, and we wasted time trying to find ways to, quite literally, get enough grant money to buy a Palm PDA for every African health worker. Like everyone else, we would never in a million years have imagined a local market for 'pocket computers' in Africa or other parts of the developing world (and, boy, were we wrong).

Lesson 5: It is easier to move electrons than molecules: it's much easier to build and scale software worldwide than hardware.

Miracle #1: Hotmail

As I was wrestling with all the difficulties our EpiSurveyor users encountered in installing our software, I happened to notice that almost all the health workers I was working with in sub-Saharan Africa had a Hotmail account.

At first I didn't think much about this, but after a while I began to see the parallels between what we were trying to do (unsuccessfully) and what the Hotmail people were doing (very, very successfully – first as an independent company and then, starting in 1998, as part of Microsoft). We were both trying to distribute software to everyone who needed it, regardless of where they were.

But all the approaches of distributing technology that I had learned within government involved flying around the world to every country. And lots of conferences, and lots of training sessions – and, by no means coincidentally, a lot of *per diem* payments, a lot of hotel bills, a lot of frequent flier miles, and a lot of contracts for trainers and consultants.

I should know. I was one of those trainer/consultants.

But Hotmail wasn't doing it like that at all. Hotmail was getting software capacity out to its users, but not flying around the world to do it. Hotmail wasn't training people, Hotmail wasn't paying for *per diem*, or hotels, or airfare.

Of course, Hotmail was just the beginning. I soon saw my African colleagues using LinkedIn and Flickr and Gmail and Google Maps, and of course *none* of those things required any training. Or programmers. Or consultants.

Lesson 6: Technology creates new business models; new business models drive technology.

This dramatic difference in approach, I realized, wasn't driven by technology but by business model. Hotmail had used every tool at its disposal to drive costs down. First, it used the web and shared 'cloud' servers to decrease hardware costs. Then, it simplified the software so that no training or support was required.

With costs close to zero per user, Hotmail was able to support itself not through training and consulting and flying out to locations where it was used (like most development organizations). Instead, it could more than recover its very low costs simply through advertising revenue.

Hotmail was also very pointedly not an 'open source' application (and neither was Gmail or Flickr or LinkedIn or Google Maps). That is, the computer source code that made up the Hotmail program was not made available to the public. Why? Because if it were, then anyone with a server would theoretically be able to deploy their own Hotmail clone, and no one would use Hotmail, and they would no longer be able to get advertising revenue to support themselves (and to support improvements to the product).

Of course, regular users are not interested in seeing source code. They are interested in simply getting their work done. E-mail, for instance. And with its free, simple e-mail program available to anyone with a browser, Hotmail spread rapidly to even the poorest regions on earth (not, yet, to the shepherd in the field, but definitely to the professionals at their desks in the capital cities).

I wasn't so much interested in supporting EpiSurveyor by advertisements, but I was *very* interested in worldwide scale. I realized that if we could move EpiSurveyor to the web it would mean that no one would need to install it anymore (you don't install websites, you just type their web address into a browser and hit 'Go'), and just as importantly no one would need to hire a consultant or trainer to use it anymore (not even me). It might even be possible that we could have people using EpiSurveyor in every country on Earth.

So in 2009, EpiSurveyor became the first Hotmail-style web application created for international development. It was also free, online in the browser, and so simple that any literate person could use it without the need for organized training.

Miracle #2: the mobile phone

The web certainly made it easier for us to move *software* around the world, but that didn't solve our issue with *hardware*. We still needed a cheap mobile computer on which to run the app – and the Palm Pilot, as I mentioned, was just not widely available enough.

This problem has famously been solved by the tidal wave of mobile phone adoption through rich and poor countries alike (see Figure 5.3). We realized that if we wrote public health software to run on mobile phones that the costs of exporting devices to poor countries would be borne by the mobile manufacturers and distributors – not by us, or the global health community.

This meant that we could piggy-back on the success of mobile, and that's what we did. As we moved EpiSurveyor from the PC to the web, we simultaneously moved the mobile component from the PDA to Nokia's common Symbian 'feature phone' platform.

Almost immediately after the move the Palm began a rapid collapse, to our shock. Had we not made the move to phones, EpiSurveyor would have died with the Palm. But as it turned out, the Symbian platform would also soon be under siege, as the iPhone and Android phones began grabbing market share. So we soon added iPhone and Android versions of our mobile app.

Lesson 7: Never rely on a single hardware platform.

FIGURE 5.3 Mobile phones per 100 People, 2005–13

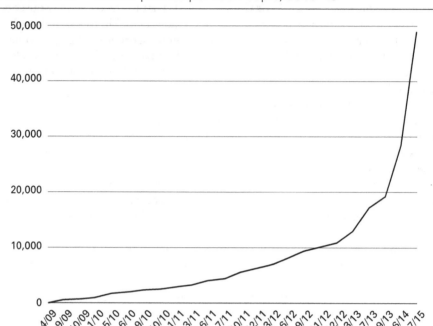

EpiSurveyor phase 2: rapid growth (2009–12)

My initial hunch that we needed to follow the technology model of Hotmail (and Facebook and Flickr) was really borne out by our experience. During June 2009 to December 2012 we saw EpiSurveyor users online rise from zero to more than 10,000. And just as predicted from the Hotmail model, those users were active in more than 170 countries – and we had never even spoken with the vast majority of them.

That was a slightly bitter pill to swallow. I had always enjoyed going out to the field, travelling in exotic places, and providing training. I missed it, and still do. But we had learned an enormously important lesson:

> Lesson 8: If your technology requires an expert on the ground every time it's used, it will never scale.

It turned out that our enjoyable training trips to the field were in themselves an enormous obstacle to widespread use, and eliminating them increased our user base dramatically. 'Self-service' was definitely the way to go.

This lesson has not tended to be very popular in global development given that it goes against the very lucrative consultant approach.

Not just for epidemiological surveys (2013)

Though we had initially created EpiSurveyor for epidemiological surveys, when we changed our distribution channel to the web we quickly found that other users were discovering the software and using it to collect data on a whole variety of things. This is probably the most amazing part of what we do and how we do it. Almost every month I learn about some other user or organization that has discovered Magpi (the new name for EpiSurveyor since January 2013) and how they put it to use doing something I never imagined.

FIGURE 5.4   Magpi users July 2009–13

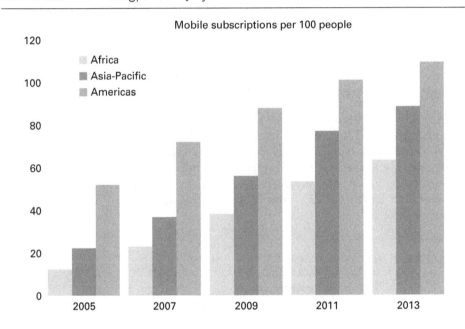

Just a few examples:

Camfed

Camfed is a UK-based charity that promotes the education of girls. With programmes in five sub-Saharan African countries, Camfed pays families to keep girls in school, and monitors school activity for the girls in its programmes.

Its old monitoring system, on paper, required a year or two before the data would even reach anything like a management report.

Then Camfed switched to Magpi for *real-time* monitoring of its programmes. Data collected on basic phones by teachers got uploaded to Magpi, then sent to Salesforce.com for analysis and display on web dashboards. All in all, an amazing use of technology – with running costs of less than $15,000 per year for all five countries combined.

JSI (John Snow Inc)

JSI is a US-based organization working in global development that has used Magpi extensively. It has also provided funding for us to add additional features to Magpi that have benefited all of our users.

JSI has pioneered the use of Magpi for supply chain management – one more thing we never intended it for – utilizing it efficiently to gather and analyse stock availability and case management data for malaria medicines at health facilities each quarter in Tanzania, Ghana, Liberia and Zambia.

According to JSI's website: 'EpiSurveyor [Magpi] has replaced paper-based data collection and, by automating data entry analysis, has improved the speed and accuracy of completing and disseminating quarterly reports. The information gathered through mobile phones provides quick, actionable information to PMI, USAID, Ministries of Health (MoHs) and in-country partners regarding stock-outs, supervision and training problems, expiring drugs, and more. It enables decision makers to intervene sooner to resolve potential problems.'

Kenya Ministry of Public Health and Sanitation (MOH)

Kenya's MoH has been a long-time partner as we developed Magpi, and it was the first place we tested the software back in the PDA days *and* the first place we tested the software using mobile phones. Now there are many experienced Magpi users at the MoH, and they use it for everything from one-off surveys to tracking polio outbreaks, to monitoring the twice-yearly *Malezi Bora* (Child Health) week in collaboration with UNICEF – and Magpi use has now spread to the Kenya Red Cross, as well.

FIGURE 5.5   Kenya MOH fighting polio with Magpi

PHOTO: Joel Selanikio

Many, many others are using Magpi as well. Physicians for Human Rights used Magpi to document sexual violence in Congo and elsewhere. Abt Associates has used it to monitor tuberculosis treatment. Researchers in South America have used Magpi for studies of the human papillomavirus. And the Canadian government used Magpi to monitor outbreaks of disease on commercial pig farms.

The message from all this, of course, is that the world population is cleverer and more resourceful than any organization or individual could be. By making Magpi simple and free for almost all users, we allow anyone – regardless of how much money or how many connections they have, or whether we even know they exist – to gain the benefits of mobile data collection.

The mechanics: it's the business model, stupid (2009–10)

Our move online to the cloud did not just allow more users to sign up – it also gave us visibility into who was logging into the software. We could see, in real time, which people from which organizations were logged in at any one time – and who was not. This led to some uncomfortable revelations.

My career as a professional PowerPoint performer

While going over our user activity logs for the online EpiSurveyor app, I quickly realized that no-one from any of our funding organizations was listed. It turned out that no-one who was supporting us had ever seen our working software.

This didn't seem to make sense. Who would pay to support software without ever looking at it? And if our funders hadn't seen the software, what information were they using when they decided whether to fund us each year?

Slowly, and uncomfortably, I realized that my idea of myself as primarily a technologist was wrong. I was not being paid to create great technology – after all, none of our funders had any idea at all whether our technology was good or bad, or even if it existed.

I was a storyteller. I was being paid to produce stories about technology saving lives in poor countries. Stories that I sold once a year to our funders, in the form of PowerPoint presentations. Stories that they then distributed to their constituents.

> Lesson 9: Your job is what people pay you to do. This is sometimes different from what you believe your job to be. Figure out what your real job is, and if it's what you really want to be doing.

I can't emphasize it enough. I am confident that even if we had produced *no software at all* my excellent PowerPoint skills could have kept the money coming. And in my experience, this is all too common in international development. Good communications skills can make bad technology, or even non-existent technology, smell like a rose – and building a good slide deck is cheaper and faster than building good technology.

Keep in mind: I'm not saying that people with great technology should not tell that story. I'm saying that in many cases I see stories about technology *substituted for* the sustained and scaled development of really useful software.

> Lesson 10: Some organizations in international development have learned that it is easier and cheaper to tell stories about sustainable and scaled technology than it is to create it – and just as effective for obtaining funding.

For me, the burning question became how to get evaluated primarily on our technological skill, rather than on our PowerPoint skills. How could we become *real* technologists, not just storytellers about technology?

Which was another way of saying, 'How do we get paid for our technology, not for our storytelling?'

The freemium is the message

During the PowerPoint era our product was stories, and our customers were grant-making foundations. Looking once again to Silicon Valley for inspiration, I identified a new business model for EpiSurveyor that I thought fitted perfectly with international development. It was called 'freemium'.

Freemium ('free' + 'premium') is familiar to most people who use Skype. Most people know there is a free version that is used to make computer-to-computer calls, and there is also a paid version of Skype that is used to make computer-to-phone calls (and vice versa).

Because Skype uses the internet to transmit its call data efficiently, its costs per call are exceptionally low, and close to zero for computer-to-computer calls. This cost-efficiency allows Skype to 'give away' computer-to-computer calls, and still make enough revenue with computer-to-phone calls to be profitable.

Even today, after Skype was acquired by Microsoft and pushed to increase the percentage of paying users, about 75 per cent of users never pay anything.

I thought this kind of model would be great for international development because, in my experience, a small percentage of organizations had huge amounts of money for technology, but the large majority had almost no money at all.

So the small percentage of organizations with money could be our customers, buying our technology product. We'd still tell stories, of course, but that wouldn't be our primary job anymore. Those organizations would be paying us for our software – and if our software wasn't good enough, they wouldn't pay us – thus making us absolutely dependent for our livelihoods not on the quality of our stories but on the quality of our technology.

As with Skype, free users get a great deal, but so do paying users. In almost every instance, the cost of paying for our software is a tiny fraction of the cost of collecting data with paper, and cheaper than other electronic systems that require technology consultants and programmers.

In international development, organizations generally tend to get the technology they can afford. Rich organizations – or organizations that can successfully attract the attention of a rich donor – can afford to build or buy great tech. Other organizations often get little or nothing.

But just as Gmail is available to everyone, no matter how much money they make, Magpi is available to every organization – from the smallest local project to the biggest multinational activities. The size of the organization, or its budget, is no longer a barrier to adoption of critical, even life-saving, technology like Magpi. In our freemium model, small organizations can use the free version of Magpi for as long as they like. And the projects with big budgets that buy Magpi subscriptions end up supporting its free use for all those other organizations.

That is deeply, deeply satisfying to all of us at Magpi.

Sharing is good. Sharing everything is suicide

You'll remember that earlier on I noted that Hotmail and our other early inspirations like Skype and Google Maps were not open source products. In other words, their core source code was protected and not made public, a decision that enabled them to compete. Skype and Google *do* share some of their code, but usually just enough to let other software connect to it. These bits of software are called APIs (Application Programming Interfaces). Google Maps API, for example, lets any other piece of software 'talk to' Google Maps. For every restaurant listing, for example, Yelp sends the restaurant address to Google Maps and Google Maps very nicely sends back a map showing the restaurant location.

Google does this in part because it makes more people use Google Maps, and see the ads they are paid to display. If they made *all* the code for Google Maps available, Yelp would just make their own copy and no one would ever click from Yelp to Google Maps anymore. Fewer ads viewed, less revenue to support Google Maps, potentially no more Google Maps.

This model – keeping your main product code a secret so it can be a revenue source, and providing an API to make your main product even more useful (and therefore more monetizable) – has proven very successful. Silicon Valley start-ups following this model have made billions of dollars, and a lot of that money goes into improving their products to fend off competition. And ultimately the user benefits; including, in many cases, users who don't have much or any money.

In international development, unfortunately, almost every piece of grant-funded technology is open source. While it is often said by proponents that this means that *anyone* can modify every piece of software for their own benefit, the problem is that *anyone* really means 'anyone who knows how to read and edit computer code'. Which is not *everyone*. In practice, this means that those technologies are:

- *Hard or impossible to monetize*
  It is hard to sell something while you're simultaneously giving it away for free.

- *Dependent on grant funding*
  As we've discussed, this makes them subject to the 'storyteller' issue, and means that their customers are in reality the grant funders, not the users of their software.

- *Dependent on consultants*
  Because of the storytelling problem, these technologies never seem to advance to the level of simplicity of Hotmail, or Facebook. Although the software is

'free', it's the kind of free that requires expensive technology consultants to be installed and maintained and made useful. Which, like a 'free' car that requires you to employ a chauffeur to drive it for you, really isn't free at all.

So, in 2010, after becoming the first web-based application for international development, EpiSurveyor also became the first freemium application. And at the same time, and not at all coincidentally, we also moved from an open source (and therefore grant-funded) approach to a standard Silicon Valley one. Today, our core code is private and we have APIs to let others connect their software to Magpi.

And because of this, Magpi also became the first (and is still one of the only) technology companies providing free technology to development and global health organizations that is completely self-sustaining, with no grant revenue. This, despite less than 1 per cent of our users paying to use our software.

Magpi here and now

Moving to the cloud and switching to a freemium, closed-source, API business model has driven further changes, including a change of name from EpiSurveyor to Magpi as our users began showing us it was useful for a lot more than just epidemiological surveys.

Also, we originally had two price tiers (free and 'Pro' for US$5,000 annually) but later expanded to include a US$10,000 annual 'Enterprise' subscription with features and capacity suited for larger organizations.

In autumn 2013 we added 'Magpi Messaging' – super-easy, super-affordable and super-fast basic messaging capabilities that lets *every* organization create an SMS-based education system, or recorded-audio vaccination reminder system, in minutes. Or just to keep their field staff organized. And in 2015 we added 'interactive SMS data collection' which allows data to be collected from *any* phone at all by means of an SMS 'conversation' (really a Magpi form deployed one question at a time by text message, as in Figure 5.6).

I suspect that Magpi Messaging will prove even more popular than Magpi data collection. After all, there are many more people out there looking simply to communicate than to collect data. But only time will tell.

What our work means for the world

Magpi surpassed 50,000 users worldwide in 2015, with more innovative uses emerging all the time. Organizations using our platform include the International Federation of the Red Cross, DARPA, CDC, the Kenya Red Cross (and many other national red cross societies), UNICEF, PACT, IRC, UNFPA, WHO, JSI and many, many others.

Back in 2011, the World Bank did us the enormous favour of documenting and measuring the effect of Magpi (then EpiSurveyor) on their data collection activities

FIGURE 5.6 Magpi 'interactive' SMS data collection

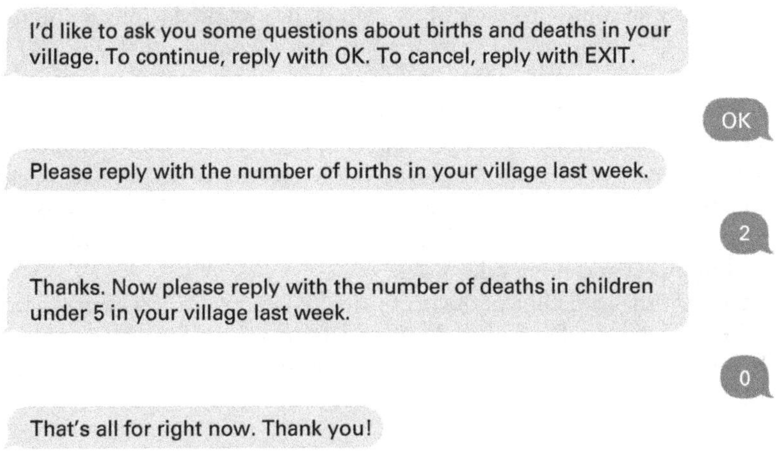

I'd like to ask you some questions about births and deaths in your village. To continue, reply with OK. To cancel, reply with EXIT.

OK

Please reply with the number of births in your village last week.

2

Thanks. Now please reply with the number of deaths in children under 5 in your village last week.

0

That's all for right now. Thank you!

in Central America. In a report titled 'Cutting Costs, Boosting Quality and Collecting Data Real-Time', they noted a 71 per cent reduction in data collection costs compared to their previous paper-based systems.

Think of the millions and millions of dollars spent each year on data collection activities using paper forms in international development, in global health, even in government and commerce. Now imagine saving nearly three-quarters of those costs and making it available for purposes other than photocopying paper forms. Think of thousands of organizations saving thousands, or hundreds of thousands, of dollars for each and every data collection activity – for a collective total of millions and millions of dollars saved, and countless lives improved by better data driving better decisions.

Probably just as important as the cost savings has been the impact of having real-time data available for making decisions. Even small organizations can now react faster to data that's collected and analysed in minutes, not in months or years, or never.

Faster data and better decisions for 71 per cent less money? That's real impact.

Magpi's benefits in time and money were shown in full effect during the 2014–15 (and continuing) Ebola crisis in West Africa. Organizations like IFRC, CDC, IRC and others have used Magpi for every aspect of their data management.

One powerful example has been CDC's use of SMS data collection for 'zero reporting' surveillance in the affected countries. The low cost of Magpi, and of basic mobile phones, has made it possible for CDC to have hundreds of health reporters in each affected country, each equipped with a basic mobile phone, to send a single text message each day reporting the number of suspected Ebola cases seen that day. In most cases – thankfully – that number will be a zero (hence the name of 'zero reporting'). This way, each country is blanketed with a large number of reporters, but the total cost of the technology is less than $10,000 per year, per country – including the cost of the SMS messaging – which is extraordinarily low for a country-wide surveillance network (normally such a system would cost hundreds of thousands of dollars annually).

Another example comes from the IFRC, which has worked to ensure dignified and safe burials for Ebola victims in several countries. As part of that work, IFRC used Magpi to record information about unidentified bodies, including their photos, in the hope that this may allow family members to find out later where their loved ones have been laid to rest. And the technology cost to IFRC is again less than $10,000 per country per year. Importantly, IFRC was able to create and deploy that Magpi-based system themselves. There was no need for expensive technical consultants or programmers, expertise that would have eaten up tens of thousands of valuable dollars just in travel and hotel bills alone.

And finally, as the lead clinical doctor at the IMC Lunsar Ebola Treatment Center in Sierra Leone between December 2014 and January 2015, I was able to devise a Magpi-based electronic health record system that may in future reduce the incredible burden of hours of daily paperwork that confronts health workers in these treatment centres.

As to the future, I don't know what comes after Magpi Messaging and interactive SMS, but I think that at Magpi we'll just keep doing what we've been doing:

1 identify a technology like mobile data collection that is useful but barely used because it's too complicated and expensive;

2 make it simple and affordable by using the cloud and mobile and freemium;

3 sit back and watch all the crazy, cool and life-saving things people do with it.

FIGURE 5.7   The author recording clinical patient data in an Ebola treatment centre, December 2014

Lessons learnt

Most of us are oblivious to the great societal and technological changes occurring around us. Again and again I have been helped in my career by being well-informed in a broad variety of fields. And I got that way by reading widely outside the field of medicine. I recommend reading at least a third of *The Economist* every week, including one of the articles about business, and a book outside your main field at least a few times a year.

1 *We don't know what you think we know.* Although our increased connectivity (thanks to the internet and mobile phone) has brought more of the world in front of our eyes, it's important to be aware that there is still plenty that we do not yet know, measure, or chart.

2 *Technical people always underestimate the scarcity, and the cost, of their own expertise.* If I had a dollar every time a programmer described some open-source software – that required me to hire them to use – as 'free', I'd be a rich man.

3 *You cannot do this alone.* Or at least I couldn't. I've been extraordinarily lucky to have had a partner in building Magpi that thinks completely differently than I do, but who has the same values – which include the understanding of how to resolve differences amicably. Thanks, Rose.

4 *It is easier to move electrons than molecules: it's much easier to build and scale software worldwide than hardware.* This is one of the fundamental lessons of our internet/mobile phone world. Others did the hard work by combining the technologies that allow mobile phones and networks to be possible, and then business models that allowed that possibility to become reality. Once those devices and networks were in place, everyone and anyone with connectivity can theoretically reach everyone else – with their art, their writing, and their software.

5 *Technology creates new business models. New business models drive technology.* I am constantly meeting people working in international development – daily users of Gmail and Facebook – who do not believe that a truly free version of Magpi exists. Then, when I assure them that it does, they struggle to understand how it could be sustainable. They swim in the ocean of internet economies of scale, but they are unaware of the water. For that, I'd recommend a weekly glance at *The Economist*.

6 *Never rely on a single hardware platform.* To me this is just common sense. Although it is admittedly harder to support multiple platforms (PC/Mac or Android/iOS), it does get easier all the time, and it's a much stronger position from the perspective of not going out of business.

7 *If your technology requires an expert on the ground every time it's used, it will never scale.* The technologies available to us, and the world, exist because we as a society have discovered methods to lower the cost of scaling them. And one of the most important methods is wherever possible to replace every human expert with software. It works for Uber (which replaces the human taxi dispatcher), it works for Google Maps (which replaces human mapmakers), and it can work for whatever you're doing.

8 *Your job is what people pay you to do. This is sometimes different from what you believe your job to be. Figure out what your real job is, and if that's what you really want to be doing.* I spent years getting paid to tell stories, while thinking I was being paid to create technology. I should have noticed all those years ago that the only thing our donors ever yelled at us about was when we were late in submitting our stories and reports. They never yelled at us for being slow to add features, or because of the quality of the user experience or the reliability of the software. That should have rung alarm bells, but it didn't.

9 *Some organizations in international development have learned that it is easier and cheaper to tell stories about sustainable and scaled technology than it is to create it – and just as effective for obtaining funding.* If you want to do more than tell stories, make sure that your organization is truly focused on its programmes, not Powerpoint. Make sure you get funding that pushes you to excel at what *you* want to do. And if that's not Powerpoint, you should strongly consider avoiding grant funding, or decreasing your dependency on it as soon as you can. Having users pay you for your product will make your success or failure dependent on how good the product is, which is really all that matters.

Discussion questions

1 How do consultant-based business models in technology, and international development, foster dependence on the part of aid recipients? Is the emphasis on 'free and open source' technologies, which require much more technical assistance than free closed source tools, a result of this consultant-driven model?

2 Given that free open source technologies in international development generally require much more technical assistance than free closed source, does this explain the preference of development technology consultants for open source? What other reasons might there be? How do you feel about closed vs open source approaches?

3 Why are simple, free, self-service apps like Facebook and Google Maps so common in consumer applications, but so rare in international development? Is this a technology issue, or a business model issue?

4 Compare the business model of Apple or Google to the business model of an organization working in 'technology for development'. For each, where does the revenue come from? What is the product (that is, what is exchanged for that revenue)? Who is the customer (that is, who provides the revenues)?

5 Technology (like mobile phones) is often paid for by the users of that technology. What changes when a third party (eg a donor) is paying for the technology? What are the pros and cons of each approach? What if the third party is an advertiser, rather than a donor? How does this affect the quality of the technology produced?

Further reading

You can find more material to do with this chapter at www.koganpage.com/
socialentrepreneurship

Munk, N *The Idealist: Jeffrey Sachs and the quest to end poverty*
Moyo, D *Dead Aid: Why aid is not working and how there is a better way for Africa*
Christiansen, C *The Innovator's Dilemma: When technologies cause great firms to fail*
My TED Talk: http://bit.ly/magpi-ted-talk

06
Food waste meets food poverty: closing the loop

FOODCYCLE – KELVIN CHEUNG AND MICHAEL NORTON

ABSTRACT

The story of FoodCycle starts with Kelvin Cheung and Michael Norton. Michael is a serial social entrepreneur and the founder of the Centre for Innovation in Voluntary Action (CIVA). He also co-founded UnLtd – the foundation for social entrepreneurs – who grant awards to individuals wishing to make changes in their community.

Kelvin was interning at MyBnk in 2007, another project started by CIVA, and was looking for something fun to get involved with. The location was London. It was 2008, and Kelvin and Michael were on a project collision path. One of the big issues of the day was the co-existence of food waste and food poverty in Britain. One might wonder how we have come to accept the existence of such a paradox around the world.

Rather than looking at the causes of these two huge problems, the idea was to shortcut both issues and instead focus on reducing food poverty *through* food waste. Could one of the problems – food waste – also act as a solution?

With a focus on student and young people's potential in the community, Michael and CIVA asked Kelvin to help incubate a programme based around volunteering, food surplus and spare kitchen space.

With three months' living expenses to research and develop what was to become FoodCycle, Kelvin set off for the United States. There he connected with The Campus Kitchens Project, a highly successful student-powered hunger relief initiative which seemed to encapsulate a new approach to an old problem. Kelvin and Michael wanted to research whether a similar model would be viable in the United Kingdom. Having done that, the next step was to try it out for a year. And Kelvin was hooked.

It was only after the initial start up that Kelvin and the team realized there was also a social isolation aspect to FoodCycle as well. It was hardly new that people received a free meal; nor was it new that people enjoyed community activities. But what *did* seem new was that food waste would be the vehicle for this initiative.

The FoodCycle journey

So how does a Chinese Canadian end up running a UK-based food charity?

Kelvin originally comes from Canada. In 2006 he came over to London with a plan to get a Masters in International Development, and a teaching degree, and go back to Toronto to get a job at his old high school to teach and inspire students there.

In 2008 he met Michael Norton, and this changed pretty much everything. Through Michael he got to visit Campus Kitchens in the United States, and saw the real potential of a similar food-based project taking off in the United Kingdom. Lily Lapenna was another key contact. Lily co-founded MyBnk, an organization which focuses on teaching young people financial management skills, and she introduced Kelvin to the friendly and passionate world of social enterprise. Interning at MyBnk for six months – at the stage they were about to take off as an organization – gave Kelvin many of the skills he needed to 'just do it' when FoodCycle started. UnLtd gave him his first official start-up grant of £5,000 to try out the idea at one location, and to give what essentially was a young person with very little work experience a chance.

Kelvin also credits his parents as a major influence on him. Their support – along with his dad's own influence as an entrepreneur – were key. It was lucky, perhaps, that he never received that often-shared parental advice to 'get a real job'.

10 May 2009 will always be remembered as 'that' pivotal day in FoodCycle's history. After six months of getting the key ingredients of food, volunteers and a kitchen together for the first FoodCycle cooking session ever – it was game time.

The moment of truth came as we all looked into a pot of brown slop. This was not the gourmet meal we wanted, but we'd come too far to quit now. We took it on as our mission to make each week tastier and better – and when you're starting from what we cooked, well, we definitely did get a lot better!

Fast-forward four months to September 2009. FoodCycle had been turning out weekly meals and was very quickly becoming dependent on a core founder team. And without buy-in it would never scramble to its feet. Drawn in by the prospect of gaining hands-on experience in a field they were passionate about, two postgraduate students jumped at the opportunity to join the FoodCycle movement.

Tory Coates and Jessie Veltman became the second and third members of the team. Says Tory: 'I started in September 2009 with Jessie. Both of us were finishing MAs and got involved in FoodCycle for different reasons. Jess was in the process of finishing her MA in Public Health Nutrition so came in with the idea of improving nutrition and starting a café project. I was excited by the simple idea of using wasted resources in a unique way. I also liked the fact that we were giving students skills beyond university degrees. Of course we both loved food, too – probably the thing that connects all FoodCyclers!'

So, from May to August 2009, while Kelvin was getting his first cooking sessions together with some friends, somewhere in London two other students were approaching graduation and looking to get their hands dirty.

Food waste and food poverty: joining the dots

It all started with food waste. Then we realized we could use food waste to feed people, and we realized that many of the hungry people out there were living in the same communities as those creating the waste. Then we noticed how volunteers could come together and build a community for themselves. And that the teamwork and innovation required to make a meal is amazing.

But let's pause for a moment and take a look at the wider issues. What is food waste and food poverty?

Food waste, food poverty and social isolation

On their own, their origins are rooted in complex socio-political factors.

The effects of the financial crash of 2007–08 led to a rise in poverty levels around the world. The United Kingdom was no exception. One symptom of the crash was escalating 'food poverty' – people being unable to get healthy and affordable food. This might be due to lack of income, lack of access, or lack of knowledge. People may also not have shops in their area, or have difficulty reaching them, or local shops might not stock much healthy food, or people might not know how to cook well enough. Today, many people simply cannot afford the cost of food along with rising rent payments, utility bills and other household expenses. Due to this complex mix of factors, people living on low incomes generally have the lowest intake of fruit and vegetables and are far more likely to suffer from diet-related diseases such as cancer, diabetes, obesity and coronary heart disease.

Surplus food is food that is fit for human consumption, but has no commercial value or its sale is restricted by the date on its label. Food may be mislabelled, damaged, have incorrect packaging, have expired its shelf life date, been over-ordered or over-supplied. Though retailers work hard to minimize food waste, we know from our collections that there is sufficient volume to provide services such as FoodCycle's.

Despite hiding in plain sight, the co-existence of the dual problem of food waste and food poverty seemed rarely, if at all, spoken about in a start-up capacity. Combining surplus food to address food poverty seemed an obvious solution to a growing problem. Perhaps surprisingly, then, the catalyst for FoodCycle to expand beyond Kelvin's group of friends came from students and postgraduates looking for all-important work experience lacking at university.

When you have no experience and no money, but a bit of time, the risk in trying something out is small and it's possible to find out pretty quickly if an idea will work. 'I think this became much more prominent in the era of Big Society, government cuts and rising food prices, and it just seems so obvious and simple', says Tory. 'Use food that would otherwise be thrown away to bring people around the table. When we first started, bridging the skills gap among young people was considered equally as important as the issues of social isolation and food waste. And as a student fresh from an MA, the competitive job market made this appealing to me.'

FoodCycle's first cooking events experimented with the conflicting problems of food waste and food poverty. But what emerged was a realization that these sessions could also address social isolation. The simple idea of combining two problems started to become more meaningful when we saw the power of communal dining as an answer to social isolation.

Social isolation is loneliness, or a lack of contact with other people and the wider community. This can affect anyone but there are particular links to physical and mental health, disability, age, unemployment, transportation, loss of a spouse, and socio-economic background. Older people are particularly vulnerable to being socially isolated after the loss of friends and family, reduced mobility or limited income. Research from Age UK in 2014 showed that over 1 million older people say they often feel lonely and nearly 600,000 older people leave their house once a week or less.

'At first we thought of the food waste, and then the fact that people in the communities were going hungry' says Kelvin. 'It was the coexistence of colossal food waste and devastating hunger in the same communities. But then we realized the social isolation aspect of it, too. We hadn't realized this at first.'

Our first cooking session

From May to August 2009, FoodCycle became a reality. Kelvin and his friends took all the food and resources they could get. They looked for the triple donations – food, time and kitchen space – and tried to fit them together.

After a major scouting exercise, following leads, online searches and cold calling, FoodCycle found Lucy at Fleet River Bakery in London. Not terribly far from where FoodCycle needed to deliver, Fleet River had a professional kitchen, available for free and perhaps most importantly an ex-start-up entrepreneur. As such, Lucy was receptive to what FoodCycle were trying to achieve and happy to try to help make it work.

The team reflected on those very early days:

> We were just a band of university students and we didn't really know what we were doing. People all had their own ideas, so things were just cobbled together. The first time we had food, in that first cooking session, we had stuff from Planet Organic and fresh vegetables from a friend's allotment. We cooked up absolute rubbish – a kind-of big stew. We didn't really think too much about the logistics – we knew we needed to deliver it the next day but we only just finished cooking at 11 pm. Everybody was pretty tired and wanted to go home.
>
> Fleet River Bakery had to be open at 5 am the next day to make bread. Needless to say, the remnants of the previous day's cooking session were still a little apparent the next morning! And so it was, we got a call from one irate baker asking 'What is all this stuff doing in my kitchen?' It's fair to say there was a lot of chaos.

Two weeks in and things still weren't running very smoothly. But that's the nature of starting up. It's not really designed to be smooth. It wasn't really designed at all. As Kelvin says, 'I think that's the process that every FoodCycler and every Hub has to go through'.

That first beneficiary group was The Choir with No Name – an amazing initiative that runs choirs for people affected by homelessness. They actually had a food service already, where they'd get ready-made sandwiches for members. But it wasn't great. A sandwich isn't really a substitute for a home-cooked meal, and we really liked the idea of getting people together and actually cooking. We were with The Choir with No Name for two months. Then we moved to Holy Cross, part of the Kings Cross area of London, and were cooking and serving every week. It was hard because we were offering two services – we also had a Hub at Imperial College London, which would deliver food to people at a refugee centre – and on a Sunday.

By this time the team wanted to make FoodCycle work so much that they were muddling through and somehow coping despite a lack of expertise. Failure was never an option.

Seeing the ready-made sandwich delivery service and its limitations helped FoodCycle adapt its strategy to focus on improving the service and experience for the diners, as well as the quality of the food being served to them.

At the beginning our pitch to potential customers was along the lines of 'what are you doing now that's costing you money, and why don't we provide that to you for free?' We'd then go in and help them create a better meal for more people, totally free of charge. This was a breakthrough moment. It was only when we started providing services that hadn't previously been there, such as this brand new community dining event, that we saw how important the communal aspect of the project was. We were beginning to realize how powerful food could be as a tool to unite people.

An initial challenge for FoodCycle in pitching to organizations was that people wanted to see a menu prepared in advance. If not that, a simple guideline or hint as to what to expect to eat. When you work with food surplus you don't always know what ingredients or foods will be available day to day, so this turned out to be very hard to do.

Kelvin, however, saw this more as an opportunity for FoodCycle, and a key component of what FoodCycle was:

> Once you see the challenge in action then you understand. It's where the creativity and teamwork and everybody coming together to solve a problem comes in. It's not your traditional cooking approach, which is deciding what you're going to make, thinking about what you have, and then buying all the ingredients.
>
> We were trying to change the way people went about cooking a meal. It was more about just seeing what you've got, thinking about what we know of food and cooking, and just taking a gamble – seeing if your culinary innovation would actually work. You don't know if it will, of course – but you have to try. And that's a big part of it.

And of course this practice remains with FoodCycle today. The 'Ready Steady Cook' element continues to be not only the best way to deal with on-the-day surplus, but a big attraction when it comes to people wanting to volunteer. We worked with The Choir with No Name for two months.

The evolution of the FoodCycle project

As mentioned earlier, by this time FoodCycle had begun working with a Hub at Imperial College London, who delivered food to people at a refugee centre. Imperial Hub's meals were better at first because they bought their own ingredients, but after a while they started to get donations from a farmer's market near Kensington. That was another key moment for us, realizing the benefits of starting Hubs with a local food source nearby. FoodCycle was still very much in experimental, start-up mode, thinking on its feet the whole time. But a strategy and approach was beginning to emerge.

Tory joined in September 2009 with a remit to expand the Hub projects. Initially the model was based around universities, which worked well because students often had free time to run a project. This sometimes ran into trouble, though, particularly during the long summer break. Beneficiaries and supermarkets needed continuity for this to work.

Despite the challenges, progress was being made. The third FoodCycle Hub scrambled to its feet shortly after at London's School of Oriental and African Studies (SOAS).

Our strategy for starting up Hubs was to find the key components all at the same time – volunteers, kitchen space and surplus food. This can be difficult. You need to identify and track down all the community spaces and talk to them, gain their trust, and then figure out where the closest market is. The days need to match up, too. The venue might want the meal on a Saturday but you can only get the food on a Sunday.

Up until this point, FoodCycle had focused solely on opportunities in London, but this all changed when Kelvin met a guy called Max on a training course. Max was a student activist over at Bristol University and he was interested in working with the model. As increasing numbers of people started talking about FoodCycle, more and more people expressed interest in what we were doing. Everyone seemed to have friends at other universities, so they'd tell them about FoodCycle. Word-of-mouth can be a powerful ally, but it all began to move a little too quickly and things spiralled out of control. By this time FoodCycle had 14 Hubs, and the team decided it was time to pause expanding and take stock. Too much growth too quickly isn't always a good thing.

Kelvin was a realist throughout all of this. Some Hubs would rise up, some would never launch, others would shut down, some take breaks, others rework strategy and approach. But this seemed to be the nature of FoodCycle, which had expanded from just two projects to a dozen in just a year.

'On reflection things went too quick. There were challenges with Hub leadership, and we still hadn't tested how different projects would work in different places', said Tory. 'At times some Hubs required vast amounts of work, especially in areas where kitchens were hard to find. Others needed financial support that we hadn't anticipated. Trial and error did mean we had to close down the Edinburgh project because of difficulties getting commitment from volunteers.'

The café project

While Tory expanded the Hub programme, Jess set up a café initiative to improve nutrition in the community. 'The initial idea for the café was to facilitate change in the food environment', explains Nicola Corney, the FoodCycle Community Café Manager at the time. 'We decided not to focus exclusively on people in extreme food poverty – those who cannot afford to eat – but to include those who do not have access to healthy food for a number of other reasons. The café provides a healthier alternative to what is on offer in Bromley-by-Bow – chicken shops and greasy spoon cafés.'

By this time, FoodCycle had already moved into east London's Bromley-by-Bow Centre and opened Pie in the Sky. It was at this point, with an expanding Hubs programme and the community café idea, that two models emerged. These two models were to live side by side, both operating under our banner of tackling food waste and food poverty – the Hubs building communities with a free, healthy three-course meal in a communal dining environment, and the cafés as an example of how affordable healthy eating can be achieved along with a successful community training programme.

The first café was based in Bromley-by-Bow, one of the most deprived wards in the United Kingdom and an area of high unemployment and poor health outcomes. There, we support volunteer trainees including young people not in employment, education or training, young ex-offenders, and people who are long-term unemployed. Serving over 50 meals per day, the café environment provided an opportunity for confidence building and the development of skills needed to gain employment in the hospitality and food industry. FoodCycle developed a structured training model, offering an induction to working in a high-pressured kitchen environment, the development of cooking and nutrition skills, and customer service and barista training. Volunteer trainees also gained a Level 2 Food Hygiene Certification. Our café also ran our catering enterprise, providing delicious food handmade from surplus ingredients. All proceeds from catering went back into the café to help support and train more volunteers.

However, despite its popularity, positive outcomes and successes in helping young people back into employment, Pie In The Sky Community Café did not make money and wasn't filling our charitable mission. A strategic review carried out *pro bono* by a management consultancy firm exposed the problems of having a deep social impact and achieving financial sustainability. In an economic climate where these two elements would strongly conflict with each other in the short term, a very real dilemma emerged. In June 2015, after four years, the difficult decision was taken to close Pie In The Sky Community Café.

FoodCycle's social franchise model

FoodCycle's social franchise system was developed to enable the FoodCycle Hub network to expand across the United Kingdom. Its objective is to increase the social impact that we make whilst still delivering the service in a high quality, consistent format. The FoodCycle social franchise system was developed by FoodCycle in conjunction with the International Centre for Social Franchising (the-icsf.org.uk).

Two different social franchise formats were developed – the organizational franchise model and the community franchise model. It is expected that most FoodCycle franchisees will come from existing groups or organizations but it is possible to establish a new community group to operate as a FoodCycle social franchise Hub. As part of the agreement, FoodCycle social franchisees are required to appoint a 'nominated individual' who will be the main point of contact between FoodCycle centrally and the local Hub.

Franchising is about the replication of a tried and tested model – business format franchises replicate commercial businesses and social franchising replicates social enterprises and charities.

To ensure quality and consistency is maintained, there must be a franchise agreement and the Hub must deliver social impact and be financially sustainable.

FoodCycle specifics

Funding

In August 2009, we received funding from the Esmée Fairbairn Foundation one year after the initial idea and just months after the first cooking session. They agreed to fund FoodCycle for three years.

Trust

FoodCycle needed to be developed as a brand to gain people's trust. We had to create something that sold, that was cool and fun and attractive. So we got pictures of people cooking, we got t-shirts and business cards and a Facebook page. And we made a brand that people wanted to be a part of. We were also very open and honest about the practical aspects and challenges of FoodCycle's work so that people would trust us, and believed we were going to do what we said we were going to.

Insurance, food safety and consumer confidence

We knew we needed this from the very beginning. It wasn't easy to persuade people that we weren't going to poison them, especially since we were using surplus food and nobody really knew what that meant. But when we said we weren't going to use meat, it was all freshly cooked and we weren't going to reheat it, they soon bought in.

Volunteer management

This was relatively straightforward. Our local Hub leaders took most of the responsibility since they were on the ground. We tried to get formal processes in place to make sure we attracted really good people, but it was mostly just a case of volunteers showing up, if we're honest. The Hubs used their own management systems – a mixture of Group Spaces, Excel, Drive or Dropbox.

Sustainability plan, structure and business model

At the beginning we didn't have a structure, sustainability plan or funding mechanism. These were all made up and evolved as we went along. Some people new to social enterprise might be surprised by this, but it's a reality for many as they seek to get off the ground.

There were a few crises along the way, but we always had belief in what we were doing, allowing us to successfully work through them. When you're on a roll you don't really think about it, particularly when the money continues to come and everything seems to be running okay. We did start thinking a bit about alternative streams of income through the alumni network.

We registered with the UK Charity Commission in February 2010. This not only helped with issues of credibility, but also with fundraising and the process of formalizing our accounts processes. Becoming official legally is another step in gaining credibility and trust.

FoodCycle today relies on a mix of individual donations, partnerships with the private sector and grant funding, plus a management fee from franchisees (see below).

Hub development

Up until this point, new Hubs had been directly delivered by the growing but still small Hub Team at FoodCycle's headquarters. Rapid growth is difficult to sustain, however, when each Hub demands so much input from a Hub manager.

A key landmark in the life of FoodCycle was the development of its Social Franchise Model. The model, developed in partnership with the International Centre for Social Franchising, means that FoodCycle projects are run and hosted by a partner on the ground – a housing association, health service or community organization, for example – meaning we can work more efficiently and with the most impact, collaborating to raise funds from businesses, grant-makers and the local community.

FoodCycle has opened five new Hubs using this model, each run by a local partner organization with an established community presence. Operating under the FoodCycle brand, these Hubs have been able to attract support from trusts, foundations, corporates and local authorities before starting up. And being part of the FoodCycle network has enabled them to attract volunteers, access surplus food and engage their local community. FoodCycle has developed strong relationships with supermarkets to safely make use of their perfectly edible surplus food.

In return for a management fee, FoodCycle provides partner organizations with a package of support, including our online Volunteer Management System, access to the brand and marketing, and training at our annual conference. This is followed by regular support and evaluation to ensure that Hubs are sustainable, of high quality and capable of delivering real social impact.

Brand and marketing

For Kelvin, one of the key elements was branding. FoodCycle was originally called FoodWorks, and it had a logo that was comparatively dull and uninspiring.

The Pip logo we have today was inspired by a post-apocalyptic space-age video game called 'Fallout Three'. Kelvin was pretty obsessed with it and used Vault Boy as inspiration. For six months he tried to convince everyone that this was the brand for us, and it turns out he was right. When the first t-shirts, water bottles and badges were produced it was one of the most exciting and inspiring moments in FoodCycle's history. Great brands bring visions to life, and this did.

FIGURE 6.1   The FoodCycle Logo

In our earlier days we never really had a marketing strategy as such. Once the new brand came through though, it sold itself. We kept an active presence on social media and made sure everyone directly involved had t-shirts and aprons to help them feel part of the brand. That's something really important about FoodCycle – it's a movement. You're part of something meaningful, and something bigger.

2015–20 – the next 50 hubs

Our model has been revised and our vision streamlined to enable us to tackle food poverty and social isolation through the delivery of healthy meals using surplus food. After our recently-undertaken strategic review, and the difficult decision to close Pie in the Sky Community Café, what has emerged is a vision that concentrates our efforts on our Hub programme. Here we cook a three-course nutritious and communal meal for people at risk of food poverty and social isolation with the help of volunteers and surplus food. Our aim is to build community through this activity. Guests have the option to make a donation if they wish, but this is not a prerequisite for enjoying a FoodCycle meal. We are already in 20 locations and our expansion plan projects we'll be in 50 locations within the next five years. What we're finding important now is to choose the right social franchise partner to grow. Having a real impact in the community can only come about if FoodCycle grows in the right environment. A bit like putting a cutting into the right soil.

So we are poised right now at a new stage in our life. And it will be more important than ever to remember who we are and where we've come from in order to navigate the next five years.

FoodCycle in numbers and impact

Since we started cooking in 2009, FoodCycle has:

- served over 105,000 meals;
- created over 1,000 communal dining events each year;
- reclaimed over 120,000 kg of surplus food;
- worked with over 3,000 volunteers;
- received 78,000 hours of volunteer time;
- expanded to 20 Hubs.

Moreover:

- 87 per cent of guests say that they feel more part of the community;
- 85 per cent have made new friends;
- 60 per cent of guests say that coming to FoodCycle has increased their confidence;
- 73 per cent of guests eat more fruit and vegetables after coming to a FoodCycle meal;
- 70 per cent of guests think more about healthy eating.

Lessons learnt

1 *Get a bunch of friends to brainstorm.* Get some ideas, keep it fun.
2 *Start small.* Do it in your spare time. Go one step at a time.
3 *If you're not a 'starter' then help someone else start theirs.*
4 *When you've got an idea, go for it.*
5 *Be clear on your mission.* The more elements there are, the more confusing it can be. Can you develop a start-up with two models? The café always struggled to define itself in relation to the Hubs. Seeing the potential of a model makes it difficult to say no. But it's vital that you learn when to say no.
6 *Financial sustainability.* Tweaking your model to align with funder aims can lead to mission drift. A slight change in your social target may guarantee funding, but weaken your long-term financial sustainability.

7 *Figure out how you are going to demonstrate your impact.* How are you going to measure confidence-boosting, for example?

8 *Rapid expansion versus sustainability.* Tread this line carefully.

9 *Reliable volunteers are essential.* For us, working across universities and the local community worked better.

10 *Create quick and easy systems* for volunteers, monitoring, finance.

11 *Maintaining good communication and relationships is essential.*

Discussion questions

1 At what point does an organic movement need to professionalize? Indeed, does it ever need to professionalize?

2 Kelvin commented on how powerful food could be as a tool to unify people. Why do you think food has this influence?

3 How does FoodCycle use food to help achieve its mission to 'build communities'?

4 For FoodCycle, food waste was a problem that was turned into a solution to food poverty. Can you think of a similar situation, where a problem might become a solution?

5 What do you think of the potential of FoodCycle's social franchise model for its future growth? Can it be applied to other organizations in different sectors?

6 How important is the FoodCycle brand in its success?

7 One of FoodCycle's pieces of advice is to start small and go one step at a time. What do you see as the first steps in your project?

8 Can two models/approaches ever be a good thing? If two models emerge from your idea, how do you deal with them?

9 How do you measure impact such as happiness, friendship and confidence? Do we put enough emphasis on these kinds of 'soft' impact in the social sector?

Further reading

You can find more material to do with this chapter at www.koganpage.com/socialentrepreneurship

About FoodCycle:
   Our homepage: http://foodcycle.org.uk/ [accessed 10 December 2015]
   Personal words from our founder and CEO: http://foodcycle.org.uk/about-us/our-story/
   Projects: http://foodcycle.org.uk/locations/ [accessed 10 December 2015]

Food poverty:

Food Ethics Council: http://www.foodethicscouncil.org/society/
food-poverty.html [accessed 10 December 2015]

Food Ethics magazine: www.foodethicscouncil.org/uploads/publications/
Food_HumanrightsHumanwrongs.pdf [accessed 10 December 2015]

Evidence to the APPG on Hunger and Food Poverty to which FC contributed evidence:
https://foodpovertyinquiry.files.wordpress.com/2014/12/food-poverty-appg-
evidence-review-final.pdf [accessed 10 December 2015]

The Guardian food poverty section: www.theguardian.com/society/food-poverty
[accessed 10 December 2015]

Food waste:

WRAP: www.wrap.org.uk/content/solutions-prevent-household-food-waste [accessed 10
December 2015]

WRAP: UK household waste in 2012 www.wrap.org.uk/content/
household-food-and-drink-waste-uk-2012 [accessed 10 December 2015]

07
Innovation in Africa's Silicon Savannah

USHAHIDI – ERIK HERSMAN

ABSTRACT

On 27 December 2007, Kenya held its five-yearly Presidential elections. Nothing but a peaceful outcome was expected. After all, until that time Kenya's most recent history had seen relatively peaceful elections and transitions of power. However, this one was going to be different. Incumbent President Kibaki was declared the winner and sworn in, despite claims of victory by opposition leader Raila Odinga. Tensions boiled over. Violence broke out across the country. To add to the confusion, reliable information wasn't available on what was happening. This wasn't helped by a certain eerie silence from the government and from the Kenyan media. The international press did a better job of getting information out, but they couldn't be everywhere. Bloggers were doing their best to fill many of the gaps. It was a time of fear and mistrust, not helped by the fact that people were being kept in the dark about what was going on, and where. Deeply concerned, and watching the crisis from a distance, was a group of Kenyan technologists and bloggers, among them Erik Hersman. A blog post from a colleague kicked into action a series of events which led to the creation, over a frantic three-day period, of the Ushahidi platform. Ushahidi – meaning 'witness' in Swahili – allowed people to use a mixture of e-mail, web form and text message to report what was going on where they lived. Information was visualized on a map, creating the most accurate picture available of the crisis. From its humble roots, Ushahidi is today used by a wide range of organizations with an equally wide range of information needs, and was central to the international community's response to the Haiti earthquake in 2010.

The view from above

The air is cool and smells with the scent that seems only to come from aeroplanes and dry cleaners. A dotted red line shows our path for the next seven hours. And I find myself fortunate today as I sit in an exit row, so the computer can actually fit on my lap without banging up against the seat in front of me.

Soon I'll land in London. There I'll navigate meetings with top executives in some of the world's largest tech companies. There I'll stand on a stage and speak to a couple of hundred people about Africa. There I'll find the funding for my endeavours. When I land back in Kenya in three days I'll take meetings with local start-up entrepreneurs, enjoy cheering while I attend the large annual sevens rugby tournament, all while weaving my motorcycle between the cars jamming up the city.

What allows me to handle both worlds?

Thirty-six thousand feet below is the land where I spent my youngest years. We're crossing over that border point, a nebulous region from above, where South Sudan, Kenya and Uganda butt up against one other. A place where a murky memory serves up images of dusty roads, a metal mabati house in the bush, lost toys in the sand river, escape from flash floods with my sister, hunting lizards, and my village dog and tiny antelope pets.

My memory flashes forward to urban Nairobi of the 1980s, right after the coup. Of soccer fields, tinkering with small electrical engines, towels draped like superman capes off of our backs, kick-the-can and van rides across town with the other missionary kids to a school where I was only interested in getting good enough grades to not get a spanking.

I remember quick flits – trips to America visiting the family by blood that I didn't know. I was good at the sports that the Americans didn't play, and was bad at those that they did. I remember cycling everywhere, learning to fish, and being grateful when our time there was done and we were heading back home to Africa.

I realized at 13 that I wanted to go to boarding school: that I was made for it. Rugby. Basketball. Soccer. The things that save a teenager from boredom while on an escarpment campus with an unparalleled view over the Rift Valley.

Learning to compete. Learning friendship. Learning to question. Learning business through action and through spoken daydreams of wannabe entrepreneurs.

It's generally good, all of it, and it is a history that I wouldn't trade. It is this uncommon past that allows me to travel, communicate and build so easily between worlds and cultures.

It is a strange mixture that formed my character. A combination of travel, mixed cultural experiences, tough education facilities, hard-fought victories and losses, trainings for a foundation of belief in something bigger than myself. All this as I touch two worlds – the raw, gritty reality of my home country, mixed with the wealth and ease of my parent's country.

When I'm asked why I do the things that I do – as the co-founder of Ushahidi, iHub, BRCK, Savannah Fund, AfriLabs, Maker Faire Africa, and others – it has to be seen through this lens. A lens that helps me see what's possible, and that allows me to bridge between cultures, business and technology to make it happen.

An unconventional childhood

My parents were linguistic missionaries in Southern Sudan. Most people who grow up as children of missionaries don't go into business. I, however, had other ideas and from the age of eight I had turned over a wooden crate, cut a hole in it, and was selling gum on the mission station in Nairobi out of my mini-kiosk. I didn't think of it as anything more than a way to get spending money, as that wasn't something that was in great supply in our family. I saved money too, for things like buying my first bicycle – as my parents didn't have the money and my dad thought it would help me appreciate its value. He was right.

FIGURE 7.1   From 1980. Each morning started with my father taking my sister and me to Juba Model School in South Sudan

Courtesy of the author

The idea of making money was natural for me, and it solidified when I was thrown together in boarding school with a Kenyan roommate who was just as enthralled by it. We hatched and executed on plans for selling old clothes, buying food in town and reselling it at school, writing book reports for less voracious readers, among other enterprises even less glamorous and not always profitable.

All this led to a discussion with my mother one day while I was home on holiday, where she told me that she was worried that all I would focus on was making money, and that there were more important things in life. This conversation set a tone for my life. Today, I still follow my business instincts and path towards entrepreneurial activities, but refuse to let money be the primary driver. Our recent launch of a tablet computer aimed at education in Kenya, powered by our battery-powered internet router, BRCK, is a good case in point.

Everything changed

2007 was an exciting year for Kenya. The economy was buoyant and we were approaching the end of a Presidential term. While there had been some unsavoury text message (SMS) campaigns in the political race to this point, the mood in Kenya was at an all-time high. Like every year, Kenyans went 'up-country' (home) for the holidays, and right after Christmas the vote was held. Then silence.

This disconcerting, gnawing silence started to make people wonder what was going on. Tensions grew. In the last election, the new President Kibaki was sworn into power at Uhuru Park in broad daylight. I was there, I saw it. This time he was sworn in somewhere at night and it was broadcast to the citizens of Kenya. The silence was eventually broken with pent up anger and resentment. Rumours of attacks, deaths, roadblocks and burnings began.

Violence broke out from the slums of Nairobi to rural Eldoret and the coast. Information wasn't available on much of what was happening, and there was a certain eerie silence from the government and from the Kenyan media. The international press did a better job of getting information out, but they couldn't be everywhere. Bloggers did their best to fill the gaps, but it wasn't enough. At the time I was living abroad, in the United States, watching all of this, concerned, from a distance.

The building of a mapping platform

I sat frustrated in front of my computer, holed up in a farmhouse in rural Georgia as news of the mounting tension and violence came out of Kenya. What a place to be, with limited internet access while the country I called home was beginning to burn.

Being disconnected allowed me time to think, time to write, blog and read what others were thinking and doing. If technology allows us to overcome inefficiencies, isn't that what I was looking at? There was definitely a shortage of information, so could we use technology to do something about it?

Fortunately, Ory Okolloh, an old Kenyan blogging friend who was using her blog as a nexus point for journalists and others to get the word out, had an idea. She wrote:

> Google Earth supposedly shows in great detail where the damage is being done on the ground. It occurs to me that it will be useful to keep a record of this, if one is thinking long term. For the reconciliation process to occur at the local level, the truth of what happened will first have to come out. Guys looking to do something – any techies out there willing to do a mash-up of where the violence and destruction is occurring using Google Maps?

I Skyped with her about the idea, then sent an e-mail out to the Kenyan technology community via the Skunkworks e-mail (a local technology contacts list), and waited. Nothing. Not right away, at least. Maybe friends and colleagues in Kenya were too busy and couldn't take the time to do anything at the moment. While I waited I called David Kobia, founder of one of Kenya's biggest and oldest online forums, Mashada. I had written a blog post about him and his organization a few months previously, so perhaps he would be open to talking about the idea I was formulating.

Later I would become familiar with a few of David's habits. For example, he doesn't often answer his phone. Fortunately, on this occasion, I was able to catch him during a long drive to Atlanta. We talked for a few minutes about the idea of creating a platform for Kenyans to report what was going on around them, and also to aggregate the news that was coming out of the country.

David was hesitant. Before he could say 'no', I asked him not to make a decision, and instead promised to supply some mock-ups by the time he arrived in Atlanta so we could chat more the next day. Three hours later I shot off some early designs to him.

The very next day David sent me a link. He had created the first version of what would later become Ushahidi.

We hurriedly organized ourselves and set up a Skype chat with Ory, Juliana Rotich and Daudi Were (all prolific Kenyan bloggers) and started discussing what we should call this 'new thing'. I remember our preference was for some easily pronounceable word, like 'kuona', which means 'to see' in Swahili. Someone else had already registered the website, so we considered alternatives whose addresses were still available. The word 'ushahidi', which means testimony or witness, was proposed. Could we get the .com? Yes, but non-Swahili speakers wouldn't be able to say or spell it. 'It doesn't matter. This will only ever be used in Kenya', one of us piped up. 'Buy it, we have other, bigger things to worry about.'

Two short days later, Ushahidi was launched to the world. The day after launch a friend donated an SMS short code allowing us to receive reports by text message. We now had a basic application allowing anyone to send a report in via e-mail, mobile phone, or web form. It was rudimentary, but it worked.

The timeline was rapid:

- Jan 3 – Idea (blog post)
- Jan 6 – Prototype built
- Jan 9 – Global launch

The most pressing issue for us was time. If we were to make any difference with the website it had to be launched almost immediately. This meant there was no room for 'it would be cool if...' discussions. We could only consider the essentials. This was software product triage.

Stepping back

Let's take a step back. What enabled five seemingly loosely-connected bloggers and techies to conceive, create and launch a new web app in just a few days in the midst of a crisis?

There were two factors. First, all of us were part of the young and vibrant Kenyan blogosphere. Second, four of us had met at what would later turn out to be a seminal event on the continent: TED Africa in Arusha, Tanzania in the summer of 2007.

In short, we all knew each other already and had a feel for our personalities through our blogs. The TED event allowed us to actually meet in person and develop some mutual trust. When things got crazy, we knew that we could reach out to each other and rely on the others for support during a rough time.

As the crisis was unfolding, Juliana Rotich was upcountry in Eldoret, a town in western Kenya. From there she gathered stories and helped verify what was coming in.

Daudi Were was in Nairobi, the capital. As a founding member of the Kenyan blogosphere, he helped get other people involved. He also gathered stories and pictures, and helped verify reports with non-governmental organizations (NGOs).

Ory Okolloh was in Nairobi at the outset, but had since returned to Johannesburg, South Africa by the time we launched Ushahidi. She used her blog to aggregate stories, push even more news and information to Ushahidi, and got others engaged.

David Kobia built the platform, creating new features and adjusting things as necessary, determined by what was happening on the day. His genius for simple solutions that worked ended up saving us.

My job in the beginning was to help David on the platform, but then quickly turned to managing the media with Ory, building our supporter base and raising awareness.

We worked throughout the nights and at weekends. We took time out from our normal jobs and put aside client work in order to create, and then run, Ushahidi in Kenya. This went on for two months, into February, until there was a peace agreement in the country. Throughout this time old friends like Ethan Zuckerman, and new friends like Patrick Meier, helped us overcome numerous hurdles along the way.

The mainstream media picked up on Ushahidi early, around 12 January, attracting considerable attention from the Kenyan diaspora. We quickly learned that many big crisis deployments were driven by the desire of those from the affected area to get information from family and friends. This would later be referred to in our lexicon

FIGURE 7.2   The Ushahidi core team – Linda Kamau, Juliana Rotich, Erik Hersman and Brian Herbert

Courtesy Ushahidi

as 'pothole theory', after we realized that 'people care about the pothole on *their* street, not the one two streets away'.

By this time, several important truths had come to light:

- The technology was nothing special. In fact, the Ushahidi platform could have been built years earlier if someone had had a need for it.

- People wanted to tell their stories. They wanted others to know what was happening in the face of media intimidation, or about their inability to gain access to a particular area.

- We caused a stir by asking ordinary people what was going on. This bottom-up approach to information gathering during a crisis was either interesting or unsettling to the traditionally top-down humanitarian industry, media houses and government.

- Many of the NGOs that we asked to help verify incidents didn't want to share information or cooperate at all. Juliana later described this as 'data hugging disorder'. It put something of a chip on our shoulders and made us question the ethos of NGOs, raising questions internally about who they actually serve.

Ushahidi for the rest of the world?

It was not long before other people started asking us whether we could 'do Ushahidi' in their country. By March 2008 there was unrest in Chad, and xenophobic attacks had started to become a big issue in South Africa. We declined. After all, this wasn't our day job. If we spent yet more time away from our paid work we would not have been able to pay our own bills for much longer.

The Ushahidi site had been built in .NET, a software development environment that David knew, enabling us to set it up quickly. We told others in these countries that they could have the code, and we gave it to them. The South Africans ended up using it to set up UnitedForAfrica.co.za

We were surprised early on that we'd failed to find software that would work for our particular situation in Kenya, and that no-one had built any type of crowdsourcing software for a map 'mash-up' before. Ushahidi had taken us about three days to build. We quickly realized that if we made the Ushahidi software freely available it would allow others to do in three hours what took us three days.

None of us could take the time off from our normal lives to do this, or to do it properly anyway, so we set about seeing whether we could find funding that would allow us to create an organization to manage it. By now it was April, and the five of us talked and put an ultimatum to each other – will you be a part of a new 'Ushahidi, Inc' organization and dedicate one year to it, if the money is found?

David, Juliana, Ory and I agreed to form the organization. Daudi decided to stick with his own web company in Kenya, although three years later he would re-join Ushahidi.

A month later we won the NetSquared Challenge, worth $25,000. This allowed David and I to put the work with our consulting companies on hold and start

FIGURE 7.3   Ushahidi in use during the 2011 Liberian elections

Courtesy Ushahidi

redesigning, finding coders and rebuilding the Ushahidi platform as a free and open source software platform for the world to use. Competitions like NetSquared are important as they give new, young, unknown start-ups an opportunity to get recognized, and winning can give validation in the eyes of larger donors who hold the purse strings.

In August 2008, Humanity United awarded us $200,000 which provided each of us with a salary, enabling everyone to work on Ushahidi full-time. When I think back to those first conversations with funders, I remember how strange it was dealing with grant funding. After all, we had been on the business side of the fence until then. There were a few tense calls where neither side could understand the other's language, but in the end we were able to find a common mission. Our pitch was that we 'simply' wanted a platform that would allow others to organize themselves and make a difference in their part of the world, with a lot less effort than we had in Kenya. Funders started to buy into that.

I also remember how shocked I was when I was told that a platform for crisis situations shouldn't mix political crisis with other types. The argument went along the lines that there was a big difference between political, environmental and other crises, and what we were doing didn't reflect that. This didn't compute for me, so I told them to think of Ushahidi as nothing more than something the Red Cross should be doing online.

This, of course, begged the question why the Red Cross – or anyone else, for that matter – hadn't already built Ushahidi. To this day, I hypothesize that large organizations have a hard time innovating, that there's just too much money and bureaucracy in the way and that it's the smaller, faster, nimbler organizations that tend to do the most interesting and meaningful innovation.

How I think about Africa

When I look at the challenges we face in Africa I see them from the perspective of an entrepreneur. Challenges are opportunities – and we are practically overrun by them.

By the time Ushahidi was born I had been writing about the use of technology on the continent for a couple of years through my WhiteAfrican.com blog. I started to get to know other early bloggers and get connected to people who were as interested in how technology could help catapult the continent forward. This led to the creation of a website called AfriGadget, a place where we showcased stories of African ingenuity, and practical innovation, in the face of problems. It's about the micro-entrepreneurs, the makers on the side of the road and the university inventors.

Through this writing I was connected to those who would later become my network for future endeavours. This is how I got to know Juliana, David, Daudi and Ory, who would become the founders of Ushahidi. This is how I started talking to Emeka Okafor who would invite me to TED Global in Arusha, and who would be my friend and co-organizer of Maker Faire Africa. This is where I met the early tech enthusiasts in Nairobi who would go on to build Skunkworks, the local techie e-mail list serve – and from where the conversation at BarCamp 2008 would plant a seed that would grow to become the iHub.

In our read/write world of the web, openly publishing our thoughts and ideas is the single greatest way to build the foundations of something that doesn't yet exist. It's a long road, it takes years, but with consistency and focus it opens doors that we don't even know are there.

I wrote about the Ushahidi idea before it was launched, helping get the concept across for quicker adoption. I wrote about the iHub idea for over a year before it came to reality, because no-one wanted to fund it. I wrote about the 'maker' culture in Africa for three years before we created an event around it, allowing interested parties to start congregating around the idea.

The opportunities that I've been a part of in Africa didn't come fast or easy. They took years to build and few were interested in paying for them at first. Some were a product of being in the right place at the right time, with the right people. Others are a product of a past track record and a network of people I know who were able to open doors that wouldn't normally open. Networks are so often key.

Ushahidi: business model and sustainability

The process of forming Ushahidi was foreign to all of us at first as we were coming from the business sector and found ourselves starting a non-profit tech company.

Raising grant money was new. I remember having discussions with people explaining that we didn't need money for a 'project' – the funding model most charitable foundations favour – because in our eyes we were building an organization. We felt we needed operating capital, not something most funders are keen to provide. We ended up with something like an 85/15 split on operational-to-project funding in those first three years, which I came to find out later was opposite of the norm. Forward-thinking funders such as the Omidyar Network, MacArthur Foundation and Ford Foundation made this possible. It remains something of a surprise, to me at least, that most donors fail to see the importance of operational support. Without the ability to pay rent, salaries and electricity bills, for example, few NGOs can survive.

Early success in winning awards and getting seed-level funding allowed us, at the very least, to build something and put a flag in the ground. With that capital and added attention we were able to build a better platform, then leverage the use cases to help find funding the following year. It was this combination, one that is so familiar to for-profit start-up companies, yet seems to be less familiar to the grant funding world, that allowed us to become successful.

We were already thinking about how to reduce our dependency on grant funding in 2009. Our plan was to work ourselves into an earned revenue model that would allow us to bring in about 50 per cent of our income through project work on our own software, with organizations globally. It started slowly, with 10 per cent earned revenue in 2010, and fluctuated from 20 per cent to 35 per cent between 2011 and 2014. In 2015 we expect to see this grow beyond 40 per cent if the launch of our new software-as-a-service (SaaS) platform works as we hope it will.

Beyond the business model, what also helped make Ushahidi successful was the fact that the founders were all good at writing and communicating. Remember, we were mostly bloggers, which meant we were already familiar with telling our stories. We simply leveraged this for our work on Ushahidi. We didn't have money for marketing or PR campaigns, but we were part of a vested and passionate community and we could reach out to them through our blogs and through Twitter. To this day, we rarely do a press release, and we focus heavily on communicating regularly, helping create a culture of transparency both internally and externally. This in turn creates an open book for the media and others to find out what's going on, and this makes us easy to reach out to for a story.

Finally, the confluence of being from Africa and applying technology to hot topics such as mapping and crowdsourcing have made it easier to get in front of the media and large organizations who are slowly trending towards this new way of thinking. Our work is visual, and there is always a crisis, election or campaign going on around the world somewhere that would benefit from our software. Because of this we remain highly visible and we have been able to communicate what we do well enough to capitalize on it for our own community's needs, and our organizational growth.

Ushahidi impact

The core Ushahidi platform has changed the way information flows in the world, and it has reached 18 million people. To date it has been used in 159 countries, has

FIGURE 7.4   Ushahidi impact infographic

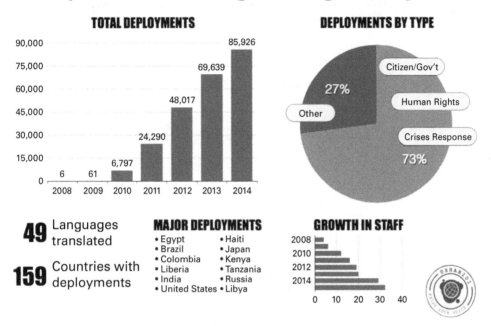

Our platform has grown globally

been translated into 49 languages and has been deployed over 85,000 times. From earthquakes in Haiti and Japan, to floods in Pakistan, blizzards in the United States, fires in Russia, and elections in East Africa and South America, it has been used by everyone from individuals, civil society groups and government. The most common use cases are for crisis and disaster response, election monitoring and civil society coordination.

Ushahidi has also been widely used by funders and governments as a way to gather information about their work in an effort to improve decision making. Ushahidi's tools allow for easy data collection and analysis for feedback on anything from projects to opinions. Ushahidi hopes to continue to support decision makers in their use of these public tools to help gather public feedback about their projects, making their public consultation process more open and transparent. For example, the Government of Paraguay (in partnership with Fundacion Paraguay) used Ushahidi to gather feedback and opinions for mapping poverty. They used it as a survey tool to gather feedback on government initiatives, poverty levels and needs, and then used this to determine how to apply resources.

After the Nepalese earthquake in 2015, the QuakeMap.com team used Ushahidi to aid response efforts, with 4,600 global mappers involved in documenting the earthquake, 2,000 reports submitted offering immediate relief and documentation of long-term damage, and 400 organizations using QuakeMap to carry out relief operations and verify that aid was received.

FIGURE 7.5   QuakeMap

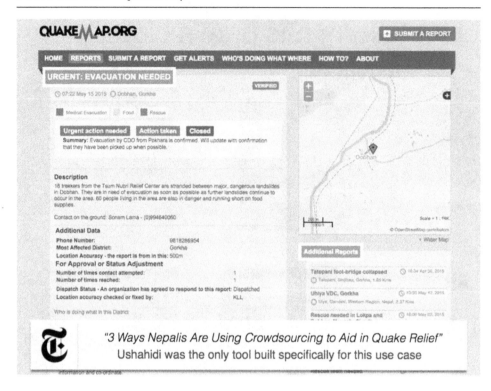

"3 Ways Nepalis Are Using Crowdsourcing to Aid in Quake Relief"
Ushahidi was the only tool built specifically for this use case

Ushahidi hopes to support more innovative initiatives such as this.

FIGURE 7.6   Ushahidi deployment data

73% of deployments are in 3 categories of social impact

Crises Response	Human Rights	Citizens & Elections

April 2011 - Dec 2014	December 2010	March 2013
5,433+ reports, XXX,XXX views	319 reports, 156,859 views	4,747 reports, 20,000 views
Tracking violence and missing, killed and arrested persons	Help bring awareness to sexual harassment in Egypt	Monitor Kenya 2013 election
syriatracker.crowdmap.com	harassmap.com	http://ke2013.uchaguzi.org/

Besides building the core Ushahidi software, the organization has been a catalyst for the creation of additional organizations and tools. Some of these, like the iHub, Popily and BRCK, have gone on to become independent organizations in their own right, while others were products and tools that have developed their own communities, such as SMSsync and CrisisNET.

FIGURE 7.7   The Ushahidi Ecosystem

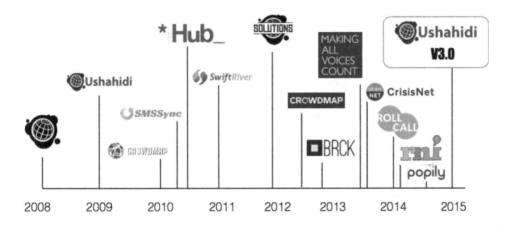

By being at the edge of technology and global challenges, we build innovative organizations

Lessons learnt

So many times I've seen people with a good idea do things in the wrong order. Here are a few things we've learnt along the way, along with some of the biggest mistakes people commonly make:

1 *Don't think of the money first.* If you do good things, money comes. I've never put it first on our list of things to think about. It comes somewhere after product discussions and user needs, but before personnel issues and travel. Yes, money is important for the long-term viability of your organization and/or platform, but it's not the deciding factor for the first six months. If what you're doing cannot be done without money, on nights and weekends, then you don't care enough, or it isn't a big enough problem to solve.

2 *Make sure you have the technical person on your team to build the tool.* You should not outsource software development. It should be a core competency for any software-related organization. If one of the co-founders isn't a strong coder, then find one before you do anything else.

3 *Don't become bogged down by organizational issues before you have a prototype.* You have nothing yet, so don't sweat the small stuff – such as organization set-up – until you have something worth spending time on.

I've seen a number of promising start-ups derailed by spats between their founders over equity, working titles and ownership issues. Go easy. If you can't trust your potential co-founders, the project is doomed anyway.

4 *Keep ahead of yourself.* Since 2008 we've tried to keep a culture of innovation alive within Ushahidi, letting everyone make quick decisions and reducing bureaucracy in order to maintain agility. This has led to some other interesting products, including the iHub (Nairobi's – perhaps Africa's – most prominent innovation hub), SMSsync (a mobile app that sends incoming text messages over to a website), Crowdmap (a simpler, more rapid-deployment version of Ushahidi which we host), SwiftRiver (which analyses news and information streams and tries to make sense of them) and, more recently the BRCK (a device which helps people connect to the internet in resource-constrained environments). Organizations often have to fight to remain nimble and open to seemingly crazy new ideas, the ones that are really different that allow change beyond the incremental.

5 *Everything needs a champion, someone that inspires people to build towards what doesn't yet exist.* If you get enough people to believe, then it becomes real. If you're not that person then the idea won't become reality. You need to really care about it. It's just as important for you to inspire your team as the wider community. My job at Ushahidi is to frame and explain what we're doing – for myself, for the team, the media and for funders so that we can punch above our weight. So that we ourselves are inspired to challenge the status quo. So that others are inspired to join and support this movement, or start their own.

6 *Traction is more important than anything else.* If you can show a little progress then others will come on board much faster and the community will grow more rapidly, and the people with money pay more attention. Sometimes you'll have to do this early by kick-starting on your own, with your own money. Remember – you need to really care about it. Our latest initiative, BRCK, is an internet communications product designed and made to work in emerging markets. I had the idea to do this side project within Ushahidi about four months before I could get the other founders to agree to it. It took us another six months to get a prototype together. The truth is, it's a miracle the transport authorities allowed me on any flights with those early prototypes in my bag. During these early stages, BRCK resembled those home-made bombs you see in the movies, with loose-fitting circuit boards connected with dangled wires and coloured lights, all packed together in a loose-fitting, taped together black plastic box. These early prototypes, though – products that were ugly and only vaguely worked but that you could touch and feel – were crucial in providing the early traction within Ushahidi that allowed us to keep going. Team members could pick a BRCK up and start imagining what it would be, which gave it enough legs to keep going as a product. We could show it to the Board to get buy-in. We were digging deep into our pockets to make it happen, but because there was something to see, something to show, it was 'real' and it was able to move ahead.

7 *Those who push harder and longer, win.* Life in Africa has a certain level of friction. I spent a year looking for someone to fund the iHub idea. It turned out that no-one wanted to put $200,000 into creating a space for the tech community in Nairobi. We knew one was badly needed – a space where the growing number of disparate groups of non-profits, technologists, business-people and activists around the country could get together, work together and meet, and share stories of their work. A focal point for Kenya's technology sector, in other words. At the time there was nothing like it, and it sounded crazy and unnecessary. The Ushahidi founders knew there was something there though, so we figured out a way to get funding to allow it to happen through our own organization. In late 2009, a couple of early believers from the Kenyan technology community came together to form the advisory board. We started kitting out a space, technologists started coming, and we realized we had stepped into a much larger vacuum than we thought. We were overwhelmed by the technology community in Kenya's desire to connect. Suddenly, the technology companies we originally approached understood and started to seriously support the idea. It all looks great today, but it took years. Again, once it came alive people began to believe, and then wanted to get involved. In the end our focus – with all our initiatives – was what made it work. We were always building something that we needed. We were scratching our own itch. It was something where we were the users and we had the drive to build it at the same time.

Framing innovation

It's helpful at this point to frame innovation – to think through why innovations happen at all, and which power structures led to them being identified as innovative. After all, innovation is just a new way of doing things.

In any industry, society or business there's a status quo at play. These are generally legacy structures, set up for a time and place that needed that design. Think big media in broadcasting and print, and how this has been disrupted by the internet, mobiles and social media in the last decade. How about government? How about the humanitarian sector? How about the energy industry?

All of these industries were seen as 'innovative' when they came into their own, decades and centuries ago. Now they are legacy in both infrastructure and design, and their relevance in their current state is in question. By their very nature they fight to maintain the power structures that keep them in the positions that they hold. Changes to the foundations on which they stand are not only scary, but deadly.

Innovation comes from the edges, so it is no surprise that innovators are found on the margins. They are the misfits among us, the fearless, the ones who see and do things differently. They challenge the status quo and the power structures that prop this up, so are generally marginalized as a reflexive and defensive action.

Think about what you're *really* looking for when you say you want innovation in your sector. Because, when you do, what you're really asking for is the outliers, the disrupters and the rebels to have their way. You're asking for a new way of thinking and doing to become dominant. And if you're in a position of power within an industry, you're probably going to find things a little uncomfortable. Just look at what happened to Kodak and Nokia, two giant companies that failed to grasp innovation and succumbed to disruptive technologies from competitors.

At Ushahidi we clearly have this healthy mix of questioning and stubbornness, and certainly jump in at the deep end without looking too often. It's this penchant for creative independent thinking within, at every level, which allows us to keep trying new things – where we keep a culture of experimentation – and being okay with something not working right away, pivoting, and then trying again.

Discussion questions

1 How important is it to have a perfect product before you launch?

2 What helps to be in place before you go out to seek funding? Why?

3 How do you grow an initial success beyond the first win and into a real, solid organization?

4 How do you hire top-quality people to work in companies like Ushahidi?

5 What is required for someone to move from idea to creation?

6 Are any industries safe from disruption? How do big companies avoid being overtaken by young start-ups?

7 Why does some of the more interesting innovation happen on the edges, where resources are often in shortest supply?

Further reading

You can find more material to do with this chapter at www.koganpage.com/socialentrepreneurship

The best place to find out about Ushahidi and our history is to see the Ushahidi blog at http://www.ushahidi.com/blog/ where you can read through the years as far back as 2008 when we started.

Patrick Meier was a key person at Ushahidi for three years. His blog at http://irevolution.net is one of the best on the making and building of the CrisisMapping community, and his *Digital Humanitarians* book tells the history and importance of it at: http://www.digital-humanitarians.com/

Get involved with the CrisisMapping community at http://crisismappers.net/

Understand more about how African technology and entrepreneurship is going through the following sites:

The iHub is one of the first and largest tech hubs in Africa, find out what's going on through the website and blog: http://www.ihub.co.ke/blog/

The *Next Africa* book helps explain where we are and where we're going in Africa from a business and technology perspective: http://us.macmillan.com/thenextafrica/jakebright

Acknowledgements

The story of Ushahidi wouldn't have been possible without the vast community that deploys the software around the world, or the many individuals who give their time to make the platform better by fixing bugs, adding features and generally coding for a better future. Five years on, the core Ushahidi team still surprises me with its brilliance and commitment. Thank you for your efforts and sacrifices in what is ultimately a crazy work environment. Finally, to Juliana, David, Ory and Daudi, the journey has only just begun, and I couldn't have asked for better travel partners.

08
Touch-based treatment for autism

QSTI (QIGONG SENSORY TRAINING INSTITUTE) – LOUISA SILVA

ABSTRACT

Autism is the most rapidly growing developmental disability in the Western world. Fifty years ago, it affected less than one in 10,000 children. Today, it affects one in 45 children and the numbers continue to rise. The symptoms appear before the age of two. Children avoid touch and eye contact and are unreceptive to social connection and communication. They display unusual repetitive behaviours and have difficulty dealing with change. Social development is delayed. Parents find it difficult to parent effectively – the usual ways of soothing and communicating with their children don't work, and parenting stress is four times higher than that for typical children. Once children reach school, developmental delay and challenging behaviour stand in the way of progress. With no known cause and no known cure, parents, teachers and doctors are struggling to know how to help.

It started with teaching the mother of a child with autism a massage treatment based on Chinese medicine, and led to researching and developing a treatment for autism – QST massage – that was effective, inexpensive and suitable for delivery worldwide. Scientific paradigms are generally based on understanding cause. In the case of autism, where the cause is unknown, research funding has focused on genetic and brain causes. The QST massage research challenged the existing paradigm for autism by investigating and treating a cause for autism (impairment of the sense of touch) that *was not* on the list of likely causes of autism but *was* on the list of rare causes of developmental delay. For many years, it was ignored by mainstream autism research funding organizations. It was only when sensory abnormalities were included in the diagnosis of autism that it received major funding and made the quick trip from theory to evidence-based treatment. Today, thousands of children worldwide are receiving the benefit.

Why me?

It's almost impossible successfully to treat a condition without understanding the cause. But sometimes, when watching a condition get better you can see what was wrong in the first place. Such was my experience with autism. As it happened, the cause was in plain view all along.

I am a doctor of Western and Chinese medicines, with a further speciality in public health. Throughout my appointment at Western Oregon University's Teaching Research Institute I have researched a massage treatment for young children with autism that is based on Chinese medicine.

I didn't start my medical career with a desire to do university-based, integrative medicine research on autism. I started with taking care of people. My first passion was working at a free clinic in Los Angeles. I love the mission of providing safe, affordable treatment to those who really need it.

My father had been a dentist in South Africa under apartheid, and I once visited a public health dental clinic that he had started for Zulu women. The women had vitamin deficiencies, but didn't like to take pills. Inside the clinic, chairs were lined up for people to wait their turn. But just outside, there was a courtyard where about 20 women were sitting in a circle, talking, laughing, nursing their babies and drinking liquid vitamins from large brown bottles. Afterwards they came inside to have their teeth worked on. There was something about that natural joyful vision of community healthcare that stayed with me.

Chinese medicine was far from my mind while I was in medical school at UCLA, but when the surgery department brought a team of physicians over from China and did a radical mastectomy under acupuncture anaesthesia – without any drugs – the seed was planted. Over the years, as I reached the limits of what Western medicine could do for my patients, I studied osteopathic medicine and herbal medicine. But it wasn't until I studied Chinese medicine that I hit the jackpot for safe and effective treatments.

After working in India, Ireland and rural Kentucky, I settled down to do family practice in Salem, Oregon. I was contentedly practising my own blend of Chinese medicine, osteopathic medicine and Western medicine, when in 2000 something happened that took my life in a totally unexpected direction.

Autism: a growing phenomenon

All around the world, cases of autism kept popping up. When I was in medical school, autism was so rare it was barely mentioned, but by 2000 it was affecting nearly one in 500 children. Autism is a developmental disability in which behaviour is abnormal, and social and language development are delayed. It is a spectrum disorder, meaning that there are huge differences between children and it can be mild, moderate or severe. Nonetheless, all children avoid touch and eye contact and are unreceptive to social interactions. And all children have difficulty adjusting to change and managing stress. Tantrums, aggression and self-injury are common and can be severe.

There are two variants of autism: the regressive form, in which children develop normally until about 18 months and then suddenly lose language and social skills; and the non-regressive form, in which development is slow from the beginning. Either way, by the time the child is two years of age the symptoms of autism are evident and early intervention can be provided. Without knowing the cause of autism, however, it has been difficult for parents, teachers and doctors to know what intervention to provide.

After two decades of genetic research, no genetic cause for autism has been found, and the search is on for an environmental cause. A plethora of treatments are available, each oriented to a particular symptom set – sensory, behavioural, language or social. Success varies depending on how much language children have, with educational methods having better success in children with language. Until recently, no treatment has been effective for all symptoms in all children.

Hearing the call: the beginnings of a journey

The son of a dear friend wasn't developing normally. He was four and had no language. He wasn't sleeping and was easily over-stimulated to the point of meltdown. Ordinary family events like meals, gatherings, or outings were major struggles. Despite the fact that both parents were skilled communicators, they couldn't communicate with him, or even reach him most of the time. It was difficult to moderate his energy or regulate his behaviour. He could not be soothed or redirected. Simply keeping him from being a danger to himself was an exhausting, all-consuming task.

I had been aware of the difficulties my friends had endured – the months they'd spent visiting specialists to find out what was wrong, how hard it was to get through each day. But when the diagnosis of autism finally came, what caught me square between the eyes was how little relief this 'answer' brought them. Instead, the information sent my friends into a tailspin of despair that dragged the whole family down.

Up to this point, it had taken all of my friends' energy to keep their son contained and safe while they waited for a diagnosis and treatment that could finally help. But when they got the diagnosis, their hope evaporated. Autism is a lifelong disability. There is no known cause, no known cure. They were told that there was nothing they could do. The only treatment was the early intervention services he was already receiving.

I couldn't just stand by and watch my friends suffer. I remembered watching my Chinese medicine professor, Dr Anita Cignolini, give a massage to a four-year-old autistic boy. Within a few days worth of massages he had begun to make eye contact and roll a ball back and forth with her. I thought that this massage technique might help my friend's son. Little did I know what I was starting.

Dr Cignolini's treatment incorporated qigong massage, a specialized form of Chinese massage that works on restoring the flow of qi (vital energy) through the major energy channels (also called meridians, or acupuncture channels) in the body. The idea that we can restore health and improve circulation by working with these energy channels has been the basis of Chinese medicine for 3,000 years.

I flew to California and typed while she dictated her protocol. The massage was a series of 11 movements. It took about 15 minutes to pat down the energy channels of the body from head to toe. The doctor advanced the course by giving the expert version of the massage 10 times over five weeks, while the parents, who learned the treatment from the doctor, maintained the gains by giving their version of it at home daily.

When I returned home I taught the treatment to my friends. We tried it on their son and it worked. He calmed down and his behaviour became more manageable. And then it hit me – there were thousands of children whom this massage could help, but no-one would believe me if I went around saying that you could treat a neurological disorder like autism with massage, even if it was a specialized massage. I was going to have to prove this scientifically.

At the time I was working on a Masters in Public Health and Preventive Medicine. A few years previously I had started a clinic to serve the local migrant population. We were integrating Western and Chinese medicine approaches to find inexpensive, effective ways of treating chronic conditions. The timing was perfect. I needed a research project for my degree, and no research had been done on qigong massage for autism. My thesis project was literally in my own hands.

FIGURE 8.1   Dr Silva working with a child

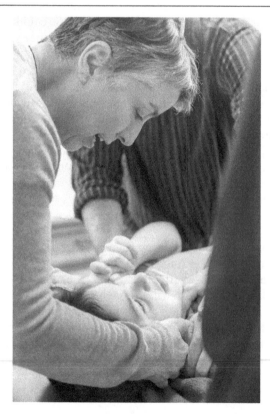

I contacted the local intervention services for the autism programme, and they helped me locate eight children. An occupational therapist and a speech therapist volunteered their services to do the pre- and post-treatment testing. I taught the parents the massage and met with them weekly to provide ongoing support.

At the end of 10 weeks children were more social, made more eye contact, were eating and sleeping better, and parents were less stressed. All of the developmental measures had improved and the occupational therapist reported that children were easier to touch. This would later prove to be a vital clue towards unravelling the puzzle of autism.

I finished my Masters programme and submitted the study for publication in a British autism journal. The reviewers turned it down, questioning my background and telling me the article wasn't up to their standards. I resubmitted the manuscript to the *American Journal of Chinese Medicine*, and it was accepted. It was my first lesson in the difficulty of publishing qigong massage research in mainstream journals.

The experience didn't temper my desire to get the word out, though. But I knew I didn't want to be sidelined as 'alternative'. The massage treatment needed to be in mainstream early-intervention programmes. I realized that I was going to have to do more than a case series. I needed to do a controlled study.

I learned to write grant proposals. Eight applications and seven rejections later, I was awarded a small grant. None of the autism granting agencies were interested – research funding was going towards genetic research and brain imaging studies. It was the local Native American casino, Spirit Mountain Community Fund, which offered funding. This seemed fitting, given that Native American culture is based on energy and spirit.

I recruited 15 children, randomized them into two groups, and carried out a small controlled study, this time for five months. Parents gave the massage daily, and I provided treatment and parent support weekly. I gave 300 massages over the course of the study. As before, testing showed behaviour and language improvement. All the senses improved, but the changes in touch were the most dramatic.

It was fascinating to see what happened with the children's hands. It was difficult to touch their fingers at first. They would pull away as if they were in pain. But within a few weeks, I could see their fingers relax. They would stretch out their fingers for more. Once their fingers stopped hurting, they started using their hands more. There was a geography of meaning on the skin. Hands were for connecting, communicating and exploring.

Autism is characterized by lack of interest in social relationships and avoidance of touch, and yet touch is where social relationships begin – in the deep mutual pleasure and satisfaction of the mother and child during nursing. Repeated countless times, the very life of the child depends upon touch. Yet children with autism were refusing touch, and parents were avoiding it. What should feel good (a kiss on the cheek) was uncomfortable and caused children to pull away. What should hurt (cuts and scrapes, for example) didn't hurt or weren't noticed.

There was definitely a problem with touch, but the research field didn't seem to be paying attention. At the time, sensory problems were classified as comorbid autism symptoms, common in children with disabilities, but of unknown cause, and having nothing to do with autism. Touch problems were outside the autism box by definition. It was dogma posing as science. I didn't want to be bounded by a definition that was incomplete, but the experts had spoken and the field listened.

I knew I was in trouble. I had a treatment that worked for autism, but it presumed a cause (abnormal touch) that wasn't considered to be part of autism. Never mind that touch is necessary for social development, granting agencies weren't interested in funding the research, and researchers weren't citing it. There were millions of children with autism, but apart from myself and Dr Cignolini – who had since retired – there were no other practitioners. Families were suffering, and treatment brought relief, but how were we going to get the treatment to them?

In Dr Cignolini's view, the massage had to be administered by a Western physician who was also trained in Chinese medicine. At the time, there were only a handful of such doctors. How could I recruit them to treat autistic children? Even if they all jumped on board, there still wouldn't be enough doctors to meet the need.

I needed a group of trainees who had experience with autism and understood the emotional territory of autism well enough to make a good connection with parents. The early intervention people fitted the description perfectly and were desperate for effective tools.

This might sound like a great solution, but it really put me out of my comfort zone. Was I really going to train early intervention therapists in Chinese medicine? In China, qigong massage is given only by doctors trained in Chinese medicine. Was it time to step off the beaten path and teach non-physicians? In order to be good at qigong massage, therapists have to be able to reason in terms of Yin, Yang, Qi and channels. Otherwise, they can't go with the flow of the treatment and get the most out of it for the child.

I decided to go for it, and developed an Applied Chinese Medicine curriculum to teach the massage to early intervention therapists. It was one of the most creative projects I have ever participated in and so much fun to bring the ancient concepts of Chinese medicine to life for non-physicians. It meant sharing the wealth and putting healing tools in the hands of people who really appreciated it.

I pulled together a group of therapists, trained them, supervised them and tested their results with children against my own. The curriculum was adequate. Trained early intervention therapists could achieve the same good results as a Chinese medicine doctor. The study was published in the *American Journal of Occupational Therapy*. We were up and running. We had identified a group of people to bring the massage to parents. We had an effective training regime. And we had published it all in a mainstream journal.

In the meantime, something else was becoming obvious. We were seeing a lot of families in crisis, and despite seeing the massage work, some of them weren't able to follow through with it. The therapy only worked if parents played their part. Without the daily massage, children didn't get better. What did parents need to have or do to be successful?

What seemed to work best were regular visits with therapists who provided a combination of ongoing support and accountability. There was no doubt that caring for a child with autism was a lonely road, and parents needed the support of a caring professional with whom they could share the daily trials and successes. And when, between the ups and downs of life, parents let the massage fall out of the routine, they appreciated the gentle reminder to pick it up again.

Casting the net wider

Every research study seemed to lead to a new one, and I kept refining the massage itself. There were now 12 movements in the sequence, each one could be done in several ways, and there were back-up techniques for specific areas. Five years into it, projects were multiplying like rabbits. I had started out doing one research study at a time, and now had several going simultaneously.

During the first three studies I had observed a lot of kids very closely under my own hands and captured hundreds of treatment sessions for video analysis. Because I was looking at the children through the lens of Chinese medicine, I was noticing predictable symptoms that were present in all of the kids but were not part of the standard definition of autism.

The symptoms I was noticing – tantrums and meltdowns, sleep problems, failure to make eye contact and pay attention, appetite and digestion problems – were also defined as comorbid symptoms (comorbidity is the presence of one or more additional disorders or diseases, co-occurring with a primary disease or disorder). The massage was improving them, and as they improved, so did the autism. It seemed to me that in that mix of comorbid symptoms was the cause of autism.

I had the massage refined to the point at which I knew which massage movement ameliorated which symptom. After looking at more than a thousand hours of video, I had come to recognize that the way children reacted to touch on different parts of the body wasn't random. It was connected to specific problems and developmental delays. Avoidance of touch on the ears translated to difficulty listening and delayed language. Problems with touch on the chest meant inability to self-soothe. Problems with touch on the belly signified digestive problems. Problems with touch on the face meant not being able to face another person.

Once I figured out how to adapt the massage techniques so that uncomfortable areas got comfortable, and numb areas started to feel, symptoms got better. So, if we didn't avoid the ears, and instead worked through the discomfort, children started using their ears to listen and language picked up. If we massaged the chest until children rubbed their eyes and yawned, tantrums decreased. We could change the direction of massage on the belly to alleviate either constipation or diarrhoea. This was wonderful and powerful stuff. At the same time, parents were commenting on how natural it felt. And it was – touch is natural – Chinese medicine is natural medicine.

The skin, the self and a theory for autism

By 2007 I had a theory for autism that I needed to test. But first, I had to create a measure for the comorbid symptoms and their response to treatment. Even though each child started out with different combinations of comorbid symptoms, over the course of five months they all improved in predictable ways.

My theory centred on the skin. Each child had a different combination of under-sensitive, over-sensitive and normal skin. A child might be numb on the back, over-sensitive on the face and normal on the leg. The skin is connected to the brain by millions of tiny sensory nerves. Sensory input from the body was confusing and contradictory. For the developing brain, the body *is* the self. Without a coherent sense of their bodies, children couldn't arrive at a sense of themselves. Suddenly it made sense that the children didn't use the word 'I' – there wasn't an 'I' – there wasn't a *sense of self*.

With massage there was a predictable progression from numbness to over-sensitivity to normal. Then, one day, the skin would start to work as a cohesive sensory organ rather than a collection of scattered parts. That was the day children acquired a sense of self. That was when children started to use the word 'I'. I remember a father crying tears of joy when he recounted finding his son rummaging through a box of toys and asking him what he was doing. His son, who had never used the word 'I', replied 'I am looking for my bear'.

Once children developed a sense of self, they would discover their will, and move into the 'terrible twos'. The previously disoriented, disconnected child would start saying 'no!' and testing boundaries! It was wonderful! Normal social development would take off from where it had stopped – it was no longer stalled.

Children with autism tend not to have empathy for other people's pain and it was always a milestone when the children felt pain for the first time. I remember a mother almost beside herself with excitement because her child had fallen down in the car park outside my office, skinned her knee and cried real tears for the first time. Once children could feel pain, they could feel empathy for *someone else*'s pain. If a sibling got hurt, they would get concerned. Before, when they couldn't feel their own pain, they didn't notice anyone else's either.

Even time was coded onto the skin. As it turned out, it was coded onto the back. The past is behind us. We noticed that children who were numb on their backs couldn't turn onto their backs when asked. These same children had no idea what had happened earlier that day. You could ask them what they had for lunch, and they couldn't answer. Once the massage restored normal sensation, the children could turn over when asked, and lo and behold, they could tell you. Once they had a past, they had a future, and they could participate in planning conversations, such as when they were going swimming. It was fascinating.

With the recovery of a sense of *self*, came *self-regulation*. It is a fact that human development rests solidly on the development of early self-regulation. I found a paper describing the first-year self-regulation milestones. Just like motor milestones such as sitting and crawling, there are self-regulation milestones. But they are far more important – they underpin the timely unfolding of development and allow the child to grow and learn. These huge milestones consist of the ability to regulate attention, to self-soothe, to have a regular sleep-wake cycle, and to have regular digestion.

Suddenly all the co-morbid autism symptoms fell into place. They were all delays of the first-year self-regulation milestones! And these milestones all required copious amounts of normal touch to be achieved. The problems children were having with face-to-face attention, tantrums, sleep and digestion were all stemming from the same cause – delays of early self-regulation milestones. They didn't need four different specialists for four different symptom sets. They just needed to catch up on their self-regulation milestones – by restoring a normal sense of touch. We felt we were in the ballgame now.

It was time to design a research measure to capture this. I developed the Sense and Self-Regulation Checklist, and learned how to conduct a validation study. Fortunately

Mark Schalock, my research partner at Western Oregon University, was well aware of how to do so, and as he had done with all the other studies, he guided the data collection and statistical analysis with a sure hand.

Damage to the sense of touch

The Sense and Self-Regulation Checklist was a home run. The validation study showed that children with autism were clearly different from other children by virtue of two main things. There was global delay of early self-regulation milestones.

FIGURE 8.2   Relationship between sensory and self-regulatory symptoms

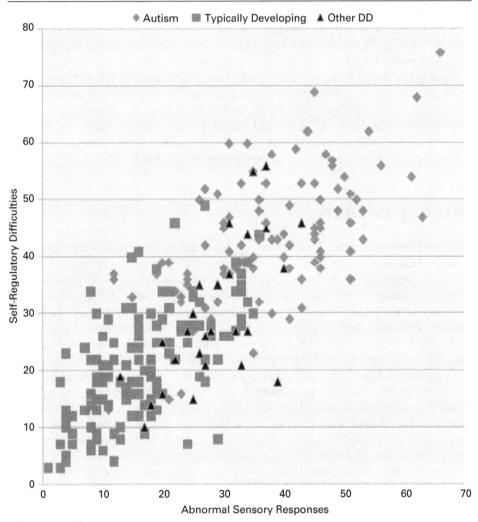

COURTESY: Dr Silva

And touch was severely abnormal, with pain and numbness on many areas, including the face, mouth, hands and feet. It brought to mind diabetic patients with neuropathy – where just the touch of the sheet on their feet at night could hurt, and yet an infected hangnail could go unnoticed.

It was appalling to think that the millions of children with autism worldwide have damage to the sense of touch. Yet there was no other explanation for the findings. There was no known brain condition, or genetic condition that gave that combination of pain and numbness on different parts of the body. These were common signs of neuropathy – the most common cause of damage to the sense of touch.

I had designed the Sense and Self-Regulation Checklist to provide built-in confirmation of the severity of touch problems. In institutions where children are touch deprived, there is severe developmental delay. Damage to the sense of touch works the same way as touch deprivation – in both there is a barrier to touch. In autism, the fact there was global self-regulatory delay meant that touch problems were severe enough to create a barrier to touch.

And if that wasn't proof enough, the severity of touch problems was directly proportional to the severity of self-regulatory delay. As the graph shows, the worse the touch problems, the worse the self-regulation problems.

I published the paper in the American Journal of Occupational therapy and issued an urgent call for an evaluation of the sense of touch in children with autism. I have to say, the article fell almost entirely upon deaf ears. It was back to the problem of reporting on a problem that was out of the autism box. Once again, the scientific community was only concerned with what was in the box. It was disappointing, but the pleasure of helping children and families more than made up for it.

Pushing onward

Over the next five years I embarked on more controlled studies and continued to train therapists and refine the training materials. We treated hundreds of children all over Oregon, published the results in mainstream journals and presented the research at national and international conferences. We developed a Qigong massage programme for children with Down syndrome and did a preliminary study with children with cerebral palsy.

I started a non-profit, the Qigong Sensory Training Institute, and named the massage QST massage. A friend put together a website for us to share the information with parents and professionals (qsti.org) and we started showing up on the first page of Google searches for autism treatment for children. The project now took up every available minute I had apart from working at my clinic and raising my daughter. Emotionally, I found it extraordinarily satisfying – it was a deep honour to be involved in this work. Physically, I found it exhausting. By this time I knew how I'd got into this work, but how was I ever going to get out?

I needed an exit plan, but I had to have something portable to give to families before I could go my own way. E-mails started coming in from all over the world from parents who wanted instructions on how to do the massage and didn't have access to trained therapists. There was only one option – to create a parent handbook

FIGURE 8.3 After five months of massage, son seeks father's embrace

COURTESY: Dr Silva

and DVD. With the support of two dear friends, Kristi Negri and Donna Read, 'Qigong Massage for Your Child with Autism: A Home Program from Chinese Medicine' was created. But what kind of results could parents achieve on their own?

We did a study in which only parents implemented the massage, not therapists, and it was clear that parents could accomplish a lot on their own. Parents of mild and moderately autistic children could achieve similar results as when working with therapists, as long as they did the massage every day and didn't miss treatment. When it came to severely autistic children, parents couldn't get the same results as with therapists and were more likely to drop the massage because it was too difficult. But regardless of severity, children derived some degree of benefit. And if parents continued the massage for one-to-two years, benefits continued.

By 2012 we had published 10 studies on treating children under the age of six. The results were consistent in all of the studies. After five months of daily parent massage and 20 therapist massages – averaging one a week – autism was about a third less severe. The severely autistic children moved into the moderate range, the moderate children moved into the mild range, and some of the mildly affected children moved off the autism spectrum altogether. It wasn't a cure, but it definitely helped.

We were ready to take the step required before a treatment can be recommended nationally. We needed to do a large replication study. We applied for a grant from the US Federal Bureau of Maternal and Child health. Our application was refused.

I leaned back to take a breather. It had been a long haul.

The winds were about to change, though. Research was showing that sensory problems made every aspect of autism worse. In 2013, a panel of experts convened to change the diagnostic criteria for autism to include sensory problems. They recognized that impairment of the sense of touch could readily account for autism symptoms, and that touch had never been fully evaluated. Our research was no longer sidelined.

Our fortunes had changed. We were astonished to be personally contacted by the US Bureau of Maternal and Child Health. Our grant that had been refused the previous year was now offered to us, and we were authorized to evaluate the effect of treatment in older children and do skin biopsies to rule out neuropathy. We would take very small skin biopsies and examine the sensory nerve fibres under the microscope for signs of loss and damage. It was an enormous break.

Now, at the time of this writing, we are just completing the replication study. We treated 103 children in Oregon with the massage and followed them for two years. In the first five months we replicated the previous results. Touch problems reduced

FIGURE 8.4   Mother and child during massage

COURTESY: Dr Silva

by 50 per cent, autistic behaviour and severity of autism improved by a third, language improved, and child-to-parent bonding and interactions improved. The treatment was effective in low- and high-functioning children and success was only dependent on the parents giving the massage every day.

The pilot study in children aged 6 to 12 has also been completed, and yes, the treatment was effective in older children. It was remarkable to see. High functioning children who already had full language made progress more rapidly than we had ever seen. With normalization of touch, they could build on their already-acquired skills and boost their development. The lower-functioning children also progressed, but more slowly, as expected.

The two-year follow-up results came in December, 2015. Touch took anywhere from five months to two years to normalize, depending on how severe it was to start with. By the end of two years, children with less severe autism had 100 per cent normalization of touch and 66 per cent decrease in autism severity; 43 per cent had come off the spectrum. The more severe group had 62 per cent normalization of touch and 40 per cent decrease in autism severity. They were at the level of severity where the less severe children had started, and they were learning language. This was very encouraging news for parents, and good reason to keep going.

Also in December, the first skin biopsies reported 50 per cent loss of small sensory nerve fibres in children with autism. These are the fibres that mediate touch, pain and the pleasure of close physical contact. For the first time there was a physical explanation for their distinctive lack of interest in affectionate touch and physical closeness, and there was tissue evidence of partial loss of the sense of touch.

Dissemination

As we move towards completing the US Bureau of Maternal and Child Health grant, it has become obvious that our work is far from done. A whole new horizon has opened up. It's one thing to prove a treatment works and explain why, but quite another to change the habits of paediatricians worldwide so that children actually get the treatment they need. What needs to happen now is that all children coming in for autism evaluation should be evaluated for touch, hearing and vision problems, and treated with QST massage as soon as touch problems are found.

The technical name for this is dissemination. When I reviewed the research literature on how long it takes to disseminate new information into clinical practice, I saw that the average time was 10 to 20 years. Well, we've now been at this 15 years, according to the research, so we have five more years to go until millions of children receive the benefit! I certainly hope so, and will continue to do my best to that end.

A last-minute breakthrough

To help the dissemination process, we refined the Sense and Self-Regulation Checklist and renamed it the Autism Touch and Self-Regulation Checklist. We had collected data on about 400 children – half with autism, and half with normal development.

In the process of analysing the data, we found something astonishing. I had asked Mark if he would take a look at the five questions concerning pain on the face and in the mouth, and see how many of the children with autism we could identify using those five questions. It turned out to be 82 per cent. It was stunning – five questions about severity of pain on the face and in the mouth – not a single question about language, social development or autistic behaviour – and we could identify 82 per cent of children with autism? We were onto a core problem in autism, and one I had been thinking hard about for a couple of years – how do we orient to ourselves, and other people?

Difficulties with touch on the face and in the mouth are present in almost every child with autism. We are born being able to orient to another person's face. It's called the orienting reflex. It's a simple sensory-motor reflex whereby the mother touches the cheek, and the infant turns towards her to nurse. Sensation to the face and mouth is provided by the trigeminal nerve. If sensory fibres are damaged, the areas will be painful or numb and instead of turning towards the mother, the child will turn away or fail to respond.

When we added the questions about orienting to the questions about the face and mouth, we could accurately identify 92 per cent of the children with autism. It pretty

FIGURE 8.5   Orienting to mother's face during massage

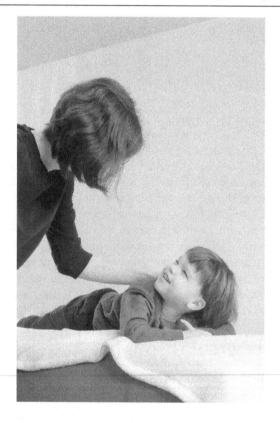

COURTESY: Dr Silva

well explained autism. The face is what we orient with. Damage to sensation on the face early in life would prevent the brain from learning to orient to another person. Being together, face-to-face, is where social development begins. It seems that in autism it is being hindered right at the source.

Keeping ourselves in business

The mechanics of how this work was accomplished were very fluid. After the first couple of studies, we knew we had something to offer that was desperately needed, but it was unknown, untraditional and inaccessible to most people. We felt our success would depend upon finding a way to explain the treatment in common-sense terms and on research establishing an evidence base. This meant doing research and publishing in mainstream research journals, but keeping quality high and holding true to our original sources. And it meant finding language that didn't turn people off with unfamiliar terms.

What were we to call the treatment? It was Qigong massage, QST massage, family-based treatment for autism, tactile stimulation of the skin to improve circulation to sensory nerves, and touch-based treatment for autism. We learned to be flexible with language, and to speak to audiences in terms they could understand. If parents are going to sign their children up for an unfamiliar treatment and administrators are going to offer it in their pre-schools, they have to be able to explain it in their own words. We had to find those words.

Initially we were operating purely on the research side. After the first study, funding was acquired on an as-needed basis. We'd get a small grant, carry out the research, and then look for another grant. But after the first few studies, we saw the need to build a base for dissemination, developing courses, training professionals and developing master trainers. That meant starting a business. The parents we wanted to reach were already drained dry by the financial burdens imposed by the disability, and we couldn't espouse a for-profit model. So we needed to form a non-profit and find a source of funding for it. After the first book was written, the publishing company was kind enough to provide us with the books at cost so that we could sell them on our website. Book sales helped to pay for a half-time administrator to take care of the website, answer the queries on our Facebook page and complete a thousand different tasks as needed.

As the years passed, more books followed, and these also went to fund the non-profit. When we started organizing training for parents and professionals, we did it so that the courses were self-sustaining – the charge for the course paid the course teachers, and gave 10 per cent back to the non-profit to support the website and other dissemination efforts. We were operating on very slim margins, but day-to-day functioning was supported.

Each time we needed to expand, we were fortunate to find a donor to support it. Funding growth spurts doesn't fall under the category of research and isn't usually covered by grants, but is incredibly important to a small organization like ours. Recently, we received the funding to translate the book and website into five languages. Once that is done, it will sustain the development of master trainers in those countries. I am grateful, so grateful, to Cliff and Delight at the Curry Stone Foundation for that support.

We probably could have made money on the assessment tools we developed – The Autism Touch and Self-Regulation Checklist and the Autism Parenting Stress Index, but we chose to offer them free of charge to clinicians in the interest of disseminating the research and expediting children receiving services. I think it was a good decision. One of the big hurdles to dissemination is any barrier, financial or otherwise, to getting information about how to implement the change. The assessment tools make implementation easy and are available as a free download from qsti.org

Did we make a difference? Looking at impact

What has been the impact of all this? Quite a lot, really. We'd brought the qigong massage treatment from theory to evidence-based treatment for autism. We'd carried out and published a dozen research studies showing that five months of treatment resulted in decreased severity of autism by a third, improved touch responses by 50 per cent, decreased parenting stress by 44 per cent, and improved social and language skills. In the process, we'd empowered thousands of parents to help their own children, seen reduced stress in the families, and helped children onto a better developmental path. We had developed onsite and online training programmes for professionals, and made them available in the United States, Europe and South America. The way autism was being thought about and treated was changing. In the process, we'd brought together Chinese medicine ideas with Western scientific ideas and introduced some of the most beautiful parts of Chinese medicine to Western families and Early Intervention programmes. Impact can't always be measured in hard numbers, as many people expect, and that certainly applies to the work we do. How do you measure in numbers a child's happiness and well-being?

Calmer waters

We've crossed a lot of bridges to get to where we are today. When we started, there was no published scientific literature showing the effectiveness of qigong massage treatment for autism or any other condition in the West or in China. There was no public awareness of qigong massage. There were no theories for autism that included problems with touch and self-regulation, and no way to measure whether treatment helped the problems. Apart from Dr Cignolini and myself, there were no practitioners of qigong massage for autism, and no training programmes for practitioners and parents. All of that has changed.

My own belief systems have been challenged and I've had to rethink three myths that I previously believed. The first is that you have to be a doctor to practise Chinese medicine and assist healing. Not true – the early intervention people are doing a great job with the massage. The second is that parents cannot provide treatment for a neurological handicap. Also not true – no-one *but* a parent can give the massage day in and day out for the length of time required. The third is that treatment for a serious neurological condition like autism must surely be complicated and expensive. As it turns out, this treatment is relatively easy to teach parents and nearly free to dispense.

I am now less desperate for an exit strategy. The really hard work of slogging away into the unknown, against the grain of a limited scientific paradigm, has been done. As it turns out, I love doing research. And I have the support of an extraordinary group of friends and colleagues to help with the work as it comes. I have learned to trust that things are unfolding exactly as they are supposed to, and I will know my part when I see it.

I'm deeply grateful to Chinese medicine and its understanding of our mysterious and amazing bodies. The knowledge is available to all of us, and is a gift from ancient China to all of humanity. It is knowledge that is very close to the bone and can guide us in helping our children and ourselves. It is as ancient as civilization itself.

Advice for others

What advice would I give to another person who hears the call? When I first got this call, I could see a path opening up in front of me. Look for that path – it is different for every project and person – and it is vital to the integrity and success of the project. I knew I wanted to develop a research base and soon after, I knew I would disseminate through a non-profit.

Here are some other practical considerations about how to stay sustainable:

- *In the early phases of the project*, get grant funding or make sure that you have a job that pays the bills and supports your family. If you are the one who is birthing the project, realize that it can take a while for a project to become self-sustaining, and it is unrealistic to think that the project will support you in the beginning. In my experience, you have to do the work *and* sustain yourself.

- *As the project grows*. There are some common-sense rules about growth. Start with small goals, get tangible results and make them visible. Then set bigger goals, realize them, and make them visible. Follow through and complete everything you commit to. Have a project budget and stay within it. There will be volunteers who will want to help you. Let them. But as soon as you can, develop a small core team of people who know the project well, and pay them a fair wage. Ask for guidance from people in the field who you respect, and be willing to modify your plans accordingly.

Lessons learnt

1 *Often the call isn't at all practical.* It's more like getting set on fire by a lightning strike, and all you know is that you are 100 per cent committed and will do whatever it takes. A call like that comes to you because you are the

only one who can answer it. It can take everything you have – body and soul – and years of your life. In return it can give you more satisfaction, pleasure and meaning than you would have thought possible. In that case, listen to your heart, and ask yourself whether this call is important and meaningful to you. If something is calling you hard, and if you really believe in it, answer it, and see where it leads you. The call is precious. It can lead you towards your life's purpose. While you are in the 'slogging uphill' phase, take care of your own health, especially when you feel tired and it seems like the work never ends. Offer yourself choices. When things got really difficult and I wanted to quit, I visualized the end of my life, and asked myself if I would be sorry if I didn't complete the work. When the answer came, I made my choice. I've never regretted it. Follow the passion and the love, and steer clear of fear and doubt.

2 *When you don't know what to do, ask for guidance, and keep your ears open.* Guidance comes at unexpected times and places.

3 *Definitely don't get attached to knowing how things will turn out.* It can be a wild ride, far beyond your imagining, and far better than anything you could have dreamed up yourself.

4 Remember what Yoda said: 'Trust the Force'. There is so much more going on than meets the eye.

Discussion questions

1 What are the strengths and limitations of modern medicine and Chinese medicine when it comes to autism?

2 What are the ethics of entrepreneurship in the context of (quality of) life-saving medical treatment for children?

3 If ethics dictate that medical treatment should be accessible to all children in need, how can a project like this be sustained, and where does the profit motive fit in?

4 How important is affectionate human touch to the health and happiness of children and adults? To your health and happiness?

5 How did the existing scientific paradigm alternatively hinder and help the progression of this work? Why is it difficult to enlarge an existing scientific paradigm?

6 What strategies might you think of deploying when you have an idea which you know works, yet others need to be convinced?

Further reading

You can find more material to do with this chapter at www.koganpage.com/
socialentrepreneurship

One of the best resources illustrating the signs of autism is available as a free download
from http://www.helpautismnow.com/physician_handbook.html [accessed 10 December
2015]. Do not be put off by the title, 'Autism Physician Handbook'. This is a handbook
for parents as well as professionals, and clearly illustrates the early signs of autism in
pictures. The website has excellent resources for parents of newly diagnosed children.

www.qsti.org [accessed 10 December 2015]. This is the Qigong Sensory Training Institute
website. We offer books and DVDs about the massage, an informational video about
autism, and resources for parents and professionals who are interested in training or
research.

Silva, L (2009) *Qigong Massage for your Child with Autism: A home program from Chinese
medicine*, Jessica Kingsley Publishers, London. This is a parent handbook and DVD with
instructions for the QST massage for children with autism.

Silva, L (2015) *The Little Chinese Medicine Book for Children with Down syndrome*, Guan
Yin Press. This is a parent handbook and DVD with instructions for the QST massage for
children with Down syndrome.

Montagu, A (1971) *Touching: the human significance of the skin*, Oxford, England:
Columbia U Press.

Field, T (2014) *Touch*, Bradford Books.

09

Reconnecting the disconnected: a story of technology, refugees and finding lost family

REFUGEES UNITED – DAVID AND CHRISTOPHER MIKKELSEN

ABSTRACT

On 20 June 2015 – World Refugee Day – the United Nations announced that the world had more than 59 million people displaced from their homes. This number has tumbled so far towards the absurd that the outside world is losing faith in our ability to solve the crisis.

These 59 million women, children and men are scattered across distinctly different scenarios, but are all partners in the same reality of fear and uncertainty. From Syria to Southern Africa, families have fled violence and persecution, drought and famine, forced to endure harrowing journeys through inhospitable climates with little or no food and water, hopeful that tomorrow will grant them a little respite from the hardship.

One of the most devastating effects of war is the separation between loved ones. Families caught in conflict flee in different directions and soon become engulfed in the currents of a mass exodus, losing track of each other while trying to find safety. Finding themselves camps apart, even countries apart, most go for years without discovering the fate of their loved ones.

We founded Refugees United (REFUNITE) after helping a young Afghan refugee find out what had happened to his family after a human trafficker had separated them. Our journey, taking us across war zones and the depths of Southern Russia, led us to understand that not only had no-one created a central data repository for information on separated families, but the most important pieces of the puzzle had been left out of the equation all together: the refugees themselves.

Building on simple mobile technologies and far-reaching partnerships with mobile operators, REFUNITE has become the world's largest missing persons network, helping more than 420,000 displaced people in their search for lost loved ones. Through text messaging (SMS) pushed out into the broader refugee populations across Africa and the Middle East, we have shifted the tracing process from being a centralized affair handled by agencies alone, to being an inclusive and dignified opportunity for displaced people to contribute to reconnecting, and bettering their own lives.

In 2005 we met a young Afghan refugee named Mansour in Copenhagen, an affable and courageous young man who had lost track of his entire family during their escape from the Taliban. Offering to help him find his loved ones, we began an adventure into the world of the human trafficker who separated the family five years earlier. Our journey took us across Pakistan and Russia in search of information to help a kid reconnect with the one thing that matters most in this world: those you love.

This is a story of two brothers helping two brothers find each other again. A story of two brothers fighting to build the world's largest missing persons network, and in the process helping close to half a million refugees in their quest to find their missing loved ones. This is the story of Refugees United.

If you don't know the rules you can't break them: why us?

When we touched down in Indonesia in 1999, we had been travelling with our wider family all our lives. Raised by an unconventional set of parents, we began our global explorations at a young age. Our father, Tom, is a scientist deeply involved in the discovery of the uses of horseshoe crabs' blood for the detection of endotoxins and other dangerous anomalies found in things such as foodstuffs, medicine, medical devices and drinking water. Our mother, Kirsten, is an anaesthetic nurse who went into business and travelled with our father as he discovered and lived out his passion, taking us kids with them as we decamped to Florida, Hong Kong, Delaware, Thailand and other places, all in the hunt for the elusive crabs. Unlike most other families, we grew up with a specific luxury: two sets of parents. Our mother's sister and her husband, Birgitte and Peter, our aunt and uncle, have equally been traversing the globe, setting up lives from Tokyo to New York and anywhere in between, with us brothers living with them in various places when our folks were off on too-difficult-for-kids trips.

We've called Hong Kong and New Jersey home with them, and to this day our little family shares life completely intertwined across the United States, France and Denmark.

FIGURE 9.1   David and Christopher Mikkelsen

We were born into adventure and with an insatiable desire to discover. Some of our first memories are of walking around the muddy flats of the Florida Keys, dodging baby sharks and barracudas, stone crabs and stingrays, eyes peeled to the silt and grassy shallows in search of horseshoe crabs.

Spirited off to faraway places, thousands of miles from our native Denmark, we spent endless days together. We fought, like all other brothers, but were always bound by a bond of closeness and curiosity, fun and, probably, plain being stuck at the end of the world, just the two of us kids. From those days, we developed a kinship that has kept us best friends and each other's keeper through travels and trials endured across most of the world, in high seas and the calmest of waters.

There was a wildness to our upbringing, a devil-may-care approach to the world where our appetite for the different, the outcasts and the pursuit of our dreams were always encouraged. These seeds, more than anything else, would take root in those early days and run through our veins as we became older, taking us further and further into the world, away from all things found on the straight and narrow, and deeper into uncharted territories.

Time flows in a special way when you're decoupled from the fault lines of everyday responsibilities. There's calmness to having nothing, no stress of deadlines or the push of a world around you to perform. It was in these moments that we had some of our deepest moments of creativity. Ideas would come flowing: thoughts on the world, inventions, books, music, family, politics and love. Everyone on this planet deserves the freedom we were granted to just be, to just think and not worry about the consequences of tomorrow.

There's a current understanding across the world that a freedom such as this would breed nothing but complacency. Maybe it would, for some. Or maybe our world has a potential waiting to be unleashed if we free ourselves from the shackles of surviving and are given the reins to a life lived, not endured. In our view it's a bet worth taking, and a conversation far too encompassing for us to delve into in this chapter.

There was a method to our madness and a reason to not wanting a formal education. In our view, an education would be a controlling factor much more than a freedom. An education seemed a statement: this is who I am, and this is where I want to go. We didn't know. Perhaps still don't. An education seemed a surrender to a system we had no desire to be part of. It was a destination defined and, to us, the purpose of this life is much less of a destination than an opportunity to get completely lost in any corner of this wonderful world.

In the years following Indonesia we moved onwards to Australia, working odd jobs at construction sites, bars and whatever came along. From there, the journey took us to Bangkok, the Thai islands, Japan, Los Angeles, Cambodia and a host of other places, immersing ourselves in the culture and life of each place.

Back in Copenhagen years later, David was commissioned to shoot a documentary film about integration in Denmark; a surprisingly difficult thing, integration, in a small homogeneous society with very limited outside influence over the past 1,000 years.

We'd both become involved with teaching young immigrants about life in Denmark, and, building the scenario for the film, a kid who stood out was a young Afghan refugee named Mansour. A great kid, top of his class, hardworking and determined to make something of himself. He was a natural focal point for us.

He quickly became a good friend, someone we'd take out to grab a bite to eat with, hang out with, a sort of little brother. He was only 17, seemingly alone and trying to make it. That's when he told us his story.

Lessons: the life of a refugee

Five years earlier, when he was just 12, he and his family had escaped the Taliban in Afghanistan, fleeing across the mountains and into Pakistan, finding brief respite in Peshawar. Peshawar is a refugee city of some 2.9 million people, many undocumented and in transit onwards to something better, as were Mansour and his five siblings and mother. Their father, a high-ranking official, had escaped earlier, leaving money and instructions for the family to follow in his path.

On the eve of their departure for Scandinavia, the trafficker arrived at their temporary housing. He explained that a bus was waiting outside with a vacant seat, and that the family was to choose one among them to go first, and the rest would follow shortly after. Mansour, the oldest child at age 12, chose to go. He took it upon himself because that's the kind of person he is. He knew, as the oldest, that this was his responsibility and, besides, his family would follow shortly after.

He boarded the bus and began a journey that would come to an end at Copenhagen Central Station many months later. In between, although the pieces of this story are stitched together from the broken memory of a traumatized child, we have been able to decipher that Mansour went by foot, train and bus, at one point staying underneath the floorboards of an apartment somewhere in Russia alongside some 20 other refugees. They were waiting for their onward bus, terrified of showing themselves for fear of being caught by the authorities, only coming out for air and bathroom breaks for an hour or so a day.

Fast forward many weeks and Mansour crosses the border between Germany and Denmark, has his fake papers taken from him by the traffickers and told that when the train stops, he's in Copenhagen and on his own.

Needless to say, Mansour's family never followed and a hardened 12-year-old took it upon himself to make something out of his life, to prepare for the day when his family *would* return to him, to be able to provide a life for them. Imagine that – such resilience, such courage at the age when most of the lucky ones among us are still complaining about having to get up for school.

We know less than we think

Hearing Mansour's story, learning that still after five years he had no idea what had happened to his family, we immediately offered our assistance in trying to find them again. This was 2005, how hard could it be to find anyone on this planet?

Our first plan of action was to speak with the well-known organizations assisting refugees in Denmark. We learned from Mansour that he'd previously filled out paper forms stating who he was looking for, the reason for his escape, where he'd last seen them, and so on, but he had never heard anything back.

With all the organizations, we were met with compassion and understanding. However, there was a lot of helplessness in a situation that was unique and special to us, but not to the more than 42 million other displaced people across the world. Everyone knew how to speak about the hundreds of thousands of people crossing borders, everyone could talk about the major crises, but when it came to the one person in the midst of it all, desperately seeking information, there was nowhere to go.

We discovered that no information-sharing system had been created between organizations. Essentially, Mansour's family could be in Sweden for all we knew, but with no direct information exchange between the family tracing offices of each country, the only way to find out anything was to write to the various individual offices. We were flabbergasted.

In the end we sent off a 10-page document with Mansour's information – a document that, to the best of our knowledge, was sent to Geneva and then onwards from there to Peshawar to check against records to see if his family had registered any kind of information. As you can imagine, having a handful of aid workers responding to a flood of 2.9 million displaced people, trying to gather personal information on people terrified of giving any information away, is a fairly tall order.

Months into the search, having knocked on all doors and used whatever goodwill and authority we could muster, we still were left with no knowledge leading us anywhere closer to the whereabouts of Mansour's missing family. So we took matters into our own hands. What followed was an adventure through some of the oddest and wildest moments of our lives. Distilled for brevity, this is a summary of serendipity that brought us to reunite two brothers and set ourselves on track not just to build a global family tracing platform, but a fight to change the ways organizations of our world collaborate, govern and innovate.

Since our search had begun, Mansour had turned 18 and had his refugee travel pass exchanged for a bona fide passport. Armed with this, we decided the next step would be for him to travel back to Peshawar to see if he could find any information on his family.

Courage his only companion, Mansour arrived in Pakistan in early 2005 and began scouring the streets, searching for clues to his past. Days were spent walking aimlessly around, his visa soon coming to an end, his desperation growing by the hour. He was close to giving up when, on his last day, he stumbled into the human trafficker that had shipped him out five years earlier, recognizing him on the street despite him having grown a beard and looking a little different. As you can imagine, this was a face Mansour would never forget.

It took guts to approach him, as he was a dangerous gangster making a living off the misery of others. But Mansour had nothing to lose and confronted him with the promise he'd made years ago – that he would ensure that the family ended up reunited.

At first he was dismissive, explaining to Mansour that he sent out hundreds of people every month, and couldn't care less. But Mansour was persistent, pushing harder and, in the end, offered what little money he had left as a bribe. The man asked Mansour to come back the next morning.

Nervous, Mansour showed up the next day and sat down with the man. He paid him more money and left with nothing but a phone number. A phone number he was informed would lead him to his one younger brother, Ali, who was nine years old at the time Mansour had last seen him.

Back in Copenhagen we began calling the number frantically, but constantly ended up with Russian-speaking people on the line, unable to understand us. But Mansour kept trying, kept calling, kept hoping.

After weeks of calling, Mansour finally had a Pashto-speaking man answer the phone and immediately spilled his heart out, explaining why he was calling, who he was looking for. The man deadpanned that the number belonged to a phone booth in the midst of an Afghan bazaar in a city called Stavropol. But ... he recognized the name of the person Mansour was looking for and proceeded to give us another phone number. Ten minutes later, nearly six years of silence was broken as Ali picked up the line and welcomed the voice of his older brother.

Over the course of the next weeks and months, we learned of Ali's predicament – a stateless refugee in Russia, de facto enslaved by a family, constantly chased out in the streets by not only the Russian authorities but also roving street gangs with a penchant for torturing refugees. The police would arrest them, beat them up, break their bones, cut them with knives and burn them with cigarettes, keep them confined until someone came to pay the bribe to have them released. This in turn would place Ali in debt, forcing him back out to work, and yet another round of sooner or later being arrested again. Imagine knowing that your little brother lives through hell while you're comfortably sitting in Copenhagen.

We arranged for Ali to come up to Moscow and meet us in early October 2005. A journey only made possible because our parents offered to subsidize the trip to reunite the two, invariably setting REFUNITE in motion.

The mission was to physically reunite the two brothers after all these years, and then to document the whole ordeal, to demonstrate to the world the insurmountable difficulties refugees were facing in trying to reconnect with their missing loved ones.

We touched down with nerves jangling and an unsettling anxiety mixed with euphoria coursing through our veins.

On 7 October at dusk, after days of traversing Moscow trying to find the mafia-protected Afghan bazaar Ali was staying at, a taxi pulled up and came to a stop in front of the Seven Sisters hotel. All three of us stood in shivering anticipation, holding our breath, hoping. The door opened and out spilled a wonderful young kid, the spitting image of Mansour, eyes wide, trying to contain himself to not arouse suspicion, until, finally, he could hold back no more and broke into running. The two brothers fell into each others arms, ending so many years of searching, so many years of pain. All of us were crying, hairs stood on our arms and necks and the intensity was palpable. It was an epiphany moment for all of us, not least for us as brothers helping two other brothers.

The days that followed were indeed to prove not just remarkable, but life changing. Crazy days; arrested by the Russian police, robbed blind by them while seeing to it that the two brothers made it to safety; experiencing the two brothers finally finding a moment's peace and falling into the inevitable discussion: what happened to the rest of the family?

Two short days later our visa was up and Mansour had to say his goodbyes. A goodbye no one should have to say, separated again after so many years of searching; separated again, knowing that your younger brother is destined to travel back into harm's way. But a connection had been made, and after giving Ali what we had of warm clothes and money, we set our sights on home and a mission to have Ali join us in Denmark as soon as possible.

Perhaps one situation more than anything else drove us to take action. Upon returning to Denmark, driving Mansour home, the last thing he told David as he exited the car was: 'For the first time in many years, I will have a peaceful night's sleep. I know where my brother is.' To this day, we have yet to find the rest of his family, although it remains a personal mission.

We reflected on what we had done. How we, as two Danish brothers with every authority at our disposal, every opportunity compared to a refugee, had found nothing. We had spoken to numerous organizations and people, committees and others, and nothing had turned up. The thoughts began to crystallize. Where was the digital infrastructure in all of this? Where was the open data system that could collect, curate and distribute information on separated families across camps, countries and organizations? Where was the collaboration in all of this? Why was it missing? In that moment, Refugees United was born.

Building Refugees United

We had not the first inkling of where to start. But in all our youthful confidence, we believed we'd deliver a world-changing system in six months. We believed it would be a system that the world's aid organizations would embrace, and show them why open data, shared knowledge and efficiency were goals we should strive for. We were wrong.

With no personal network, we started speaking with every person who'd listen to us and pitch our idea of creating a global platform of information-sharing amongst the refugee agencies.

The people we *did* have access to were creative types: people in the film and fashion industry, musicians and writers, art directors and the like. And they were the people we first spoke with, and from whom we drew the first and probably most important lesson in the future success of REFUNITE: The power of storytelling.

The first months of the project's life we simply toyed around with the idea, vacillated, circling the issue and finding out how, when and if to make the full jump. The more we got into it and the more we thought about the challenge of helping millions of refugees, the more the idea began to take hold until it could be ignored no more.

We soon quit the jobs we had working as substitute teachers. We'd still work the odd days here and there to maintain a bit of income, but REFUNITE consumed everything we were. Living in a tiny studio, sharing a bed for the next years to come, we made a living off very little, save for when our parents came by on a thankfully very frequent basis and stocked up our fridge and saw to it we had something to live on. We couldn't have got this off the ground without their support, and their insistence that we pursued our dreams.

In 2007, before the first signs of a global financial meltdown, we persuaded Danske Bank to give us a loan. We borrowed $35,000 and lived off this, while feeding into the organization whatever we needed. We were hustling and proceeded with determination to make everything either free or reduced to nothing. This bootstrapping was liberating because at every meeting, the first thing we said was: 'We have a great idea, but absolutely no money. But you should still help us, and here's why.' Using our growing network, we sought support for everything. Mind you, the first years were spent with an 'office' in a shutdown, run-down factory, where an underground nightclub ran their weekends of craziness, and our office consisted of a backroom with four milk crates and an old door for a table. But it was free. Being this down-and-out taught us a lot about frugality and, especially, the value of partnerships – a skill that would come to shape our mission in the years to come.

A wonderful character that joined us around 2007 was the actor Mads Mikkelsen. A committed and sincere person, we had met him by chance a few years earlier and developed an excellent friendship. It was not a light moment for us asking him to use his considerable fame to help us advance the cause, but thankfully he didn't hesitate for a minute in joining us. He was responsible for opening many doors to begin with, travelling with us from Uganda to New York, promoting our joint cause and sharing more than a few cold beers.

Curiously, the one place we received the least support was the non-profit sector. We genuinely thought that an industry that was built on the premise of teamwork and a dedication to helping others would be open to us and our ideas. What we found was the very opposite – an industry that seemed not only driven by competition, but a particularly insidious one at that. This kind of competitiveness was not openly so, for the sake of appearance when living off donations, but nonetheless deep-rooted and driven by a safeguarding attitude towards maintaining a comfortable status quo within the ecosystem of humanitarian aid.

As our network expanded into more influential circles, the first person we drew into the organization that had a truly deep impact on our work was a movie producer named Vibeke Windelov. Vibeke was a charismatic and eccentric lady with an illustrious career behind her, known for having a sharp tongue and even sharper

Rolodex. When we first came to see her in her palatial apartment in the centre of Copenhagen, we'd been forewarned of a force to be reckoned with, and to expect a harsh welcome. Nothing could have been further from the truth. We entered the holy sanctuary of her kitchen, a kitchen blessed with the presence of most of the movie and rock stars that have passed through Copenhagen over the years, and were greeted by a lovely woman who immediately took us under her wing. Vibeke became the first chairwoman and co-founder of the Refugees United Foundation.

With Vibeke, we went to the Foreign Ministry after first connecting with the Minister of Justice. She was so moved by our mission to help refugee families reunite that she liaised with the Minister of Development, who called not only her immediate department heads to a meeting, but also executives from a wide range of NGOs operating in Copenhagen who were financed by the Danish International Development Agency (DANIDA).

The tension in the room was palpable. One of the first people to shake our hands proceeded to shake it with such force that it hurt, and then leaned in and hissed: 'If you ever try to force a situation such as this on us again, we will see to it that you're never helped!' That set the stage for the next few hours. A few hours where each of the representatives of organizations took turn in explaining how a tracing system based on IT and collaboration could never work. We knew we had hit on something, given the response.

We later met with DANIDA and pitched our project with a potential view to get funding. The meeting was nothing but friendly and accommodating but exposed, to us, the inherent flaws in the systems at play. While there was talk of a possible project, there would first have to be a pilot project in Myanmar two and a half years down the line. We thanked them, got up, left and realized that we would never succeed with this approach. In reality, what we were looking to do was disrupt the humanitarian aid sector, and we were asking the very people we were trying to disrupt for advice and financing.

In that moment we settled our minds on building our portfolio of private sector partnerships, and to seek private funding from individuals, foundations and corporations. The irony we found in all this was that the doors of every single CEO always opened to us. The world of business was open to our idea; open to explore how they, through the power of their networks, products and personal influence, could help us leverage others to help refugee families reconnect. Who could turn down the opportunity to extend themselves by just a little, and thus help the many?

The alchemy of a tech non-profit

As we continued to find zero traction within the aid sector, we began building aggressively in other parts of the world. Early in 2007, a woman named Alexandra Aparicio joined us from Brazil. An executive with the global PR firm Ketchum, she sought us out, compelled by the mission of Refugees United, and became a volunteer in Sao Paulo.

Still hoping to engage in partnerships and dialogue with the non-profits, we worked with Alexandra to sign up Ketchum offices to support us globally. The company's global network had already selected an official non-profit cause to support, so it was up to the individual country offices to choose whether or not to support us. In the course of the next 14 months, led by Alexandra, the three of us managed to sign up Ketchum offices in 36 countries, having them represent us in the media, help with strategy in delivering our messages, and broadening the footprint of Refugees United from local to global. This was a crucial step in our continued search and struggle to find the supporters necessary to take our venture to scale.

Natural storytellers, we framed our challenge and perfected our pitch. The beauty of REFUNITE is the simplicity in the mission. There are a finite number of refugees, a finite number of family separations, and a solution to the problem. Obviously there will continue to be new refugees, but still, the message remained that this is an inherently solvable problem. In a world where many have grown tired of the ever-ballooning overheads of NGOs, this purpose-driven mission that has an end-goal was tantalizing.

We wrote down a number of 'truths' that would guide us from the start. One was to only work with the best we could find. Secondly, to always seek the win-win, understanding that engaging with a willing corporate sector would only work if they were in it for more than just the feel-good story.

The first significant funding we received came in 2008 from Peter Mads Clausen, of Danfoss prominence (Danfoss is a global manufacturer of products used in cooling food, air conditioning, heating buildings, and so on). It also came in from another charismatic individual named Mads Kjaer, founder of MyC4, an online micro-investment platform in Africa. They, together with Vibeke and us, became co-founders of the Refugees United Foundation.

Between 2008 and 2010 we had a trifecta of partners join us who would change the trajectory of the organization. The Maersk Foundation donated $1 million to us after months of us pitching them on the innovative visions of Refugees United. It was an enormous donation at the time, one which enabled us to create the first true team, and the first true mistakes, in the months to come.

We soon created what would become our most significant operational partnership with the Swedish mobile network leader Ericsson. Having met the CEO of Ericsson Denmark, Lars Tofft, he brought us to Stockholm to meet with Elaine Weidman, Ericsson's Corporate Social Responsibility (CSR) and Sustainability executive; a charming, driven and sharp-witted young American who immediately understood the power of REFUNITE. Despite not knowing exactly what we needed to do together, a kinship was shaped that would lead us down a joint path, and a shared vision, of helping families reconnect. Hans Vestberg, who had more or less just taken the CEO position at Ericsson when we engaged with them, was to become an important champion of our work, and a friend we have shared many-a-stage with across the world since. Ericsson and REFUNITE have been through thick and thin together, battling the ups and downs, achieving massive wins and taking a few losses, but continuously focused on building our partnership towards higher impact. We've always been indebted to Ericsson, who took us in like their own, betting on two brothers and an idea with all they had.

In the midst of this early progress, an employee of Refugees United, Rikke Juel-Brandt, introduced us to the IKEA Foundation and their new CEO, Per Heggenes. At the time – it was 2009 – we had already realized that trying to convert traditional multinational organizations into believers of refugee data, and the sharing of that data, was going to be a hard sell.

Knowing that if we were ever going to get traction we needed to be on-ground in the right places, we met with Per, bringing with us an ambitious plan for global scale, starting with a strategy in Kenya, getting access to the two large refugee camps, Dadaab and Kakuma; two camps holding a combined 600,000 refugees from Somalia, South Sudan, DRC and Ethiopia.

Strategically, we were weak without a critical mass of refugees on our platform. All we had was a good idea but little data and little experience. At this stage we had perhaps 8,000 to 9,000 refugees on refunite.org and found it near impossible to reconnect anyone. It's a numbers game, and while we had already had our first few successes of reconnecting loved ones, we needed to step up our game.

We continuously ran into dead ends in Geneva with various organizations, getting caught up in committees and endless meetings. No traction, despite also having enlisted serious firepower in the form of Madeleine Albright, whom we'd met through a connection with former president of Costa Rica, José-Maria Figueres. She argued on our behalf with the powers that be, but to little avail. We knew we had to build ourselves into a force that could not be dismissed. So, we quietly left the stage and took our first real pivot.

Who needs us, anyway?

As it became clear that we weren't going to make a dent in the non-profit universe without more persuasive power, it was time to take a different approach. We vowed to return with a global coalition of private partners, and to spread our influence so widely, and our reach so deep, that no-one would be able to dismiss us.

This decision led us to pivot not just our approach, but our entire reason for existence. We went from seeking to cluster the global aid community around a web platform, to move the responsibility from the few and into the hands of the many. Enter the mobile phone.

Our vision was that, in a refugee camp, assisting families was bottlenecked around a few overburdened case workers helping thousands of people each. And something became obvious to us – the failure to invoke the powers of the distributed knowledge found amongst 600,000 people. Why have two people assisting 600,000, when you can have 100,000 people assist them?

We had found that people, despite barely having clothes on their backs or food for their children, would still have access to a mobile phone. And with this knowledge we began to move away from being an organizational-centric agency to becoming a distributed hub of empowerment for refugees by equipping them with access to critical information at their own behest.

This was to prove crucial, moving our project from being defined by just helping families reconnect faster and more efficiently, to changing the very nature of how aid is delivered: from an active–passive relationship where a refugee is expected to wait patiently for others to help, into a service that urges the people in question to move beyond the confined limits of what others can do for them. The key thing we discovered, the one thing that is almost as important as when two people find each other again, was the dignity this brought back to the lives of people: giving men and women the respect to make informed decisions on their own behalf, in their own time.

This was the vision we brought to the IKEA Foundation, and this was the vision they immediately saw as the future, kick-starting one of the most significant partnerships of our existence. One thing that makes it so important, over and above the funding, is the absolute belief of the Foundation in the people they invest in. They made it clear that of course they were investing in the success of Refugees United but, in many ways, they were investing in us as founders, with a clear sense that we had it in us to succeed and that taking roads less travelled was okay. This freedom to explore, the freedom to fail and to pick yourself back up and honestly to analyse and report on what went wrong was paramount to our success.

And so we set out with Ericsson to build a mobile platform, and an alliance of mobile operators, to help end the problem of refugee families being lost from each other.

The first of many iterations of our mobile work were fairly challenging. We were trying to discover and make sense of not just new technologies, but entirely new work forms in places few had focused on – refugee camps.

The first partnerships we ran in Kenya were enormously helpful in terms of lessons learnt, but they came at a high cost. Partnering with a local organization, we got our first lesson in the inefficiencies we've found amongst many NGOs since – their primary focus and expertise seems to be in acquiring funding. Many organizations are funded by pots of money that seemingly come with very little oversight, insight and accountability. Success is metered out in percentage graphs with little to no hard data on what has actually been accomplished. Every year is about growth, not the dwindling of the problem. With no real market forces at play, organizations that deserve to fail are artificially kept alive, jostling to stay relevant while sucking up resources from others who might be able to do genuine good.

One of our proudest achievements is how far we have come without needing a single taxpayer dollar. We look our private donors in the eyes, fully in the knowledge that we're spending someone else's money, and report directly to them what we have achieved with the money we've been entrusted with. This has been painful at times, but we believe there's a healthy mechanism at play in dealing directly with the people who give you the opportunity to wrestle with some of the world's problems. It keeps us very real, and true to ourselves, and focused on one thing – running REFUNITE like a business where the bottom line is families reconnected. Our shareholders are the refugees, and the people, foundations and companies enabling us to do our job.

Another important ally and supporter has been the Omidyar Network (ON). Founded by Pierre and Pam Omidyar (Pierre was one of the founders of eBay), ON invest in high-impact organizations, their mission to amplify the effect young organizations can have on the world, often through technology solutions to age-old problems. Investing not only financial resources in REFUNITE, the Omidyar Network brought us into their circle of significant brain trust, which included both their employees and the family of other organizations receiving their help.

Building networks

Through the partnerships we've created, one key thing that has emerged is a hybrid funding model that comes with handling multiple opportunities. Given we've always been reliant on private donations and partnerships, funding and sustainability have been at the forefront of our minds from the very beginning. Working closely with partners such as Ericsson, Delta Partners, SAP and so on – as well as a plethora of mobile operators – has enabled us to have a global footprint with the budget of a local organization. Through leveraging each other's strengths, we've built what we believe to be a future model for solving global issues in a concerted manner, by working in teams and in structures that are mutually beneficial and with a positive social outcome.

Alongside (and with) Ericsson, we began to focus especially, and aggressively, on the mobile network operators (MNOs) to build out our scale and reach.

The mission with the MNOs was to build a global coalition, one which would join us and provide not only free access for our systems, be that through text messaging (SMS), USSD (a series of codes, characterized by hashes and asterisks, typed directly into the phone), or toll-free calls, but also join us in the difficult process of reaching our constituents and informing them of the availability of our services.

MTN Uganda signed up first, soon followed by Safaricom in Kenya. And with Safaricom began some deeply interesting projects, one of which involved the targeting of individuals based on their location through a million-strong SMS campaign. Using this technique, which is based on the sending of messages to phones connected to specific mobile base stations, we could target camps like Dadaab and Kakuma, and send out large-scale information pushes across the 20-mile surrounding area, offering people the opportunity to reply back to us if they were looking for lost family.

Replicating this model in multiple markets, we've partnered with MNOs across most of Africa and the Middle East: Vodacom in Democratic Republic of the Congo (DRC), Zain Group in South Sudan and Jordan; AsiaCell in Iraq; Hormuud in Somalia; Telesom in Somaliland; MTN in Liberia; AVEA in Turkey; Etisalat in Afghanistan and Pakistan, and many more to follow. Essentially tapping into most major refugee countries of origin and destination through these partnerships, we're able to engage with millions of potential users by leveraging the win-win partnerships we've created.

The Holy Grail of sustainability

Sustainability should always be at the heart of what you do. To generate a genuinely impactful project, you need to figure out two things. Firstly, how quickly can you solve the problem you're tackling, and at what cost? Then, how do you raise the money you need, based on an expectation that you'll solve it? Secondly, if this is an ongoing problem, how do you build into your project revenue streams that can either entirely replace donor funding or supplement it in a significant way? Organizations that are 100 per cent donor funded walk a fine line, regardless of how good the work they might be doing.

Building a sustainable, diverse income model is not a simple thing. The great bulk of the aid industry is built on a foundation of donor funding that has, for the most parts, rarely had to consider or build self-sustainability into its projects. Some projects never will, nor should, become sustainable, of course, such as child vaccination programmes. But increasing numbers of newer, disruptive organizations are entering the non-profit sector, leveraging emerging technology in ways incumbents often struggle with. Many also have sustainability at the forefront of their minds, something – again – that older players struggle with.

By being small, agile and not entrenched in 'traditional' ways of doing things, these new organizations can reimagine entire ways of solving global problems. Smaller organizations are able to home in on specific problems solvable with the application of new technology, create partnerships and develop proof of impact, and slice the pie into bite-size chunks which can be tackled with new perspectives.

A word of caution, though. It's easy to write off the aid industry, labelling many of its institutions as archaic and out of touch, but that would be a mistake. While certainly challenged by its very structure, the sector harbours incredible numbers of smart, dedicated and forward-thinking people and programmes that are keen to adopt new ways, and infuse them with the wisdom of their experience. The experience and knowledge residing within the aid sector is crucial, as technology is not a panacea. What you build in Silicon Valley likely won't work in Somalia. Technology exists to optimize performance and impact. Build partnerships; learn from each other; inspire each other – there's too much at stake to engage in competitiveness and NGO warfare.

Taking it to the field

In 2010 we finally launched ourselves into the wider world, and did so with President Clinton, Ericsson, Delta Partners, MTN Uganda and the UN High Commissioner for Refugees (UNHCR) at the annual Clinton Global Initiative in New York. We kicked off with the ambitious target of helping 120,000 refugees find loved ones through our platform. We had little idea whether we could pull this massive feat off, but we soldiered on in the belief that if anyone could do it, we could.

We developed a new model of working, distributing the workload so we could help more people, and for that we began searching for volunteers inside the camps – typically young people, such as community youth leaders or other notable and well-known people – who we could take through an intensive training course, teaching them how to engage with fellow refugees who have lost track of their family members. When they found people searching they would engage with them and register key details about their circumstances, sending the data straight to our platform through a simple 'dumb phone' service. Capturing their name, who they're looking for, place last seen, tribe, clan and gender, our system can then take over and begin the search process for them, collating and distributing knowledge when possible matches have been found. The key is that the refugee is the owner of not just the data, but also the process.

Designing for everyone

The typical user we design for is a 58-year-old Somali woman who is semi-literate, distrusting of outsiders and, while having a $10 phone, uses it for receiving calls only because of cost. She hasn't seen her two children and husband in five years, becoming separated from them in Mogadishu before making the perilous journey to Kenya.

The point here is if we can build tech that works for her, we've built tech that can work for everyone.

Key for us is to establish a rapport, a trust, which is bound by the very people of the Somali woman's own community helping her onto the platform. Next is for us to capture as much reliable data as we can, so we can begin the electronic search. Then we send her a select snippet of potential matches through the system, and see to it she reads it, understands it and reacts to it. Lather, rinse and repeat – for the South Sudanese, Congolese, Burundian, Ethiopian, Syrian and many other refugees in need of help.

Impacting the world around us

Because little of our work involves the use of smart phones, which are often too expensive for people to afford in the developing world, it can be difficult to measure actual engagement. Our service is provided through more primitive SMS, USSD and phone calls because that's the only way to reach and engage the vast majority of refugees. How do you measure churn, active usage and referrals when using this approach?

Beyond the analytics and measures of success, there were multiple upfront problems in our methodology that needed to be solved. For example, the sending of SMS and making phone calls can be prohibitively expensive for our users, and it's no good only connecting one half of the family to the platform. You need both to make a connection.

We've processed millions of searches, hosted more than 2 million calls to our call centre, registered more than 400,000 individuals who have sent more than 875,000 messages across the platform in numerous countries, and we're just getting started. But all that's for nothing, really, when all you want to know about is how many families we've reconnected. It's a good question, and one we can't give a full answer to just yet.

As a small tech non-profit, developing the capacity to handle complex and rather large datasets is still a challenge; especially deciphering information without compromising the privacy and security of already persecuted people – but we're trying very hard. What we can say though, is that what we do know is that we've reconnected thousands of families. Moreover, we're currently reconnecting on average 100 to 150 families every single month.

Readers accustomed to a digital world where we speak of billions of users, billions of interactions and terabytes of data, might stop here for a second – but we offer you this. Think of the DRC, a country that has been in conflict for several decades, claiming millions of lives. A country where the literacy rate is around 60 per cent (way lower with the displaced populations), where mobile phone penetration is 23 per cent spread across 75 million people in over 2.4 million square kilometres of land. A country where hundreds of thousands of families have been separated by conflict. It is an immense challenge helping a displaced population on this scale, but it's a challenge we're more than willing to take on with our partners at Vodacom and Ericsson.

Reflections on a journey not yet complete

When you're suddenly flush with cash and the world is looking at you, the pressure quickly mounts. This is often when start-ups begin feeling the foundational quivers, echoed by the frailty of inexperience. There are many things that cannot be solved only by the hardened resolve and the die-hard optimism of founders. For some things you need wisdom only obtained by having been through storms – and still weather – with a team.

Of the many failures of ours, two in particular stand out. The first was not building REFUNITE with a technical co-founder. We simply didn't know better, and coming from a world as far removed from technology as we did, we viewed our grand fight as political, neglecting to understand the importance of growing our tech products internally within our own team.

In light of this, early iterations of our platform from 2009 onwards were built in partnership with a variety of web agencies, which was, by all accounts, a tough call. Yes, there are great agencies out there, but in our experience, trying to build anything complex with them, especially concerning refugee settings in Africa from a Western office, is impossible. This took us far too long to learn. Choose wisely when you decide who you work with – passion, alone, is not enough.

There's a saying that your first three employees determine the outcome of your organization. The first batch of hires will help shape the culture and define your success – so it's up to you to choose the right ones. These are the stars that will help you navigate your path, and without them your nights will be dark.

When we received our first round of significant funding, we hired the wrong people. Going up against the data practices of the NGO world, and our view of their approaches, we reasoned that to beat the machine we needed people who understood the structure of what we were fighting. As a result we ended up hiring former employees of NGOs hoping they would be able to help us move forward. What happened was the opposite. While all lovely, smart people, they brought with them the very organizational mindset that causes so many NGOs to misfire and malfunction. In short, we had ended up hiring people who *try*. Never hire people who *try* – hire people who *do*. This was our fault entirely as founders. Our fault for not recognizing it, and our fault for not leading them better and for not making the necessary staffing cuts fast enough.

Battle-hardened from the ever-present fight with the system we were striving to change, we never let down our guards, and never took off our shields. We fought everyone around us, feeling at times like returning soldiers finding it impossible to adjust to the quiet of home. We did not yet have the maturity to truly lead at that time, and perhaps we should have turned our anger and frustration into something more positive. Sometimes your strengths are also your weaknesses.

Many of the storms we weathered would have probably taken lesser people down, but we had each other as brothers. There are times that feel so soul-crushingly hard when you're trying to build a global movement that you all but hang on to each other. It hurts, and the brick walls so many organizations hit will bring you down unless you brace yourself for some of the roughest and most emotionally draining roads you'll ever experience. The rewards may be great, but the journey will test your resolve, for sure.

While our tenacity was the key catalyst in our early moves, the countless passionate and smart people who have brought their expertise to our mission have unquestionably driven the success of Refugees United. There are far too many to mention here, but you know who you are. One of our key talents has always been to find brilliant people and persuade them to help us out, and this is no less so today.

Our first key hire was a young woman named Claudia, who joined us in 2011. With a career at eBay and different consultancies behind her, she brought to the table the focused, results oriented thinking we needed. With her, the three of us began the arduous task of building an organization that could genuinely match our mission.

Lessons learnt

Some of the key takeaways we've gathered over the years can be neatly summed up in a relatively few points:

1 *Know your customer.* Far too many products and projects are built without any user involvement. We failed to understand this well enough during our early years, until our pivot.

2 *Create a compelling narrative around your work.* Why is your work critically important to the world? Why should anyone care, and how *can* they care and move with you, and support you? Few people remember statistics and details, but everyone remembers a great story. Find your own great story.

3 *Think about what kind of funding you're seeking.* For us, 'investment-style' donations were best, giving us the freedom to experiment and be supported by people and foundations who not only understood the importance of financial support, but also human resources, risk and the nature of tech development.

4 *Build great, big partnerships.* Because it is infinitely more fun, rewarding and impactful when done right. Sharing the burden, the costs and the successes will get you further than if you decide to go it all alone. Just choose the right partners!

5 *Define what you are, and aren't, as you set out.* It's important to be clear in your own mind who you are, what you want to achieve, and how far you're willing to go to get the job done. Once you know that, communicate it as clearly and succinctly to others as possible.

6 *Surround yourself with the smartest and most driven people you can.* Integrity + motivation + passion + experience = a winning team. You know you've succeeded in building the right team when you're the least smart person in the room.

7 *Culture is crucial.* You need to create the right environment for people to not only thrive, but to experiment and move forward with their own big ideas. This was one of the most significant barriers for us to cross as founders – letting go. It's great being the captain, but without someone to help you set the sails, navigate the oceans, cook the food and help lift the heavy cargo, your ship might look awesome, but it will never leave the harbour.

8 *Build the right team.* Define the problem you're looking to solve, and educate yourself on the market before you. What succeeded and what failed? Why? And think long and hard about the smartest three people you can find to help you build those early foundations of a team. Find someone you trust who has extensive experience in hiring people and ask for help. Make sure the person you're asking for help understands you, your objectives and your approach.

9 *Boards or advisers?* Building on that, find a few key advisers, not necessarily a board (it can be difficult to get the right calibre of people to commit to at first, but try). You need people you can call up or meet up for coffee when you need to talk things through.

Further discussion

1 What is the role of the private sector in social good projects?

2 The aid industry is a $157 billion a year industry, having grown tenfold in the past decade. This is not sustainable, and is often ineffective. How should this be changed?

3 Is creating a profitable business based on helping others morally acceptable?

4 Should the developed world accept as many refugees as neighbouring countries to the conflicts? If so, how can we provide the best possible life for them in their new homes?

5 The aid industry has largely been a top-down exercise for the past 50 years, with donors engaging with 'passive' recipients. With the advent of mobile and internet technologies, this is beginning to shift to two-way dialogue. How might this change the way the aid sector works? What benefits, and challenges, might it bring?

6 How do you see technology embracing, changing, disrupting and inspiring the humanitarian aid industry in the next decade?

Further reading

You can find more material to do with this chapter at www.koganpage.com/socialentrepreneurship

Robert F Kennedy, *To Seek a Newer World* (1967)
Ash Maurya, *Running Lean: Iterate from Plan A to a plan that works* (2012)
Alistair Croll and Benjamin Yoskovitz, *Lean Analytics: Use data to build a better startup faster* (2013)
refunite.org [accessed 15 December 2015]
'Refugees' on Wikipedia: https://en.wikipedia.org/wiki/Refugee [accessed 15 December 2015]

10
Let a billion readers bloom

PLANETREAD – BRIJ KOTHARI

ABSTRACT

Same language subtitling (SLS) is Bollywood fortified with subtitles, for mass literacy. Conceived in 1996, while watching a Spanish movie with English subtitles, SLS is a simple idea of subtitling mainstream TV content in the 'same' language as the audio. What you hear is what you read. Several research studies have found that SLS causes automatic and inescapable reading engagement among all viewers, including weak readers. Especially on song-based content, SLS is known to more than double reading skill achievement.

India has nearly 800 million TV viewers already and is slated to cross 1 billion by 2018. Over half of them cannot read a simple text, although they may be 'literate'. The average Indian watches a little over two hours of TV a day. Content is available in a mix of more than 20 languages, on 600 channels. Bollywood produces around 1,000 movies a year, each with an average of five to six songs. Bollywood songs are a dominant force on TV in India. If all the songs were to be shown with SLS, it would make a phenomenal contribution to raising the reading skills of a billion people.

From 2002–13, the Indian Institute of Management, Ahmedabad and non-profit PlanetRead ran several SLS pilots in partnership with Doordarshan, India's national/state TV network and, from 2013–15, a major scale-up in Maharashtra state with Zee Talkies. SLS has been implemented in India on song-based programming in eight major languages: Hindi, Bengali, Gujarati, Marathi, Telugu, Tamil, Kannada and Punjabi.

In 2010, following a decade of engagement, the Broadcasting Corporation of India (Prasar Bharati) accepted SLS 'in principle' for a national scale-up. However, 'in-principle' acceptance is yet to translate into practice. A national scale-up of SLS would cost only $1 million, annually and give daily reading practice for 15–30 minutes to an estimated 300 million weak readers.

This is the story of a simple, but perhaps not simplistic, idea that I've been irrevocably married to since 1996. If I can't shake it off, it is because SLS has the potential to make a billion people read in India, and another billion in other countries.

Conception

What does *Women on the Verge of a Nervous Breakdown*, Pedro Almodóvar's zany award-winning film, have to do with mass literacy in India? Nothing, and yet … everything! In early 1996, after almost a decade of student life at Cornell University in Ithaca, NY, I was finally in the home stretch of writing my doctoral dissertation. That is precisely when, I believe, the desire to watch movies peaks.

So there we were, a group of friends watching this hysterical movie in Spanish. As students of Spanish, we had discovered that watching movies in the language was not only effective, but also great fun. Those were pre-digital and pre-DVD days when foreign language movies in the United States came on videotapes with English language subtitles.

In an ambience of hilarity, I blurted out during a bathroom break: 'Why don't they put Spanish subtitles on Spanish films. We'd catch the dialogue better.' My friends agreed. So I casually ventured an extension, without worrying too much about its linguistic narrowness in a country that has 22 official languages and over a thousand dialects: 'Maybe India would become literate if they simply added Hindi lyrics to Hindi film songs.'

'I think you're onto something', a friend reacted. Coming from a fluent Spanish and Hindi speaker who had grown up in India, who understood Bollywood's hold on Indian passions, it was the sort of nonchalant affirmation I needed in order for a synapse of an idea to become a lifelong obsession. The idea couldn't have had a more serendipitous beginning. But before I could get too excited about it, I had to confirm the novelty of the thought. The idea seemed ridiculously simple to have not been thought of, or tried, for mass literacy.

I found that most of the literature on subtitling was coming out of the United States and Western Europe. One major stream dealt with the use of subtitling for access to audio-visual content across languages or translation subtitling. Considerable attention is devoted to how translation subtitling contributes to additional language acquisition (second, third, foreign, etc). Some even suggested subtitling in the 'same' language for improving one's pronunciation and listening comprehension. The other major stream, Closed-Captioning (CC), leveraged subtitling for media access among the deaf and hearing impaired. A trickle of articles talked about subtitling as karaoke in the limited context of entertainment in bars or on increasingly popular home-based karaoke machines.

The bulk of the literature made one crucial assumption; subtitling was only for functionally literate viewers. Still, there was an occasional mention of the potential of subtitling to support reading skill development, lost in the cacophony of subtitling for other purposes. The idea of 'same' language subtitling was articulated in some cases with academic terms like 'unilingual', 'intralingual' and 'bimodal' subtitles, in the context of language acquisition. The odd piece, however, would also refer to subtitling and its potential for literacy. Subtitling in the 'same' language for literacy, albeit in a limited classroom or research context, had at least found a passing expression.

It would be fair to ask about the original contribution we were making. The first thing that occurred to me was that the idea of 'sameness' tying audio and text was somehow lost in the many monikers floating around in literature, like, unilingual, intralingual and bimodal subtitling. The tight bond I wanted to forge between audio and subtitles needed a more fitting term that brought 'sameness' of language front and centre. The term 'same language subtitling', and its very own acronym (SLS), thus came into being.

Concocting SLS felt a bit like sweet revenge for all the academic jargon I had endured in my coursework in graduate school. Now I had my own term to inflict upon others. My literature review made two things patently clear. SLS had never been used on television or other mass audio-visual media, anywhere in the world, expressly for the purpose of improving mass reading or literacy skills among functional non-literates. Research on the potential impact of SLS exposure, or subtitling generally, on the reading skills of early-readers, was rare. An aspiring academic trained in development communication and education could want nothing more than to stumble upon a novel idea, as yet unproven, at the crossroads of these two fields.

By the time I had finished writing my dissertation, titled, *'Towards a praxis of oppressed local knowledges: Participatory ethnobotanical research in indigenous communities of Ecuador'*, a mouthful that couldn't be further from subtitling and literacy, I had been offered a faculty position at the Indian Institute of Management, Ahmedabad (IIM-A), in its Ravi J Matthai Centre for Educational Innovation. The centre was created in honour of IIM-A's first full-time Director who had a vision of establishing an institute of management dedicated to the application of management principles, not just to business, but also to the public and social sectors. Although I did not realize at the time, SLS could not have found a more suitable base than here at one of India's most prestigious institutes. The year was 1996. Within nine months, SLS would go from conception in a living room in the United States to its first tiny steps in India.

Life before SLS

While most of the SLS story developed in India after 1996, it would be remiss of me not to outline the part played previously by the Sri Aurobindo Ashram, Indian Institute of Technology, Kanpur (IIT-K), Cornell University and Ecuador in shaping my motivations to pursue this idea.

I had the fortune to grow up from ages 6 to 20, literally in one long sweep, at the Sri Aurobindo Ashram in Pondicherry, India, entirely schooled at its Sri Aurobindo International Centre of Education (SAICE). In a country where fierce educational competition and specialization is the norm, it was unusual to experience an 'integral' system that aimed for a broad-based education, including a strong emphasis on languages, literature, performance arts, music and especially a physical and spiritual education. The medium of instruction was English and French. Every student picked up an average of three other Indian languages and had considerable flexibility to choose subjects, teachers and even the time one wished to allot to particular subjects. There were no exams, from kindergarten to college, and therefore no degree(s) to boot.

The first exam I ever took was for my Master's in physics, at IIT-K, arguably the pinnacle of competition in India. How a degreeless student got into IIT-K is another story, but once I was there, a two-year stint allowed me to acquire my first real degree and join the educational mainstream. It also humbled me by bringing me face to face with some sharp minds and a timely realization that it would have been a loss to physics had I continued any further in the field. Nevertheless, that degree served as a launch pad for my dream of studying in the United States. As my train changed tracks from physics to communication, little did I fathom that it would be for a decade-long sojourn in Ithaca, NY.

More than any other place, Cornell University brought to bear a focused desire for international development, through two years in the department of communication followed by eight more in education. It was stimulating to be around student colleagues, many of whom I encountered in cross-departmental courses, cafeterias and graduate student parties, who not only spoke eloquently about how to change the world, but also had clear-headed strategies to achieve their goals. You just had to catch them early enough in the party. People were dazzlingly adept at making connections between seemingly disparate ideas, which sometimes provided great comic relief, but sometimes what felt like 'eureka' moments.

I realize now that I must be drawn to serendipity. The topic for my doctoral research came to me initially in the form of a $99 coupon from Continental Airlines (now part of United Airlines), for a round trip from anywhere in the United States to Ecuador. My trip started as an opportunity to see Ecuador, Peru and Bolivia. A chance encounter in a Sunday market with Mr Juan José Simbaña, the president of an organization representing seven communities in Andean Ecuador, led to a two-year immersion in Imbabura province. Simbaña and his people were concerned about conserving their knowledge of medicinal plants. I was enamoured of participatory action research. Together we conceived and executed, with two *campesino* volunteers from every community as co-researchers, one man and one woman, a project to document their knowledge of medicinal plants, for themselves.

Although all *campesinos* selected as co-researchers were literate, the majority of their own community members, for whom they were documenting their knowledge, were not. Low literacy achievement in rural schools further exacerbated the problem of how to conserve knowledge in the absence of basic functional literacy. To bridge the literacy gap, we decided to represent every medicinal plant and its administration visually. We devised an icon-based representation of medicinal plant preparation and usage, resulting in the publication of a bilingual, Quichua–Spanish book.

My dissertation documented the action research process, including a critique of extractive forms of ethno-botanical research among indigenous peoples. While watching Pedro Almodóvar's movie that winter night in Ithaca, NY, my thinking was already a ferment of Paulo Freire and his approach to literacy, Bob Marley and his songs of freedom, and a newfound passion for Spanish and Latin America. Subtitling Bollywood songs for mass literacy was hardly a stretch. That same year, in September 1996, I accepted IIM-A's offer, the first and only real job I've ever had.

SLS: the first five years (1997–2001)

As a new arrival, my immediate motivation was to publish and get tenure. So I began putting together a research agenda based around SLS. The early hitch was that I was in an institute of management, albeit within a centre for educational innovation. Admittedly, this is my reading of the situation. At least some of my faculty colleagues valued a research focus on innovation in educational management, with the focus on 'management'. My proposed research was at the intersection of literacy and media. I credit the academic freedom of the institute and some faculty colleagues who encouraged me to pursue any direction of research that seemed meaningful to me and not be overly preoccupied with others' expectations.

Do viewers like SLS?

After crudely subtitling some Gujarati film songs, in Gujarati, at a local videographer's studio that specialized in covering weddings, we set out to test receptivity to SLS among our target viewers. In villages and slums, at train stations and bus stops, wherever it was easy enough for curiosity to gather a crowd, our small research team would set up two identical TV sets, connected to VCRs, synchronously playing the same film songs. One showed the songs with SLS, the other without. The onlookers' reactions were recorded on video.

Everywhere, it quickly became clear that most viewers – literates and weak-literates alike, children, youth and adults – preferred songs with SLS. Surveys later confirmed that around 90 per cent preferred SLS. The top-of-mind reason was usually that SLS enhanced the entertainment value of songs, although around 20 per cent also mentioned that it was good for literacy. The karaoke effect is what viewers enjoy foremost, including the ability to sing along, and know the song lyrics. A majority of non-literates wanted SLS, not because it was beneficial for them, but because it was perceived to be good for children in their family and social networks. Some also saw in SLS the

FIGURE 10.1   Author interacting with viewers in Gulbai Tekra slum, Ahmedabad (2002)

Photo Jaydeep Bhatt, Copyright PlanetRead

primary benefit that is attributed to closed-captioning – media access among the hearing impaired, to which one might also add improved access to the audio in a strident Indian television viewing context characterized by group conversations and ambient noise.

A few who did not prefer SLS seemed not to mind living with it. In other words, SLS did not provoke a strong rejection. For the literates in this camp, SLS had nothing special to offer and, if anything, served as a distraction from the visuals. The karaoke benefit was insufficient to offset the diversionary effect of SLS. Fortunately, though, most literates also took to SLS. We were aware all along that the idea, even though it was targeting the weak-literates, could not succeed on mainstream television without also winning over the literates. In the long run, it had to be established that SLS did not hurt ratings and, ideally, improved them.

Do viewers read along with SLS?

The overwhelming preference we found for SLS was a necessary first step, but did it lead to automatic reading engagement? To explore this question we bought an eye-tracker that could tell us, 60 times per second, where exactly a viewer was focusing on the screen. The focal points, when plotted, paint an accurate pattern of a viewer's eye movement. We brought into our lab several weak-literates, showing the same person a film song, first without and then with SLS. Unlike the standard Bollywood song without SLS, the resulting focal pattern from a song with SLS had two distinct bands. The bottom band visually and precisely captured viewer engagement with the subtitles. SLS was evidently not being ignored by the weak-literates, an observation consistent with a similar finding by a Belgian professor, Géry d'Ydewalle, whose ground-breaking research on subtitling was undertaken predominantly with literates. Whereas he concluded that, if the subtitles are there they will be read by literates, our conclusion with weak-literates, at best, could be that if subtitles are there, they will be attended to.

The eye-movement pattern alone did not allow us to ascribe reading engagement, let alone reading improvement. A noteworthy weakness of our eye-tracking research was its artificiality. The weak-literate viewers, already edgy from being in an institutional lab, had to position themselves on a chin and head support and undergo a process of instrumental calibration before actual data collection could begin. The instrumentation required that only the eyes could move while viewing. Overall, it was a far cry from enjoying film songs on TV at home. Still, it brought us another small step closer to proving the scientific merit of SLS. Weak-literates, like literates, simply could not and would not ignore SLS.

Through qualitative interviews captured on video in the villages and slums of Gujarat state, we determined that people claimed not merely to look at the subtitle band, but also to try to read along. The popularity of SLS, and the fact that people were attending to it and asserting that it was inviting reader engagement, were expected to result in measurable improvement of reading skills.

Our first real study on the impact of SLS was conducted in 1998/99 in a municipal school in Ahmedabad, serving low-income children.[1] Half the students in Grades 3 and 4, the stage at which the Hindi language is introduced in such schools, were regularly exposed to Hindi songs with SLS. The other half saw the same songs, but without SLS. After three months of exposure, three times a week for roughly 30 minutes in each session, we found that the SLS group was, measurably, further along in reading Hindi. This was the first real piece of evidence that SLS had a positive impact on reading skills. Arguably, however, the value of SLS had been found in a controlled setting wherein students were artificially and regularly required to watch songs with SLS. Nevertheless, that study laid the groundwork for piloting SLS on mainstream television. With that began the protracted battles for mindsets.

The slog begins

Armed with the study and videos of people's reactions to SLS, I wrote to all the directors of regional/state television networks, known as Doordarshan Kendras (DDKs) and several private channels, seeking permission to try out SLS on an existing song-based TV programme. Doordarshan is India's national/state television network. The only reply I received from state regional channels was from a Mr Satish Saxena, who appreciated the idea. His only regret was that he was the Director of All India Radio (AIR) and not television.

To my surprise, private channels did not pick up on the idea either. Our proposal that SLS would not hurt their programming, and if anything help it a bit, did not cut ice, even if it meant the nation would benefit substantially in terms of literacy. Private channels were very clear – they wanted to be paid for allowing SLS because their medium was contributing to literacy. Not only would the SLS project have to raise funds to cover the cost of SLS, it would have to implement SLS and pay the channel handsomely for permitting SLS. Literacy was clearly not on the agenda of the several private channels I contacted. The state seemed a better bet. Doordarshan is a public service broadcaster and historically has had a greater proportion of weak-reading and low-income viewers in rural India, although this is changing with increasing penetration of private networks.

I met seven of the DDK directors personally, in Jaipur, Trivandrum, Chennai, Mumbai, Hyderabad, Bangalore and Ahmedabad. They were all certain that SLS would detract from the entertainment value of song programmes. Video testimonies and surveys to the contrary, whenever it was possible to share, did not persuade them otherwise. SLS was rejected based on a personal hunch that viewers would not like this 'intrusion'. Close to my institute, the then Director of DDK Ahmedabad rejected SLS, too. When I requested that he see the video testimonies, he refused, citing years of experience and understanding of what viewers would or would not like. In Mumbai, a private producer of a popular film song programme, *Chitrahaar*, similarly rejected SLS saying that he was convinced it would be a distraction. I discovered early on that data were necessary, but clearly not sufficient in themselves to dislodge strong convictions, especially among people with power.

Then something fortuitous happened. DDK Ahmedabad appointed a new director, the same Mr Satish Saxena, previously responsible for radio. He agreed to allow SLS on four episodes of a Gujarati film song programme, *Chitrageet*. Letters of support came in from several viewers. Mr Saxena agreed to allow SLS on *Chitrageet*, as long as it was a free service to DDK Ahmedabad. The challenge then became financial. We had to find the necessary funds to keep SLS on air for at least one year, long enough to conduct a meaningful research study on the impact of SLS on literacy.

The scramble to fund the first ever SLS pilot on mainstream television, for mass literacy, led me to Mr BS Bhatia, Director of the Development and Communication Unit (DECU) at the Indian Space Research Organisation (ISRO) in Ahmedabad. He happened to be an IIM-A alumnus. In a timely manner, he came up with the necessary funds to continue SLS on *Chitrageet* for one year, making it possible to conduct a proper baseline and impact study.[2] The impact results of the first TV pilot were again positive and compared well with the earlier school experiment's findings. The evidence was available as early as 2000 that SLS on film songs on broadcast television contributed positively to reading skills.

Officially, there are an estimated 778 million literate people in India (2011 Census). Studies have found that over 60 per cent of the so-called 'literates' – over 450 million people, including school children, youth and adults – cannot read, for example, newspaper headlines or a Grade 2 level text.[3]

Naturally, we approached the National Literacy Mission (NLM) to consider SLS for scale-up and financial support. The NLM referred the matter to an internal 'expert' who, in essence, gave an opinion that it was not a new idea and, by implication, a tried and failed one. There was no dialogue about where, when and by whom anything like SLS had been implemented for mass reading. Having worked on SLS since 1996 and scoured the literature on subtitling and its uses in education, I could say then, and still maintain now, that the expert's opinion was just that – an opinion, not supported by evidence. Nevertheless, it had the effect of setting back my conversation with the NLM and its parent Ministry of Human Resource Development (MHRD) by several years.

Unable to find a toehold in education, I decided to approach broadcasting. Backed by research evidence and the fact that viewers in Gujarat had responded positively to SLS on DDK Ahmedabad, I approached Doordarshan Directorate in New Delhi. A Deputy Director General (DDG) there heard me out patiently. A few weeks later, a brief letter informed me summarily that Doordarshan had reviewed our tapes and were not interested in SLS. No reason given. It did not matter that SLS had just had a successful run on DDK Ahmedabad, one of Doordarshan's own regional channels.

SLS: the second five years (2002–06)

An international breakthrough

The strategy and challenge for the SLS project became one of achieving international recognition in order to overcome domestic indifference. As happens sometimes in India, our policy makers are swayed more by international credibility than the intrinsic merit of an innovation. In early 2002, the SLS innovation proposed by IIM-A won the top prize at a global innovation competition, 'Development Marketplace', conducted at the World Bank in Washington, DC. The honour came with a grant of $250,000 to take SLS forward and that changed Doordarshan's perspective on SLS.

The Development Marketplace success made it possible to approach the DG, Doordarshan, Dr SY Quraishi. At my request, the Director of IIM-A, Professor Jahar

Saha, flew in with me for this meeting in New Delhi. Dr Quraishi was quick to recognize the potential of SLS and immediately gave permission for one year of SLS on *Chitrahaar*, one of the longest running, nationally telecast programmes of Hindi film songs. This was a breakthrough moment.

Lower down the Doordarshan hierarchy, however, a peculiar challenge emerged despite Dr Quraishi's approval at the top. One of the directors given charge of handling the SLS project laid down one strict condition. IIM-A would be allowed to add SLS for a year, after which the expensive broadcast editing equipment, paid for by the Development Marketplace grant, and therefore belonging to my institution, would have to be handed over to Doordarshan. We suggested that might be possible if Doordarshan agreed to continue SLS. This resulted in a stalemate that nearly derailed our efforts even to start SLS on *Chitrahaar*. The Development Marketplace grant was at risk of lapsing. Six months into the one-year grant, the matter came to Dr Quraishi's attention and he overruled the director's condition.

SLS debuts on a national programme

With permissions in place, SLS was implemented on *Chitrahaar* for one year, starting in September 2002. As a requirement of the Development Marketplace grant, data for the baseline and impact studies were independently collected from four Hindi-speaking states and Gujarat, by ORG-Centre for Social Research. The sample was composed of randomly selected weak-reading and non-literate people in TV-owning households. The identical battery of tests to measure reading and writing skills were administered to the exact same individuals, first at baseline and then a year later. In the interim, SLS was implemented on *Chitrahaar*. The surveys captured the regularity of viewing *Chitrahaar*. The analysis compared reading/writing skill improvement among those who watched *Chitrahaar* regularly with those who did not.

Like the previous two studies, we found yet again that SLS exposure improved reading skills. The impact size, as expected, was small, in view of the short period of implementation and low exposure in broadcast mode, but it was measurable and statistically significant. We concluded that SLS did cause reading skills to be practised, on a mass scale. More than a year's exposure was probably required to convert the average viewer from weak-reading to functional reading ability. We tackled that question next. A baseline of reading skills across Hindi-speaking states was already in place. We just had to keep SLS alive on TV in the same states, long enough to revisit our baseline sample. This was mostly a financial challenge, but not without its moments of political angst.

A first brush with power

Buoyed by the international recognition of Development Marketplace and the partnership forged with Doordarshan to implement SLS on a national programme in Hindi, I approached the then Union Minister for Information and Broadcasting for a meeting to see whether SLS could be scaled up through her ministry. To my surprise, I secured a meeting rather easily. As soon as I began showing her a Hindi film song with Hindi subtitles, and before I could present our research findings, she cut me off, saying: 'I don't think this can have any impact on literacy.' Less than a minute into the meeting, the Minister's opinion from the gut had pre-empted any further discussion. It was my first brush with raw power and its ability to quash ideas. I didn't dare mention that SLS was already on TV for fear that a phone call from her might kill whatever progress we had made with Doordarshan. Fortunately, that phone call was never made. I recall my elation a few weeks later when a cabinet reshuffle gave the Minister another portfolio.

A pilot stretches

From 2003 to 2013 we were able to keep SLS running, not on *Chitrahaar*, but *Rangoli*, a weekly one-hour programme of Hindi film songs, telecast nationally. From 2003 to 2006 the SLS project was able to stretch Development Marketplace support and buttress it with three separate research grants from MHRD, each overseen by a different Union Secretary at the Department of Elementary Education and Literacy. MHRD was slowly warming up to SLS at the highest levels of bureaucracy.

On the broadcasting side, I approached Mr KS Sarma, CEO of the Broadcasting Corporation of India, better known as Prasar Bharati, an autonomous body that sets policy for television and radio nationally. I learned that Mr Sarma was visiting DDK Mumbai on official duty, so I put in a word with the DDK director there for a meeting but was told that I could not be accommodated. Feeling like a member of the paparazzi, I waited at the exit from his conference room. The CEO emerged finally at the end of the day, with a retinue of officials, and walked straight to a car waiting outside. I introduced myself as a member of the faculty of IIM-A and requested a couple of minutes to share details of an innovation. He was in a rush, but said that I could ride with him to his hotel. I discovered, that day, a rare benefit of Mumbai traffic jams.

Mr Sarma saw my presentation in his car and by the end of the ride he suggested that SLS could be tried in regional languages and on the songs in feature films, not just on song programmes like *Chitrahaar* and *Rangoli*. His suggestion turned out to be good from a couple of perspectives. Feature films attract on average four times the viewership of song programmes, and the songs therein are operationally easier to subtitle. Song-based programmes are prone to last-minute changes. Films are not. I imagine a phone call from Mr Sarma is all it took for us to begin SLS on the songs of the Telugu feature films on DDK Hyderabad. Both Dr Quraishi's and Mr Sarma's support at the helm of Doordarshan and Prasar Bharati set the tone for people lower down the broadcasting bureaucracy to allow SLS on more programmes, for years to come. The only condition was that SLS had to be kept on air at zero cost to the broadcaster.

In August 2003, I was awarded a one-year fellowship to join the Reuters Digital Vision Program (RDVP) at Stanford University. One of my concrete goals alongside the fellowship was to set up a legal mechanism in the United States to receive US charitable contributions for SLS work. The RDVP and Stanford connections put me in touch with Scott Smith, then a lawyer at Bingham & McCutchen in San Francisco. By the time my fellowship ended, they had set up PlanetRead (US) as a non-profit, free of charge. With PlanetRead (US) in place we quickly set up PlanetRead (India), another non-profit based in Pondicherry, India, so that funds could pass between them to support work in India.

The entrepreneurial spirit at Stanford inspired me to participate in the 'Social e-Challenge' a business plan competition on campus. Our team of four undergraduates won that year. We additionally roped in Stuart Gannes, the Director of RDVP, to co-found BookBox, Inc, a social venture that produces animated stories for children in many languages, using SLS. But that's another story. Immediately following RDVP completion, Ashoka stepped in to offer a fellowship. As any Ashoka fellow knows, the fellowship came at a critical time, allowing me to throw caution to the wind and focus 100 per cent on SLS.

During my RDVP days, I had occasion to present our SLS work at several conferences in the bay area, including at UC Berkeley and Stanford. Somewhere in those presentations SLS caught the imagination of someone at the then recently formed Google Foundation. It was a surreal moment when someone from Google Foundation called me to ask whether the SLS project might be interested in receiving some funding. Conversations relating to funding generally move in the opposite direction, so I found it impossible to explain to others hoping for Google Foundation support exactly how PlanetRead, a little known entity, had swung such a prime association. PlanetRead (US) received $350,000 over two years to scale up SLS on eight weekly TV programmes in India, in as many languages.

Immediately, we confronted another challenge. PlanetRead (India) could not receive foreign currency from any entity without permission under India's Foreign Currency Regulation Act (FCRA). Securing a one-time clearance for transfer of funds was relatively easy, so we did that first. We were told, however, that a 'permanent' FCRA permit for PlanetRead (India) would exact an unofficial price, which we were not willing to pay, on principle. After many trips to the FCRA office in New Delhi, often requiring me to deal with minor technicalities that the officers were clearly using to delay granting of FCRA clearance in the hope of extracting something more, we finally prevailed. As on so many previous occasions, membership of the faculty at IIM-A helped. Nevertheless, I couldn't resist but calculate which was costlier – paying for the many trips to New Delhi or paying the unofficial rate. The latter might have been cheaper if a compromised conscience were not a factor.

SLS: the third five years (2007–11)

An unexpected shuttering

Part of the funding we received from Google Foundation was for measuring the impact of SLS, after five years of exposure, by revisiting our 2002 baseline sample in 2007. Data collection for the study was again commissioned to Nielsen's ORG-CSR. The results this time were more than encouraging.[4] Regular SLS exposure from Grade 1–5 was found to more than double the rate of functional readers in Grade 5 and halve the high rate of complete illiteracy also found in Grade 5. SLS exposure raised the rate of newspaper reading among 'literate' youth from 34 per cent to 70 per cent. Many so-called literate youths, who were actually functionally illiterate, had reading practice with SLS and, over time, became functionally literate and picked up newspapers. We concluded that it took anywhere from three to five years of one-hour-per-week exposure to SLS, for most weak-literates to progress from weak to functional literacy.

The results of this important study were first shared as raw findings with an evaluation expert who had recently joined Google Foundation. Surprisingly, given the positive findings, that meeting did not go well. I was not sure what the expectations were from a draft report, but she took a position from the outset that the study did not meet Google Foundation's gold standard for an impact study, with quibbles about the reported statistics. My response was that it was a first draft, just to share the general direction of findings, and that a proper research article would follow. It did not persuade her. Two of her main objections to the study were, in my view, unfounded. One, the sample was not random and, two, the study was not independent. The fact is that Nielsen's ORG-CSR did draw a random sample, as was mentioned in the draft report, and the data were collected by them independently, but the analysis was done by us (Dr Tathagata Bandyopadhyay, a well-respected professor of statistics, and me). What made it independent was that the data set would be made available openly, after we had a chance to publish the findings. Whatever feedback she gave internally at Google Foundation, effectively shut off Google Foundation's further communication with the project.

The research article, with all the required academic rigour, did get published in Information Technologies and International Development, a leading journal in the Information Communication and Technology (ICT) space. We met the gold standard of academic peer review. That study is, today, one of the SLS project's most valuable assets to move policy, because we were able to measure impact after five years.[5]

PlanetRead remains eternally grateful to Google Foundation for supporting SLS for two years. It allowed us to establish a strong SLS presence in India. But it is a pity that a project that had delivered so well was brought to an abrupt closure. If there was something missing in Google Foundation's process, they had over-empowered an inexperienced person to pass unilateral judgement on a study, with little account-ability. It was particularly frustrating that no written comments were shared with us on why the study supposedly did not meet Google Foundation's gold standard, to which, I could have at least tendered a response.

Funds, bureaucracy and ministers

Since the Google Foundation grant in 2006, PlanetRead and IIM-A's strategy has been to maintain SLS on 8 to 10 weekly TV programmes in as many languages, in the belief that it provides an effective national cover from under which to influence policy. Maintenance of SLS at this level has not been easy. Every major funder who has supported PlanetRead has done so for around two years. That includes, in chronological order, Development Marketplace, the Google Foundation, Sir Ratan Tata Trust and Dell Giving. Our horizon of funding assurance has never really extended much beyond a year or two. A couple of times the SLS project has come critically close to shutting down for lack of resources, but somehow we have been bailed out, sometimes from unexpected sources. Since 2008, for example, an anonymous donor has been sending, through an intermediary, an annual cheque for $50,000. Thank you, anonymous donor, for this highly valuable unrestricted support, which allows PlanetRead to bridge inevitable gaps in funding and push SLS in policy. Almost all the other funding PlanetRead has received so far has been for specific projects.

Over the years, our SLS operations have been streamlined to a point where getting tapes from channels, subtitling them without spelling errors and sending them back to the broadcaster is the least of our challenges. That aspect of our work runs efficiently on autopilot. Other than maintaining a steady fund flow, our biggest challenge is without doubt convincing transient policy makers to support and take ownership of SLS long enough to advance it in policy, within the limited window of opportunity presented by their short tenures in specific positions. Building institutional memory of the progress has not been easy in a situation where one senior officer's decision in a position of power is easily supplanted by the next, while everyone below in the hierarchy tends to tow the line.

In our case, the support of three successive Union Secretaries at MHRD was neutralized easily by subsequent secretaries. After the SLS project enjoyed support from Union Secretaries Mr MK Kaw, Mr Kumud Bansal and Champak Chaterjee while they were at the helm of MHRD, it entered a phase where it was difficult to find any clear support from officers in similarly high positions. Since 2004–14 my interactions with Union secretaries and joint secretaries serving as DG, NLM have remained either neutral, meaning that I could not read their position, or in some cases clearly unsympathetic.

My second ministerial encounter was on 11 August 2009, again with the Union Minister of Information & Broadcasting. This time, however, it was a different Minister, Ms Ambika Soni. In contrast to my earlier meeting with the previous Minister, this one went well. She heard me out patiently and appreciated SLS. When I finished my presentation, she called in her assistant, and explained to him what we were doing. It was clear that she had grasped the concept. She then asked me about the budget to scale it up nationally. I told her that it would be around $1 million annually, to scale up on 50 weekly programmes. She told her assistant that since it was Doordarshan's commemorative year – it had just completed 50 years – she could think of considering SLS as a part of that.

Minister Soni asked me to follow up with the then DG, Doordarshan. The next day I was in the DG's office. Her entire tone was one of action, giving me a feeling that a message might have gone to her from the Minister's office. At the DG's request, a proposal was sent to her, with a copy to the Minister. I received a letter from the Minister's office several months later to the effect that, while SLS was a good idea, there were no funds to support the proposal for a national scale-up. What seemed like a window of opportunity in policy was once again proving to be a glass ceiling.

In 2009, I was invited to the Clinton Global Initiative (CGI) where Bill Clinton personally endorsed SLS in a plenary session.[6] The video of his endorsement has become the most powerful tool we have to enhance the credibility of SLS. India's Union Minister of State, MHRD, responsible for literacy, was present in the audience and met me at CGI subsequently. At her suggestion, I followed up with a meeting in New Delhi, growing increasingly confident that SLS was close to acceptance at MHRD.

I was asked to present to the Union Minister, MHRD and senior MHRD officials, including the Secretary, DG, NLM and other senior officers. My presentation was the last one scheduled that day. Before I could start, the Minister said: 'Tell me what you're going to tell me.' Sensing that he might be in a rush, I offered to keep my presentation to five minutes, down from the allotted 15 minutes. The Minister simply reiterated: 'No. Tell me what you're going to tell me.' So I simply told him that my presentation was on SLS, an innovation that could potentially deliver regular reading practice to over 300 million weak-literates in India, if implemented widely on television. He shot back: 'This has nothing to do with literacy. You should talk to some other Ministry.'

I suggested that he see a small clip of a song with SLS. By then he had already made up his mind and had turned to his cadre of senior officers to move to the next agenda item. I had no choice but to leave the conference room, no doubt feeling crushed and left wondering, what was it that made him slam the door so hard on an innovation backed by over a decade of research and development, at one of the country's most prestigious institutions? SLS had by then won many international honours and had been presented at conferences in some of the world's most prestigious universities. How does one fathom that it could be dismissed as 'nothing to do with literacy' in less time than it takes Usain Bolt to run the 100 metres?

The same month, the Schwab Foundation and United Nations Development Programme (UNDP) gave me the Indian Social Entrepreneur of the Year Award for 2009 at the India Economic Forum. As a Schwab social entrepreneur the World Economic Forum (WEF) network – including Davos – became accessible to me. At the following year's award ceremony the chief guest happened to be the same Union Minister. I approached him after the day's events to see whether the conversation on SLS could be restarted. He looked at me, then my business card, and walked away. If I had not realized it earlier, it was now patently clear that SLS had gone from a potentially soaring possibility at MHRD to dropping off a cliff. Clearly, nobody was likely to touch SLS at MHRD until a new Union Minister took over.

A strategic turn

With no headway in sight at MHRD, I decided to turn my attention to broadcasting policy. In June 2010, I met the recently appointed Chairperson of the Prasar Bharati Board, a respected journalist, Ms Mrinal Pande. In most policy interactions, the power differential is quickly made apparent. This was different and felt like a conversation between mutually respectful professionals.

Within a month, she made it possible for me to make a presentation to the full Prasar Bharati Board. During the interactions it was obvious that the Board appreciated the SLS concept and the research supporting the innovation. A question was raised on whether SLS might hurt the ratings. It was answered by another board member, who argued correctly that it actually works the other way. SLS contributes to ratings by 10–15 per cent. For the first time, SLS was recorded in policy as an innovation that the national broadcaster could consider implementing widely.

Meanwhile, in February 2011, the National Association of Software and Services Companies (NASSCOM) Foundation selected SLS for the NASSCOM Social Innovation

Honours for 2011. Ironically, the chief guest who presented the honours happened to be none other than the Union Minister, MHRD who could not see SLS' link with literacy. Of course, the real award would have been if he had suggested that I meet him some time to present our work. That did not happen, even though national literacy falls squarely under his Ministry. In the media glare he simply said: 'Good work. Keep it up.'

SLS: the fourth five years (2012–16)

Good idea, no money

More than five years have passed since my presentation to the Prasar Bharati Board. The first two years saw nothing but turmoil for Prasar Bharati. Several complications arose from the handling of the broadcasting rights for the Commonwealth Games. A Presidential reference followed by a Supreme Court directive led to the suspension of a CEO of Prasar Bharati. The DG, Doordarshan at the time was unceremoniously sent back to her state.

Toward the end of 2011, after a considerable gap, a new DG, Doordarshan was finally appointed. I met Mr Tripurari Sharan a couple of days after his appointment to restart the SLS conversation and handed him a proposal for a national scale-up. Soon after, in February 2012, a new CEO, Prasar Bharati, Mr Jawhar Sircar, was also appointed. They both expressed a willingness to take SLS forward in policy.

During his tenure as DG, Doordarshan from 2012–14, Mr Sharan demonstrated the proactiveness for SLS that Dr Quraishi once had in the same position. In what I see as a highly atypical move by a senior bureaucrat, Mr Sharan immediately opened up several channels of communication with me, the most significant being e-mail and mobile. He wrote to the Planning Commission requesting a special fund allocation for SLS, given that it is an innovation and, therefore, not easily accommodated under existing budgetary heads.

Mr Montek Singh Ahluwalia, the Deputy Chairman of the Planning Commission, who reported directly to the PM (Chairman, Planning Commission), wrote in response – and I paraphrase slightly – that same language subtitling is an important literacy initiative that should be supported as a Central Sector Scheme as and when posed by the Department. Somewhat ambiguous, perhaps, but it was a strong policy endorsement for SLS, not least because of who it came from. Mr Ahluwalia was popularly perceived as PM Manmohan Singh's right-hand man.

It took six months to understand and meet the 'as and when posed by the Department' condition. Doordarshan put up its own proposal on SLS to the Ministry of Information and Broadcasting (MI&B). Between Doordarshan, MI&B, Prasar Bharati and Planning Commission, the proposal entered a protracted policy labyrinth. I have finally understood at a deep level what Prof Jagdeep Chhokar, my dear friend and former colleague at IIM-A meant when he once told me, 'Delay is the deadliest form of denial!'

As long as Prasar Bharati has been in existence, it has mostly been in the red, with the bulk of its budget going toward salaries and broadcast infrastructure and very little left for programming.[7] The institution with the ability to mandate broadcast policy, perennially facing political pressures to raise more revenue to reduce its large financial dependency on the state, is possibly not the ideal institution to make the small but necessary funds available to scale up an innovation like SLS. A national scale-up of SLS requires either 0.2 per cent of Prasar Bharati's budget for Doordarshan, or 0.01 per cent of MHRD's budget for school education and literacy. The chronic funding shortage at Prasar Bharati has led to a peculiar situation. Prasar Bharati, now committed to scaling up SLS in principle, decided to come up with a rate card for SLS services at around one-fourth the rate at which it is actually viable for any agency. That has achieved two things in a bureaucratic masterstroke. One, Prasar Bharati has put a mechanism in place to scale up SLS nationally (there is a rate card!). Two, no agency has come forward to provide SLS services at the prescribed rate, which effectively means that Prasar Bharati is unlikely to spend anything on SLS. In theory, Prasar Bharati has put something in place to scale up SLS nationally. In practice, not a single song has been subtitled with Prasar Bharati resources, over the last 20 years.

Mass literacy programmes in India typically budget around $3 to $4 per learner, per year. Effectiveness apart, it would cost $1 billion to reach 300 million weak readers, although that would be operationally impossible, year after year, through direct teacher-learner approaches. SLS would achieve the same reach, with proven effectiveness, at a cost of $1 million per year and can be sustained lifelong as a support for all stages of reading. A 1,000x return on investment is a venture capitalist's dream, and should be for any government committed to its people's development. One can nitpick about the details in this maths but the big picture on return on investment is in the ball park, and a more sophisticated analysis might actually show more bang for the buck.

The Prime Minister knows about SLS

On 29 June 2013, I had the opportunity to make a detailed presentation on the SLS project at the Young Indian Leaders' Conclave in Gandhinagar, organized by the Citizens for Accountable Governance (CAG), an organization that had recently been formed then by successful young professionals. Remarkably, Dr Abdul Kalam, former President of India, delivered the opening keynote and the then Chief Minister (CM) of Gujarat, now Prime Minister (PM) of India, Mr Narendra Modi, delivered the closing keynote. Throughout the day-long proceedings, Mr Modi sat in the front row listening to speakers and panel discussions.

I was thrilled that Mr Modi heard my entire 15-minute presentation on SLS and, to my utter delight, mentioned it in his closing keynote, 'Just as the professor was saying, there should be more work on innovation', before shifting his attention to examples of innovations by his government in Gujarat. Ironically, I can claim that India's PM has spent more time listening to a presentation on SLS than any bureaucrat or minister. A small technicality, of course, is that he was the Chief Minister then.

Although speculation was rife at the time, Mr Modi had not yet been anointed as his party's PM candidate. Neither was it a foregone conclusion because of internal churn within his party pitting old timers against the younger politicians. I recall opening my presentation with a statement that India's future PM could be in the room. The audience broke into a thunderous applause with chants of Modi, Modi, Modi ... So, on the spur of the moment, I said, 'Wait a minute. As a professor my job is to question assumptions. What I really meant was that one of you "Young Leaders" could be the future PM of India.' Thankfully, the audience and Mr Modi responded with laughter.

This aside is important because even if Mr Modi forgets my SLS presentation entirely (highly unlikely, if people are right about his legendary memory), I'm confident he will remember the professor who predicted, albeit in jest, his eventual election and swearing in as PM on 26 May 2014.

An important policy lever we now have is Mr Modi's passing, but noteworthy comments on our SLS work, on video.[8] We have shared this clip with top bureaucrats and it seems to start a conversation, but has been insufficient to take it to the stage of fund allocation. Meanwhile, the Planning Commission that had been instituted in 1950, under India's first PM, Mr Jawaharlal Nehru, and was seriously considering a special fund allocation for SLS, has now been disbanded.

In July 2014, Mr Sharan, who had by then understood the power of SLS and helped its advance in policy, was relieved of his DG responsibility in New Delhi and transferred to Bihar, his administrative cadre state. Since his transfer, there have been two Acting DGs at Doordarshan. Acting DGs typically don't act on major policy decisions. It is perplexing why important positions, like DG, Doordarshan or positions on Prasar Bharati Board, lie vacant for months and sometimes, over a year.

Bureaucratic transfers generally don't bode well for an innovation's advance in policy, unless it's the transfer of a resistor. In any ministry, the first major challenge is finding someone at the top willing to make the time to understand an innovation and then wanting to support its progress. Typically, this can take several follow-ups before a senior bureaucrat agrees to send any signal down the hierarchy that it is worth considering. If the bureaucrat is transferred prior to that, and this happens more often than not, all the efforts to win over the senior bureaucrat can evaporate instantly.

A door reopens

At the end of 2014, Ms Vrinda Sarup was appointed Union Secretary at MHRD for School Education and Literacy. This came as a stroke of luck for the SLS project because she had had a long association with MHRD, was superbly informed about the country's big educational challenges, was highly respected by national and international agencies working in education, and had specifically shown an interest in SLS. With Prasar Bharati unable to allocate the funds for a national scale-up of SLS, I approached her within a couple of weeks of her appointment.

The bureaucratic wheels at MHRD began to turn for the SLS project, after a five-year jam caused by the Union Minister in the previous government. Suddenly, it was again possible to meet officers in the ministry, so much so that SLS was also discussed in a couple of group meetings. The top bureaucrat had sent a subtle signal.

But something happened overnight. Within six months of Ms Sarup's appointment, an unusually short tenure, she was transferred in June, 2015 to the Department of

Food and Public Distribution. She could now fortify food staples like wheat and rice with micronutrients to solve nutritional deficiencies, but she could not fortify Bollywood with literacy!

While the policy story continues to unfold in uncertain ways, we find ways to see any twist and turn, even setbacks, as progress. It's the only way to last emotionally in a decades-long run. PlanetRead enters and sometimes wins competitions, small amounts of project funding and regular media attention, enabling us to keep SLS, now practically 20 years old, alive.

More international affirmation

There have been some non-policy victories too along the way. At Davos in 2013, Gordon Brown – the UN Special Envoy for Global Education – took some time out to understand SLS and has given it valuable airtime, for example, at the MIPTV conference in Cannes.[9] Thank you, Mr Brown. That was a wonderful plug! But, on a minor detail, could you not have called SLS a 'small project?' Or is that a euphemism at the UN for a billion people?

Later in 2013, PlanetRead got the inaugural 'International Prize' for literacy from the Library of Congress in Washington, DC. This was the most prestigious prize in our trophy chest. Awards and prizes are wonderful morale boosters, and can sometimes help secure the next round of funding, but are proving to be weak drivers of policy change.

In September 2012, PlanetRead won a major global grant competition, the All Children Reading (ACR) Grand Challenge, run by USAID, World Vision and Australian Aid. It allowed us to scale up SLS massively, for the first time, in a well-defined geography, India's second most populous state, Maharashtra (pop 114 million). Another first was that we implemented SLS on a private channel, Zee Talkies, a leading 24 x 7 Marathi movie channel in the state. Under the terms of the project, SLS was implemented and telecast on all the songs (not dialogue) of 10 weekly Marathi movies, shown in prime time. Zee went further by repeating the song-subtitled movies in other non-prime-time slots on Zee Talkies and another popular general entertainment sister channel, Zee Marathi. For those with access to these channels, it was the strongest SLS cover that has ever been achieved.

Impact and potential

The unprecedented two-year scale-up from 2013–15 was a precursor to our advocacy for all of India – every song in every language on TV, shown with SLS. Data collection for the baseline (2013) and endline (2015) was commissioned to a reputed and independent agency, Pratham. For a decade, Pratham has been conducting nationally, the widely cited Annual Status of Education Report (ASER) to measure the basic reading and numeracy levels of rural school children. Using its well-developed approach, Pratham's ASER team drew a large random sample of school children aged 6–14 at the baseline, measured their reading skills with a range of tools and remeasured them again at the endline.

The academic in me would say that the preliminary findings are encouraging. The social entrepreneur in me sees them as stunning. While intuitively obvious, our findings confirmed that SLS is most effective when available in parallel with early grades, from the beginning of formal reading instruction. One way to assess the impact was to take a snapshot of different grades in our Maharashtra sample, at the baseline and endline.

Take, for example, Grade 3 (Figure 10.2). At the baseline, 37.9 per cent in Grade 3 could read a Grade 1 level text. At the endline, 68.4 per cent in Grade 3 could. The availability of SLS on TV at home, from Grade 1 to Grade 3, had a strong impact on reading achievement. That 30.5 per cent more children advanced to basic reading ability, with just a two-year scale-up of SLS, is remarkable. During the same period, in the neighbouring state of Gujarat, the corresponding improvement was just 2.1 per cent. Similar jumps can be reported for children in Grade 4 at the endline, who had the possibility of SLS exposure since Grade 2. At the baseline, 28.9 per cent Grade 4 children could read a Grade 5 level text, whereas at the endline, 48.4 per cent in Grade 4 could. Nearly 20 per cent more children had advanced to functional reading ability as defined by their ability to read a Grade 5 level text.

FIGURE 10.2 Percentage in Grade 3 able to read at Grade 1 level

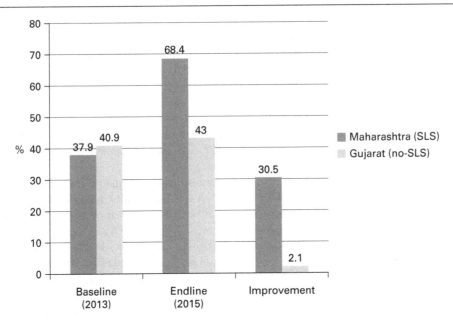

Within Maharashtra state, we compared children who had direct access to SLS at home (SLS-group), with those who did not (no-SLS-group) due to the availability or non-availability of Zee Talkies on which SLS was implemented. We analysed the same cohort of weak-reading children falling behind in Grade 2 at the baseline, to see how far they had advanced in reading by the endline, when they were in Grade 4 (Figure 10.3).

FIGURE 10.3   Baseline non-readers in Grade 2 and their ability to read by endline

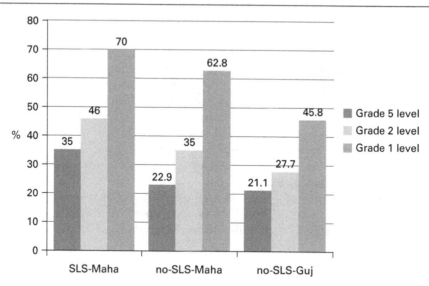

At every reading level measured, the SLS group in Maharashtra did markedly better than both the no-SLS groups, in Maharashtra and Gujarat, respectively. Within Maharashtra, which is a tighter comparison, 12.1 per cent more at-risk Grade 2 children, at the baseline, advanced to Grade 5 level reading ability by the endline; 11 per cent more children in the SLS-group transitioned to Grade 2 level reading; and 7.2 per cent more children in the SLS-group transitioned to Grade 1 level reading. The impact of SLS is even stronger when the SLS-group in Maharashtra is compared to the no-SLS-group in Gujarat. As expected, SLS had a stronger impact on those who were in the earlier grades at the baseline.

PlanetRead is committed to publishing the findings in academic research articles. If a two-year massive scale-up can deliver such positive results in Maharashtra, one can only imagine the reading and educational returns of a lifetime of SLS exposure, seamlessly woven into mainstream entertainment.

Mr Subhash Chandra, Founder and Chairman of Zee, had acknowledged the enormous potential of SLS when I first met him on April 25, 2011 in Mumbai.[10] That conversation is the seed that led to the scale-up in Maharashtra. I now believe that the Maharashtra impact study will turn out to be enormously influential in moving education and broadcast policy, not just in India, but in other parts of the world.

Zee has already tasted the viewership benefits of SLS on songs and is considering a Maharashtra-like scale-up in other states/languages on their regional language channels, possibly supported under their CSR. USAID embarked on the ACR Grand Challenge to scout for innovative ideas from around the world, in children's reading development. They now have a proven, scalable and cost-effective new idea, backed by strong evidence, ready to travel to other countries. No matter where USAID has operations, TV will have a large enough presence and viewers would almost certainly be watching song content in their local language(s).

The potential of our 'small project', as Gordon Brown framed it in Cannes, is to deliver lifelong reading practice to 2 billion weak readers worldwide. There is sufficient evidence that Bill Clinton was right when he commented in New York several years ago that SLS is, 'A small thing that has a staggering impact on people's lives'. And who can argue with Narendra Modi when he said in Gandhinagar after listening to a presentation on SLS, that, 'There should be more work on innovation'. With three former heads of state having green-lighted SLS in one form or another, how much longer can policy makers in New Delhi resist an idea whose time has come?

Lessons learnt

Strategically, our primary goal has been to move policy on SLS. Despite a long engagement, I am not able to offer a clear recipe for moving the Government of India. But that it moves slowly over time is a certainty, if one can just keep chipping away. I did so, and learned some things along the way.

1 *Evidence is necessary but insufficient.* Without evidence, and independent corroboration, it is easy for policy makers to send any idea back to the drawing board. The force of a social entrepreneur's experience and account, however genuine and authentic, is a poor substitute for driving systems-level change. Evidence takes many opinionated objections of policy makers off the table. In our case we had to build an evidence-based argument for each of these objections: People will not like SLS, the ratings will go down, weak readers will ignore the subtitles, they will not be able to read along even if they tried, merely SLS exposure cannot improve reading skills, it is a logistical nightmare to send tapes for subtitling and get them back in time for telecast, and so on. For each of these objections, as and when we encountered them, we established a regimen of monitoring, evaluation and data collection. Most policy makers today cannot easily bring up these objections to SLS. Evidence has moved the needle on SLS from rejection to resistance to acceptance in principle. The policy conversation has progressed to finding the right mechanism to pay for and scale up SLS, nationally. Evidence-based policy-making remains a distant chimera in India. There is a systemic lack of mechanisms to independently and rigorously weigh the evidence. Game-changing, good, and not-so-good solutions are all stirring in the same policy pot, and very little to separate them other than the personal predilections of people in power.

2 *Bureaucracy.* Bureaucrats overseeing ministries in the social sector – health, education, social justice and empowerment – are willing to engage in a conversation more readily with academics than they are with representatives from civil society organizations or corporations. The general direction of any key decision is first set at the top and then the details are worked out by the second and lower rungs of the bureaucracy. Bureaucrats have batch loyalty. Bureaucrat to bureaucrat communication, especially at the same rank, across

and within ministries, is highly influential. A reluctant bureaucrat will practise 'death by delay' which does not commit him or her to either a 'yes,' or 'no', because a clear decision is always open to challenge. A bureaucrat can never be wrong with indecision and it is a prerogative that is exercised more often than not. Only the minister can effectively drive a policy decision forcefully through the bureaucracy. Although senior bureaucrats have the power to resist or block a ministerial push, they are not likely to interfere unless it compromises them directly – legally, ethically, or otherwise – given the powers of transfer that a minister has over a bureaucrat. It may be tempting to bypass the bureaucracy and approach a minister to push an innovation through policy. Unless there is a strong personal rapport with the minister, or a referral via someone who has one, it is a high-risk strategy to approach the minister directly. If the minister does not like the innovation at a gut level, and that happens mostly within a few minutes of the interaction, the bureaucracy will not touch the innovation later, at least until the minister is in power. If the minister does like the innovation, you might be lucky to be referred to a senior bureaucrat to consider it. But at the first hint of resistance in the bureaucracy, and there is bound to be some, you may try to return to the minister but he or she will probably not be willing to meet a second time nor have the bandwidth to push for something, for which, there was no real ownership to begin with. 'Good for the country or society' is a weak argument to enlist a minister's sustained engagement with an innovation.

3 *The sweet spot.* The sweet spot of policy movement is when the bureaucracy has considered an innovation long enough and come around to accepting its intrinsic merit. However, the allocation of required funds for the innovation requires other forces to step in. Ministries generally don't have funds for a new idea; the new idea has to fit into an existing fund commitment. But rather than do that, bureaucrats prefer to water down the vision of an innovation drastically. A ministerial blessing in that context can push an innovation through policy, with the necessary financial backing.

4 *Awards.* There are far too many awards in the social entrepreneurship space that end with a medal of honour, a token prize, media coverage or even access to networks. That's helpful, but award-givers generally have an exaggerated sense of their award's influence to advance the cause. The role of organizations and juries that give away awards needs expansion into sustained engagement with the awardees. Maybe this is happening in a few cases, working with the awardee to remove their pain points or overcoming their challenges, but generally the engagement is transient. The Tour de France model of the individual social entrepreneur riding the ups and downs of change-making, while others cheer on the sidelines, is too inefficient. We need more and longer tandem bikes that people can hop on to, for a tour de force.

Discussion questions

1 The SLS project simply combines long-existing elements like subtitles, Bollywood and television. So where is the innovation? Why did it take until 1996 for its conception?

2 What are the pros and cons of implementing SLS on film songs vs dialogue, from a weak literate's perspective?

3 Besides literacy, to which other social development goals, and specific groups, can SLS contribute to and how?

4 If SLS is a win-win for television and literacy, because the ratings and reading skills go up measurably, why is there so much resistance to scaling it up, in the government and in the private sector?

5 The SLS project has pursued a strategy of evidence-based policy advocacy. When the state system's capacity to evaluate evidence is weak at best in India, is that a good strategy?

6 Pick a country where SLS might be relevant. What would be your strategy to scale up SLS nationally there, on all the existing songs on TV, in all the languages?

7 What are the wider barriers to implementing any literacy-based project in developing countries? How might you overcome resistance to an idea, even though the evidence might be clear that the project will succeed?

Further reading

You can find more material to do with this chapter at www.koganpage.com/socialentrepreneurship

How SLS works in Indian villages:
   www.youtube.com/watch?v=tOsWToI2Piw
   www.youtube.com/watch?v=K7XDMzsLd5o
Research articles:
   http://itidjournal.org/index.php/itid/article/view/1307/502 [accessed 10 December 2015]
   http://itidjournal.org/index.php/itid/article/view/191/61 [accessed 10 December 2015]
   Library of Congress, Washington DC, presentation on PlanetRead's work
   www.youtube.com/watch?v=ZljyLqfUkVU?v=ZljyLqfUkVU
BookBox, multilingual animated stories with SLS for children www.bookbox.com [accessed 10 December 2015]
PlanetRead www.planetread.org [accessed 10 December 2015]

Acronyms used

DG: Director-General
DDK: Doordarshan Kendra (Regional/State Broadcast Network)
FCRA: Foreign Currency Regulation Act
IIM-A: Indian Institute of Management, Ahmedabad
IIT-K: Indian Institute of Technology, Kanpur
MHRD: Ministry of Human Resource Development
MI&B: Ministry of Information and Broadcasting
NLM: National Literacy Mission
PM: Prime Minister
SLS: same language subtitling

Acknowledgements

The pursuit of a social innovation often requires a heavy dose of irrationality. I am eternally obliged to Burny, Azul, Akash and Tara who are having to live every day with my madness, but are doing it with grace. A social entrepreneur's roller-coaster ride needs a core nucleus of emotional sustenance. To my extended family in and from Pondicherry, and some dear friends scattered around the world, I just want to say, you are that core.

Notes

1 Kothari, Brij, Joe Takeda, Ashok Joshi, and Avinash Pandey (2002) Same Language Subtitling: A Butterfly for Literacy? *International Journal of Lifelong Education*, 21(1): 55–66.

2 Kothari, Brij, Avinash Pandey, and Amita Chudgar (2004) Reading Out of the 'Idiot Box': Same-Language Subtitling on Television in India, *Information Technologies and International Development*, 2(1): 23–44.

3 Kothari, Brij and Tathagata Bandyopadhyay (2010) Can India's 'Literate' Read? *International Review of Education*, 56: 705–28.

4 Kothari, Brij and Tathagata Bandyopadhyay (2014) Same Language Subtitling of Bollywood film songs on TV: Effects on literacy, *Information Technologies & International Development*, 10(4), 31–47.

5 Download from: http://itidjournal.org/index.php/itid/article/view/1307.

6 Bill Clinton on SLS: https://www.youtube.com/watch?v=juZOlmf9APk.

7 Sevanti Ninan analyses Prasar Bharati's budgetary woes at http://www.livemint.com/Consumer/3EfRLMzIRmLKA5FewN4yKO/Prasar-Bharati-Where-is-the-money-for-programming.html.

8 Narendra Modi, briefly on the SLS project: http://goo.gl/KzJ2zX.

9 Gordon Brown on SLS: http://goo.gl/nP1I7E.

10 That meeting was made possible, thanks to an introduction by Prof Anil Gupta, a faculty colleague at IIM Ahmedabad who is a globally recognized stalwart in the field of grassroots innovations and the founding Vice Chair of the National Innovation Foundation.

11

Keep calm and Dream in Tunisia

DREAM IN TUNISIA – SARAH TOUMI

ABSTRACT

Sarah Toumi – named in January 2016 on the fifth annual *Forbes* '30 Under 30' list of young entrepreneurs – is a French-Tunisian social entrepreneur and the founder and CEO of Dream in Tunisia, an NGO that aims at supporting sustainable development in rural areas of Tunisia and North Africa through empowering programmes for youth, women and farmers. Desertification is destroying 75 per cent of the land in Tunisia, and it is even worse in Morocco, Libya and Egypt. Desertification directly impacts billions of people who are already facing huge poverty and unemployment issues. These issues were what led to the Tunisian revolution, but nothing has really changed since and there is still an urgent need to address desertification before it irremediably affects the whole society.

Sarah is an Ashoka Fellow and an Echoing Green Climate fellow for her idea 'Acacias for all'. 'Acacias for All' aims to empower the farmers of North Africa to adapt to climate change through education, reforestation and commercialization. At the same time, her team is also managing an after-school programme for rural youth and a training programme on the valorization of traditional handicraft for rural women. Sarah started designing her vision at the age of nine when she discovered Tunisia and the sad impact that the gender gap, poverty, low access to high-quality primary education and desertification were having on rural communities. It became her life's purpose after her father passed away in 2012.

Sarah's personal journey

I was born in Paris, to a French mother and a Tunisian father who was a big dreamer. From an early age, I was immersed in a wide world of possibility and empathy. My father had left Tunisia at the age of 18 to study engineering in Paris and created an NGO for children of the Middle East when I was a baby. When we were not at protest marches, we were organizing fundraising events. Due to political issues, my father spent 28 years away from Tunisia and I think that this is why I fell so much in love with it, as a way of bringing him back to his roots. I was nine years old when I went to Tunisia for the first time with my sister and mother. We discovered another world, far away from our daily habits and reality in Paris. The village of my grandparents was still following tribal habits and there was no running water or mobile phones. It was a patriarchal society where girls stopped school at the age of 9 or 10. One of the pillars of this traditional society was the girls' reputation and modesty, on which the honour of the family depended. I was a nine-year-old girl and I discovered that my body was not mine in this environment; it was the family's, for their purpose and their honour. At the same time though, I also discovered a strong community where each person had a role and was required to follow certain duties. My aunt's wedding was taking place during my visit. This was a seven-day party where the families prepared the union of the two people by carefully following traditions. It was seven days of dancing, singing and learning about love and care. In this same year, I discovered the very advanced cities of La Marsa and Tunis. I was shocked by the huge development gap existing between the villages and these big cities. This was the Tunisia I discovered in 1996, when Ben Ali was President, and this was the Tunisia I fell in love with – and the one I decided to change.

Back in Paris, I spent two weeks having nightmares, thinking about the children I met who were stopping school and losing their future because of ignorance. My father, moved by my strong reaction to this injustice, decided to empower my solution-oriented-scientific brain and we created our organization: the Association for Cooperation and Prevention, Water for All. Our first action was to buy a few pens and go back the next summer to entertain our cousins. Then we bought two computers. Then we brought 783 books and managed to obtain premises to open a library. This then led to a youth centre. In 2004, my father finally came back to Tunisia, to lead this NGO. Political pressure meant that it was not easy, however. In 2007, our treasurer was imprisoned in retaliation for the fact that we had provided libraries across Tunisia with 300,000 books and more than 300 computers. It was forbidden to talk about poverty or illiteracy in Tunisia.

The level of pressure and corruption was so high that in 2008 I decided to leave the project and create my own NGO in France, where I was a student at Sorbonne University in Paris. I ran DREAM – an incubator for social and environmental student projects – for four years until my father passed away in 2012. On this day everything became clear: my purpose was to work in Tunisia to lift up rural communities, in the wake of the benefits from the impact of the 2011 revolution. Dream in Tunisia was born.

Conservation: a never-ending tension with economic development

In 2012, the agricultural sector accounted for 9 per cent, 15 per cent and 9 per cent of GDP in Algeria, Morocco, and Tunisia respectively. It employs 40 per cent of the population in Morocco, 11 per cent in Algeria, and 16 per cent in Tunisia. However, as of 2011, the availability of arable land per capita represented just 3.2 per cent of Algeria, 17.8 per cent of Morocco, and 18 per cent of Tunisia. The most commonly cultivated crops are olives and almonds, which consume large amounts of fresh water. Fruit and vegetables are also commonly produced, but in smaller quantities. Farmers in the Arab Maghreb sub-region have been planting these crops for hundreds of years. The main source of irrigation has always been rainwater, which used to be plentiful in the region.

However, recent global climate changes and disruption of the environmental ecosystem, predominantly from deforestation, has led to rainwater becoming very scarce, especially in desert areas like North Africa. The average annual rainfall, as of 2014, was below 300 mm in vast areas of the Arab Maghreb sub region, creating an arid to semi-arid climate. Water scarcity has reached a critical point in the region, and severe drought is expected in the future. The agricultural sector is considered to be the largest consumer of water in the Maghreb sub region, as the annual freshwater usage in agriculture represents an average of 76 per cent of total freshwater usage in the region. The Maghreb region depends primarily on rainfall and groundwater as sources of fresh water. The dependence on rainfall makes this region very vulnerable to climate change, which can have a strong impact on crop production. The recent environmental changes require an accompanying shift in farming practices to preserve rural land and compensate for the depleting water resources.

Due to a lack of knowledge, a concentration on short-term gains, and a lack of focus on sustainability among farmers, rural communities in the Maghreb region continue to intensively cultivate the same crops inherited from their parents. Farmers continue to plant olives and almonds, irrigating them with ground water, 80 per cent of which in Tunisia is salty consisting of 4–6 grams of salt per litre of water. This level of salt damages commonly cultivated crops (seawater has 12 grams of salt per litre of water). Irrigating land with salty water increases the salt content in the soil, rendering it acidic and infertile after three crop cycles of this practice. This allows desert sands to invade the infertile soil, and then desertification occurs. It is expected that by 2020, 80 per cent of the land will have become infertile and there will not be enough water for daily consumption in the region.

The effects of desertification not only disrupt the environmental ecosystem, but studies of the United Nations Convention to Combat Desertification have also shown that there is a link between desertification and hunger and poverty. It affects poverty levels and food security, resulting in a decline of food yields per capita in the affected areas, as well as negatively impacting the economic returns of the agricultural sector.

Tunisia is a country of 12 million inhabitants, the smallest country of North Africa. Unlike Algeria and Libya which are gas and petroleum producers, Tunisia has nothing except human brains to support its own development. That's why the

President Habib Bourguiba invested in education when the country became independent in 1956. However, this great idea led to a big problem in the 1990s: a lot of highly educated people entered the job market, but there weren't enough enterprises to employ them. From 1987 to 2011, President Ben Ali led Tunisia under a dictatorship and the associated corruption and clientelism badly damaged economic growth and job creation. A young person finishing university will often have to wait one to three years before getting a position. This means that many of today's youth are keen to leave the country to find better opportunities, but it can also open the door to extremism and radicalism. (See the 2013 Annual report of the National observatory for employment and qualifications.)

Tunisia's economy has three strong sectors:

- agriculture: Tunisia is the second largest producer of olive oil in the world and organic farming is increasing;
- industry: representing 30 per cent of GDP;
- services: information and communication technology, and tourism representing 60 per cent of GDP.

However, in 2015, Tunisia is facing a new challenge: terrorism. After two terrorist attacks in March and June 2015, the tourist industry, which had already suffered as a result of the revolution, is in a state of crisis. At the same time, desertification is advancing and will cover 75 per cent of the land by 2025. This is also combined with a huge water crisis, as Tunisia is located between the Sahara desert and the Mediterranean sea, meaning that there are major variations in precipitation between regions (between 1,500 mm in the north and 50 mm in the south). This crisis is causing foreign investors to flee, which in turn has a negative impact on the development of industry and the job market. Access to finance is one of the major issues faced by Tunisian entrepreneurs, as the bank sector isn't able to support them. There is a lack of infrastructure in rural areas and a gap between what is taught to university students and the skills needed by businesses.

This post-2015 Tunisia needs innovation and resilience to solve its economic, social and environmental problems.

This is the context in which Dream in Tunisia was born. Focusing on rural areas, our aim is to support an holistic and sustainable development of communities filling gaps in a system which has set aside rural areas for more than 25 years, creating social and economic disparities at the national level and a sense of injustice among youth. What would your attitude be if you were living in a place where corruption and clientelism excluded you from any kind of opportunity? Tunisia is the land of lost dreams – the opposite of the American dream where anybody can have a chance. During the 2011 revolution, a new sense of hope existed in the country; but it only lasted a few months until the political debates were once again focused on power, instead of national development.

For me, this context was epitomized in my grandparents' village, Bir Salah. A high rate of unemployment meant that the young men were spending all their time in coffee shops and the young women were spending all their time at home sewing shoes for a German company that paid them just $2 for every 10 shoes. It was a community of farmers living on their laurels, with no access to scientific knowledge or willingness to seek new information. 70 per cent of teenagers were leaving the school system before the age of 16 with no access to any kind of fulfilling occupation or assistance for those wishing to improve their living standards. When we created the NGO, we were surrounded by all the female graduates of the village area who wanted to work and earn a living. Thanks to a partnership with the ministry of vocational training and education, we were able to employ eight of them. But we soon became aware of the lack of professional skills we needed, and we started to teach them how to send e-mails, how to work in a team, how to develop organizational skills and how to follow a plan.

At the same time, uneducated youth asked us for opportunities. They had land, but no money or knowledge. We planted 1,000 acacia gum trees thanks to an online crowdfunding campaign and started developing our knowledge on desertification and community development. We chose the acacia tree, because it can flourish in the desert and generate incomes on a market with a high demand.

Because we couldn't ignore the needs of children and teenagers – the future of this country – we partnered with Orange Foundation. We designed the 'Village Orange' programme in Tunisia, and set up the first prototype in Bir Salah in 2013–14. This programme had only one aim: to offer rural communities access to the basic infrastructure (water, education, health) and the tools to become empowered (women's centres, youth centres, entrepreneurship centres), thus attempting to bridge the gap between services in these communities and those of the big cities.

Our approach is holistic because everything is connected; you cannot fight unemployment without improving the entrepreneurial and educational eco-system; you cannot fight terrorism and illegal emigration without offering opportunities and hope to the communities by fighting corruption; you cannot build a better future by ignoring the children and teenagers of today. We are not just fighting desertification or poverty or gender inequality – we are fighting them all at once.

Timeline

1996

The idea of creating an NGO to support the development of rural areas in Tunisia was born after I travelled to my grandparents' village in Tunisia.

2003–12

The Association of Bir Salah was created and the idea implemented by my father, Ajmi Toumi, my sister Myriam, and me. This included the opening of the youth centre of Bir Salah, the distribution of 340,000 books and 300 computers in public libraries all over Tunisia, the opening of the women's centre of Hencha and the youth centre of Bir Salah. In 2008, during my university studies, I presented my idea to the Ministry of Environment in Tunisia, who refused any sort of collaboration. Initially, I had wanted to cooperate with the ministry to plant acacia trees in desert areas in order to create a green belt to protect rural lands from the sand and wind. Despite being rejected by the government, an entrepreneurial spirit pushed me to find a more strategic entry point.

Continuing to work on this idea, just a few months later I was nominated as a young Changemaker by Ashoka's Youth Venture, who supported me in creating a professional business plan for 'Acacias for All'. From this time collaborating with Ashoka, I learned how working to create change through citizens and farmers would be more strategic and scalable for implementing the vision. I then won the Youth Venture prize in 2009.

2012

The death of my father led me to come to Tunisia and take the leadership of the organization which became Association Ajmi Toumi – Dream in Tunisia – in his memory. A few weeks later, I was in Sweden in the She Entrepreneurs programme for female social entrepreneurs of MENA. This programme helped Dream in Tunisia to focus and strengthen the vision to implement Acacias for All.

To change farmers' production practices, I began working with female rural farmers in the village of Bir-Salah in Tunisia in 2011. I recognized that women represented a strong entry point into the agricultural sector, as they are typically more receptive to change. Additionally, most women own small pieces of land and have no adequate access to education or markets. I regularly met with the women, discussed their problems, and offered solutions. I conducted field visits to speak to the women and built a demonstration centre in Bir-Salah in 2012. The demonstration centre contained a seed nursery where sustainable farming practices were used by our team.

An online crowdfunding campaign to start the programme Acacias for All, raised €3,000. I planted 1500 trees but, due to water access being cut in the village that summer, these later died. It was a huge disappointment, but I didn't give up. The seed nursery was there, the team was there and the crowdfunding campaign had demonstrated that the idea was strong. Motivation was what we needed, more than ever before, to continue with the project.

Following extensive market research into the consumption trends in the Mediterranean region, regarding sustainable products and services, I decided that our strategy needed to focus on changing farmers' practices and ideas regarding the sustainability of their land. I wanted to offer new alternative seeds to replace commonly cultivated crops, open new channels for farmers through research on desertification and enable them to think sustainably and create higher economic returns by organizing them into cooperatives.

Having studied possible solutions to desertification, I introduced acacia plants into the farming communities of Tunisia as an alternative to the commonly cultivated crops of olives and almonds, which cannot withstand salty water. The acacia is a tree characterized by very long roots that extend up to 100 metres underground, providing the soil with nitrogen and bringing fresh water to the surface. Thus, the roots keep the soil free of salt while also re-fertilizing it. Acacias can be irrigated with water that has 8 grams or less of salt per litre, as opposed to other traditional crops that cannot be cultivated with water that has more than 3 grams of salt per litre. Additionally, acacias are adaptable to desert conditions and, when planted around a farm, they create a green belt, preventing the invasion of sand and wind.

FIGURE 11.1   Panorama showing the impact of acacias on desertification. The acacia trees are on the left and the desert area is on the right

Copyright Sarah Toumi

This allows for the growth of fruit and vegetables inside the farm. Moreover, after three years, acacia trees produce gum arabic and Moringa oil, which have economic value. Gum arabic is incorporated into many global industrial processes, such as the manufacture of yogurt, cosmetics, fizzy drinks, medical products and agro-products. Moringa oil is used for massages and relaxation.

2013

Orange and the French Embassy in Tunis helped the NGO to support the women's centre of Hencha, and to achieve the project for the autonomization of Bir Salah's population: 'Village Orange'. However, at the same time, I was facing many disappointments as my leadership was continually being questioned: I was a 25-year old, half-French woman who wanted to reset the habits of an entire community in Tunisia. This was also the period of my pregnancy and the birth of my daughter, Balkis. It was challenging to be recognized worldwide for my vision (receiving the Women for Change special prize or the '100 innovations for a sustainable Africa', recognition offered by the French Ministry of Foreign Affairs), but simultaneously doubted at the local level, even by my very close family, for being a working mother.

I made the big decision at this time to close the women's centre of Hencha, without renewing the contracts of my father's team, to focus only on the Village Orange and Acacias for All programme. This allowed the organization to focus on its objective and follow its plan. The women's centre of Hencha, and the old team, were following the vision of Ajmi Toumi, which was no longer compatible with the new organization's goals.

As part of Acacias for All, we planted 5000 acacia trees but, again, half of them died and the other half were stolen, due to neglect by the team who were still working according to my father's methods and didn't recognize me because of my youth. It was not only important that farmers were receptive to the idea of changing their traditional crops to acacias, but also that they adopted an approach to agricultural practices that focused more on the long-term sustainability of their land. To achieve this, we started to train farmers on permaculture and sustainable farming techniques. I went to meet the Observatory of Sahel and Sahara to obtain tools and then started the training around the process by which small land areas can be used to yield large financial returns by employing sustainable practices. Examples of sustainable practices on which farmers receive training are: developing homogeneous sustainable crops; use of safe irrigation water; new technologies for water treatment; and maximizing the use of natural products and fertilizers rather than pesticides.

At this time, Village Orange employed more than 25 workers for one year, offered about 800 school bags to the students of Bir Salah, renovated the school for its 50th anniversary, renovated the small hospital in the village, providing it with a desk for the midwife, and offered ultrasound equipment to the nearby hospital in Hencha. This was the first step of Village Orange's programme to offer basic infrastructure to the community.

2014

With a new team recruited, based on the goals and short/mid-term objectives of Dream in Tunisia, we inaugurated Village Orange with Orange Foundation and Orange Tunisia. The opening of the women's centre, youth centre and entrepreneurship centre was mentioned in all the national media. Paradoxically, this led to a reaction of mistrust in the community and even rejection for the early months of work. In a country where the civil society only started to have power from 2011, social work is something that needs to be explained. Tunisian citizens had been living under a dictatorship for 24 years. Everything and everyone had been censored: the media, the internet, our teachers, the country's entrepreneurs. It was also very difficult to get an accreditation to create an NGO. Each NGO group had to ask the permission for the Governor and then had to be seen by the Ministry of Interior. The community was used to clientelism and corruption and we had to prove that we wanted to create positive change for all with financial transparency. Social support had been like a carrot used by authorities to keep citizens quiet. Sometimes they offered food, clothes, and children's school materials but only to justify their politics, based on corruption and censorship. We were also receiving a lot of demands for pay from young graduates who didn't understand our work and thought we were just distributing salaries for people staying at home. They didn't understand the purpose or the vision, as they had been told that dreaming is not something you can do in Tunisia because, in Tunisia, there is no opportunity or possibility to fulfil dreams. Due to community pressure, we took 12 graduates and trained them. We planted 1,000 trees and, finally, half of them survived. Following the recommendations of the local farmers we trained, we also planted 500 more trees as a test: a mix of olives, almond, date palms, pomegranate, figs and lemon which were taken care of by a local widow. It was a success. Ashoka recognized my work and supported me as an Ashoka Fellow. This gave me renewed energy to continue, with my aims in sight.

2015

This year was a new beginning. Half of the team was new and we had a new strategy and goal: to plant 1 million trees by 2018 with 1,000 farmers. I learnt a lot from previous failures of tree planting, and in May 2015, the planting of 1,000 trees led to a survival rate of 70 per cent. Tree planting depends on many different factors, including the quality of the seeds, water quality, access to water, the qualification and dedication of workers and the plantation calendar. Some 10,000 trees were planted in 2015, not only acacias or moringas, but also olive, almond, figs, date palms, pomegranate, aromatic herbs, peppers and tomatoes. The idea is to create sustainable ecosystems. With Houcem Nabli, a specialist in organic farming in Tunisia, we organized a one-year programme of training for farmers coupled with tree planting and the development of value chains.

FIGURE 11.2   Organic farming training given by Houcem Nabli, a Tunisian expert in organic farming

Photo courtesy of Houcem Nabli

The chain we started with was olive oil. It was simple because it already existed inside the community, so we just worked on the packaging and marketing. We inaugurated the creation of our first olive oil production 'Dream Olive Oil' and also produced honey, hot peppers, almond pastries as well as moringa powder and gum arabic. Echoing Green selected me as a fellow for the climate programme, further important recognition that strengthened my leadership position in the organization, Tunisia, and the Maghreb as a whole, as well as confirming Dream in Tunisia's position as a major actor for the region.

It took us three years to learn and develop our vision, through collaborating with people on the ground and matching my social entrepreneurship skills with local initiatives, creating a grassroots innovation initiative which could be replicated and could inspire other people in North Africa.

FIGURE 11.3   Dream Olive Oil, one of the products of Dream in Tunisia

Copyright Sarah Toumi

Making it work: the structure, model and sustainability of Dream in Tunisia

Dream in Tunisia is a non-profit organization, and Acacias for All is the only one of its programmes aimed at generating incomes. It is funded by crowdfunding and foundations.

The organizational structure is democratic. We have two legal representatives: myself, the founder and President, and Latifa Ismail, the Treasurer. We then have members who join for a membership fee of US $10 a year and who vote for the legal representatives. The team is paid by the Tunisian Government and is composed of young graduates who spend one to two years working with us, receiving training and improving their professional skills. The team of employees working in the seeds nursery comprises five people who are paid by Dream in Tunisia.

To finance our organization, we have access to various funding mechanisms:

- Crowdfunding. Available on the web; anyone can support us by sponsoring tree planting via our partner Women Worldwide Web at **https://www.w4.org/en/project/empower-women-combat-climate-change-tunisia/**.

- Foundations. Donors such as Orange or Roi Baudouin have supported us.

- Partnerships. With the ministry of vocational training and education to finance the salaries of volunteers.

- Selling. Products of Acacias for All, online for customers and directly via business-to-business (B2B).

Sustainability

Acacias for All is changing the agricultural industry in the Arab Maghreb sub-region, starting with Tunisia. In this region, desertification and dwindling water resources are major environmental concerns that negatively impact agricultural communities and lead to increased levels of rural poverty. It is combating these environmental and economic challenges by creating a movement that shifts the focus from commonly cultivated crops to alternative seeds that are more sustainable for the environment, creating greater opportunities for income generation.

Furthermore, the organization is introducing farmers to sustainable farming practices through training and education that shifts their attitudes regarding their land. To complement this approach, it offers farmers new opportunities through alternative crops – mainly Acacia trees, which have a positive environmental and economic impact. They revitalize the land, create a greenbelt to prevent desertification and consume much less water than the traditionally cultivated crops, olives and almonds. Acacia trees additionally produce gum arabic and Moringa oil which provide large economic returns when sold. Acacias for All couples the introduction of new crops with empirical research and studies on new potential opportunities that can be used by farmers to fight soil erosion, desertification and water scarcity.

To complement this, Acacias for All is creating a movement throughout the Arab Maghreb sub-region in which farmers not only practise sustainable farming techniques and use alternative crops, but also take ownership over sustaining their practices and thinking long term about the land. Farmers are empowered to become self-sufficient economically and to access the market. The NGO enables the farmers by organizing them into agricultural cooperatives which market their products to meet international market needs. These practices provide new economic opportunities that shape the future of the agriculture industry and lift farmers and their families out of rural poverty.

The Acacias for All idea is applicable to all the arable lands of North Africa and countries with desert regions. Starting in Tunisia, it plans to expand geographically in order to combat desertification, a major environmental concern throughout the entire Arab world.

Other programmes of the NGO, such as Village Orange, have for the moment been developed only around Bir Salah because a lot of money and human resources are needed. We are waiting for communities to replicate the model themselves, because it is not possible to go into communities we don't know and carry out programmes which are not fully connected with people's needs and purposes.

Our long-term vision is to be able to fund a scale-up thanks to the benefits generated by the commercialization part of Acacias for All. This will allow us to plant more trees, train more farmers and create a bold change. Acacias for All commercializes farmers' products, after conceiving value chains that allow farmers to sell value-added products and get a living wage. If our assumptions come to fruition, we could then create a seed funding to support social entrepreneurship in Tunisia.

Measuring our all-important impact

Our impact operates on different levels. We are a young organization with high expectations and ambitions. We set a series of standards to measure our impact. As our approach is holistic, we set social, economic and environmental impact measures to be able to follow our impact. Our impact is still limited to the area of Hencha, but we have ambitions to scale up in Tunisia in 2016, and in Morocco in 2017. We will work hard to achieve this.

For Acacias for All, we set our ambitions on the surface of restored soils, the number of trees planted, the number of trees that survive, the number of farmers trained, the number of female farmers trained, effective sales in euros, number of business clients, number of online customers and number of sponsored trees.

Here are some of our impacts in 2012–15:

- restoration of 1.5 km^2 of soils;
- planting of 19,270 trees, 12,270 of which survived;
- training of 50 people on smart farming, 80 per cent of them women.

All this information is available on our website, along with our annual report.

For Dream in Tunisia's other activities, we set our ambitions at the level of community participation and impact on youth employment.

In 2014:

- 27 children aged four to five attended our pre-school programme in Bir Salah;
- 33 children, of which 45 per cent were girls, attended karate lessons in Bir Salah;
- 41 women took part in the training programme for sewing, handcraft and pastries;
- 12 volunteers were employed;
- three paid positions were created for the workers in the seed nursery.

We also found that we sometimes got unexpected insights. For example:

- Of the 12 young female volunteers recruited in 2014, five got married during the first year of activity with us, and two got engaged.
- 40 per cent of the parents bringing their children to our youth centre are men.

These unexpected pieces of data show that things are improving for working women, and that men are also becoming involved in taking care of their children's education. The world is better for our innovation for a few reasons. Firstly, our organization is Tunisian youth-led, and is the first to empower both men and women at the same level of involvement in farming in Tunisia. We also opened up a public debate on the problem of desertification, a word which is now used by many organizations and by the government. It is no longer taboo. We were also the first organization in Tunisia to talk about coupling agro-forestry and sustainable rural development with an approach based on peer-to-peer exchanges. Of course, the fact that the founder and CEO is a young woman is an impact in itself, providing a role model and a success story for many young Tunisian women who dare to dream of a better future.

We are just at the beginning, but we expect to plant 1 million trees in Tunisia by 2018 and to expand to Morocco and Algeria where we want to plant 1 million trees every year thanks to a strong value chain process and a big marketing effort, the empowerment of at least 1,000 new farmers every year and partnership work with governments to create a green belt in North Sahel.

Lessons learnt

I would give the following tips to anyone wanting to start their own enterprise:

1 *Always challenge your ideas.* Sometimes the best ideas on paper cannot be adapted to local contexts. Don't be afraid to be wrong and adjust!

2 *Transparency is key for long-term partnerships.*

3 *Don't work alone.* Find the people who will be able to lift your idea up.

4 *Money will come if you can show your dedication to your idea.* Nothing is more attractive than a person convinced, and led, by a dream.

5 *Always be empathic.* Everyone is facing life challenges and we need to stay humble and remember that we are all humans – just humans.

6 *Don't be afraid to fail.* Learn from each failure, as failure is what leads you to success. If I hadn't failed in planting a few thousand trees, I would never have learnt the best way to do it.

7 *Humility is a key attitude for a leader, but your vision must be strong.*

8 *Be happy.* Balance your personal life and your entrepreneurial life by exercising, giving time to your relatives and to yourself. Who will follow your dream if you get burned out before you've started to realize it?

9 *Have faith.* Believe in yourself and your vision.

Discussion questions

1 Dream in Tunisia is currently a non-profit organization with a commercial component. Is it sustainable for scaling up?

2 Every day 15 *billion* trees disappear from the planet. How can Dream in Tunisia have a wider impact?

3 Acacias for All plans to scale up in Morocco by 2017. What kind of organization could support this expansion without losing the vision of the social enterprise?

4 What kind of metrics could be used to focus more on the impact on poverty of Acacias for All?

5 What are the key success factors of Dream in Tunisia? What are its weaknesses?

Further reading

You can find more material to do with this chapter at www.koganpage.com/
socialentrepreneurship

Official websites: www.acaciasforall.org or www.dreamintunisia.org
[accessed 10 December 2015]
Tunisian history, the revolution and the social and economic developments:
Gana, N (2013) *The Making of the Tunisian Revolution: Contexts, architects, prospects*
– Edinburgh University Press
Perkins, K (2004) *A History of Modern Tunisia*, Cambridge University Press
World Bank Report on Tunisia www.worldbank.org/en/country/tunisia/overview
[accessed 10 December 2015]
African Development Bank Report on Tunisia www.afdb.org/fileadmin/uploads/afdb/
Documents/Publications/Tunisia%20Economic%20and%20Social%20Challenges.pdf
[accessed 10 December 2015]
Encyclopaedia Britannica online on Tunisia Jasmine Revolution: www.britannica.com/event/
Jasmine-Revolution [accessed 10 December 2015]
On desertification in Tunisia and Africa:
Social, Economic, Financial Challenges of the Desertification in Tunisia: www.un.org/
esa/sustdev/sdissues/desertification/beijing2008/presentations/aloui.pdf [accessed 10
December 2015]
Strategy to combat desertification in Tunisia: www.academia.edu/3421162/
STRATEGY_TO_COMBAT_DESERTIFICATION_IN_TUNISIA_OBJECTIVES_AND_
CHALLENGES [accessed 10 December 2015]
UNCCD Africa website: www.unccd.int/en/regional-access/Africa/Pages/africa.aspx
[accessed 10 December 2015]
Observatory of Sahel and Sahara researches: www.oss-online.org/fr/publications
[accessed 10 December 2015]

12
The reluctant geneticist

GENETIC ALLIANCE – SHARON TERRY

ABSTRACT

By their very nature, few people beyond sufferers and their families would be expected to know much about the world of rare diseases. Despite this, it is estimated that over 7,000 rare diseases exist around the world, affecting some 300 million people, often genetically. This lack of awareness isn't the only problem, either. Rare diseases are often plagued by a lack of research, a lack of funding, and a sense of 'going it alone' among sufferers and their families. It was this very feeling which led Sharon Terry to expand Genetic Alliance, her attempt to bring some collaboration and coordination to the sector after the shock discovery that her own children were suffering from a rare, genetic condition. From unexpected roots, Genetic Alliance is today one of the world's leading non-profit health advocacy organizations, coordinating a network which includes more than 1,200 disease-specific advocacy groups.

An unexpected journey

There are those moments in life you know you will remember forever. They constitute a clear and delineated threshold. For me, it was the moment our children's lives took an unexpected turn – into the land of genetic disease. The build-up to that moment was a particular kind of rollercoaster ride, sometimes called the diagnostic odyssey. Our response was shaped by years of facing small adversities. Still, we had no idea of the journey on which we were embarking.

The start was rather innocuous. My husband, two children and I were at my niece's first birthday party in 1993. It was the first happy event since the death of her father, my brother, about four months before. It was a hot September afternoon in Connecticut. I noticed, in the softening afternoon sunlight, three small dots on each side of my daughter's neck. I thought about this discovery for a moment, feeling a little flip of fear in my stomach, before letting it go and returning to the quest for equilibrium in our extended family in the face of the large hole left by my brother's death at 31 years old.

But the dots did not disappear. Over the next few months, I asked our paediatrician periodically: 'What are these dots? Why are they only on the sides of her neck? Why are they slowly increasing in number over time? Are they important? Should I ignore them?' She repeatedly reassured me that I was needlessly worried. She suggested it was a laundry detergent allergy. I wasn't convinced and silently baulked – why weren't these dots all the way around her neck? Then, to reassure myself, I would agree with her that I was neurotically suspicious of the slightest thing since my brother's death and that perhaps I should be in therapy to mitigate that neurosis. But, if these dots weren't really progressing, why did photos from month to month look so different?

I finally decided that I needed to put my questions to rest. My husband Pat and I decided to go 'out-of-pocket' and 'out-of-plan' to a dermatologist (meaning we would pay for the visit to a physician that wasn't approved by our particular insurance plan). I set up an appointment, told Pat he needn't come since I would undoubtedly hear that it was an allergy of some sort, and off we went to see the doctor on 23 December 1994. That defining moment was looming up ahead and we marched into it, oblivious.

FIGURE 12.1   Elizabeth and Ian Terry at the time of their diagnosis

Courtesy Sharon Terry

It all happened in what seemed like a split second. Dr Lionel Bercovitch glanced at Elizabeth's neck and said 'She has pseudoxanthoma elasticum'. As my stomach began to churn at the sound of the syllable 'oma' (weren't there cancers like melan*oma*, and lymph*oma*?), he glanced at Ian and added, 'Oh, and he has it too.' Then he turned off the lights and looked in her eyes with an ophthalmoscope. I wanted to scream, 'What? Just stop right here!' This was a skin problem – what was he doing looking in her eyes? I felt like I had crossed a kind of threshold in the sudden dark: I was frightened and did not know where I was. Yes, her eyes were affected too.

Dr Bercovitch turned the lights back on, explained to me that he was trained in dermatology and ophthalmology and could assess both the skin and eye effects of pseudoxanthoma elasticum (PXE). I could not absorb the words he was speaking: something about this being systemic, an autosomal recessive disease and there not much being known about it. I just saw my gorgeous children and heard him speak about wrinkly sagging skin and blindness.

I went home, called Pat and sobbed about the disfigurement that our children would be facing in their future. How foolish to worry about their skin and appearance, when blindness was a strong possibility! I then called our paediatrician. She pulled a book from her shelves and read to me. This was a disease that would cause skin, eye, cardiac and vascular problems.

Dr Bercovitch called us after dinner. We thought this extraordinary, but were even more astounded to learn that he lived just a few houses away. He offered to speak with us the next evening, Christmas Eve, at his house, while another neighbour came and watched Elizabeth and Ian. That night, we struggled to understand what he was telling us and realized we knew too little to digest it. We would need some basic references and then some time to get up to speed.

Elizabeth and Ian remember that Christmas, when they were seven and five years old respectively, as the best Christmas of their lives. They got every toy they wished for and more. They were joyful and happy little kids, unaware that anything had changed. As they learned about the condition, they learned the long Latin name. They began to name spiders and plants – '*Pseudoxanthoma elasticum*' – believing it sounded sufficiently scientific.

Making sense of the unknown

The weeks following Christmas were difficult ones. I went to two medical school libraries and photocopied every article on PXE that I could find, pawing through the card catalogue in those pre-internet days. I brought home 400 articles, and couldn't understand any of them – only that there were grotesque photos of sagging skin, and descriptions of early blindness and premature death. Pat and I eagerly and anxiously combed through the articles, and though we were clueless as to the details, we began to see patterns.

The first pattern: there was no pattern. These authors were writing from a hundred different perspectives, only reporting one case, and then drawing conclusions about the disease from the single case. We did not understand how one could characterize a disease with only one case, something we later learned is called an 'N of 1'. The next pattern that was apparent to us was that seemingly unrelated things were associated and supposed to tell a story. As an example, there was a paper on a 13-year-old who died 'from PXE'. However, she also had a seizure disorder and had attempted suicide several times. We couldn't tell whether PXE was the cause of her death, so could the author be certain? Who were we to question the author of a scientific paper, published in a journal?

PXE appeared to be characterized differently in different geographic locations, and while it is certainly true that geographic isolation or ancestral origin could produce variations in the disease, there seemed to be extreme differences between similar populations. It was also troubling that all of the reports were positive – there were no failed experiments reported. How would researchers learn if the failed experiments were not made public? Another pattern that emerged was a lack of collaboration. In the few cases where an author wrote multiple papers, it seemed that those papers were with the same group of authors. There was no cross-over, no cross-fertilization.

The issue of collaboration, or actually competition, became poignantly clear for us in the days following the diagnosis of our children. A few days after Christmas, a scientist from Harvard called to ask whether he could have a sample of our children's blood for a study seeking to find the gene associated with PXE. We readily agreed to the visit from the researcher's assistant and the kids' blood was drawn. Two days later a researcher from Mt Sinai Hospital called and asked the same. We told him: 'Sure, the researcher from Harvard took several vials and certainly he would share. No-one would ask little children to have blood drawn twice!' He chuckled: 'No, they won't share with us, we are racing each other to find the gene.' This was astounding to us. While of course we had seen competition in many areas of life, it was unthinkable that there was competition in biomedical research. Wasn't everyone focused on solving these issues as soon as possible, with the highest degree of collaboration since the stakes were huge? No, that was not what was happening. We were shocked.

Another pattern that emerged was that nothing was being done systematically about this disease. There was no learning from one paper to another, experiments were repeated, and no one was mapping the scientific patterns that might be found in the data. And finally, a strange and horrible pattern became evident. People were called subjects in these papers. They were not collaborators, and certainly not empowered to participate.

Within a month of Elizabeth's and Ian's diagnosis, we had to let go of the misconception that every disease had *some* treatment. We needed to step away from the illusion that this was the medical equivalent of a delicatessen counter. No-one was going to call our number, so there was no use waiting hopefully until someone got to the 'P's. We also had to figure out a way to make order out of the chaos that appeared in the papers we read, and in the competition we experienced in the blood collections for research.

Accepting the calling

Trained as a teacher and a college chaplain, I was ill-prepared for the piles of medical journal papers. I was as clueless about research as my engineering husband, who is fond of saying 'we didn't know a gene from a hubcap'. It was not obvious to us or to those around us that we had it in us to change the system. But we had no choice.

As we fell asleep each night amid piles of photocopied papers and enormous medical dictionaries, we knew we had to take the bull by the horns. I remember an evening when we looked at each other, and thought, no, no, no – we don't want to do this – we do not want to create a system for this disease. Wasn't it enough to live with it, to cope with it, to walk our kids through it? Couldn't someone else make sense of it, fix it, give us a call when the cure was in? I begged the universe to please take care of us. No. Reluctantly, we had to admit that this was our burden. There was no-one else.

That decision made, we rolled up our sleeves and plunged in. Using skills I had acquired organizing the homeschoolers and counselling college students, we created PXE International in early 1995, an international foundation dedicated to the research of PXE. Of course, there were other organizations dedicated to other diseases, so we sought them out and met with them through the umbrella organization then called the Alliance for Genetic Support Groups. These other groups told us *not* to try to research the disease, or even influence biomedical research – stick with supporting patients and leave the rest to the professionals. We didn't wait for more than a minute before spurning this advice. We were also told that if we were going to influence research, it should only be by raising money, and we wouldn't make a dent until we raised hundreds of thousands of dollars. We ignored that too, and made our first grant of the entire $10,000 we raised that first year to the Jackson Laboratories in Bar Harbor Maine, to look for PXE eye signs in mice. They did not find PXE, but did find a naturally occurring mouse model for cataracts. The researcher won a Howard Hughes grant and went on to discover wonderful things in that disease.

Always very hands on, we determined that we needed access to a laboratory. Initially, we asked the Harvard researcher who had come to take the kids' blood whether we could 'wash the test tubes in his lab'. We began to go into the lab at about 10 pm each night and stay for four or five hours, eventually running experiments designed to clone the gene. Concurrently, we pondered the problem of competition and wondered how we could persuade the researchers to collaborate. We had no idea that this was such a vexatious problem – one to which I dedicate a significant amount of my time today.

When I described our vision for collaboration, we were repeatedly told: 'You can't herd cats.' That did it! Yes, you can, if you move the food! Clearly, blood, tissue and clinical information from individuals affected by PXE was coveted in this age of gene discovery. All we had to do was to amass this resource in an orderly way, and then the cats would come to us. We could set the rules – to eat you must 'play well with others'. And so, the PXE International Registry and BioBank was born. This was, as far as we know, the first lay-owned blood bank. By the middle of 1995, we were collecting blood and tissue from affected individuals throughout the world – reaching out through newspaper ads, billboards, and physicians.

The combination of increasing knowledge about the human genome and our hard work through many nights (thanks to our neighbour Martha for watching our kids all those nights) resulted in our discovering the gene. I co-authored the gene discovery paper with not one, but two labs, in back-to-back publication in *Nature Genetics*.

Disappointingly, I couldn't persuade the various labs to collaborate in the end, so this was a creative solution that at least resulted in a tie. I then participated in patenting the gene, as a co-discoverer, and all of the patent holders turned all rights over to PXE International. At that time, I was the only lay person to patent a gene – and that may still be the case. I consider myself a steward of the gene, shepherding it through to creating diagnostic tests and trial therapies.

During these years, we were also characterizing the disease. We developed the first lay-designed and managed registry. We wanted to know how PXE progressed, how long people lived, what the major and minor symptoms are, how fast the symptoms progress and why we were seeing extreme variation in the symptoms in people. Some had lost their vision, some had not lost their vision. Some had very baggy loose skin and looked 80 years old at 30, some had almost no skin manifestations. We realized later that many diseases have these same problems: they are not well-characterized, their progression is unpredictable and there isn't a good understanding of how to alleviate symptoms.

Between 1995 and 1999 we did a great deal of work to characterize the disease by asking people affected by the condition many questions. In fact, we asked 900 questions in a survey. We were able to discover critical aspects of the disease. For example, at a variety of support group meetings, women would tell us over and over that they had had a mammogram and then been called in for a biopsy straight afterwards. Mammography specialists would see calcification in the breasts of these women that worried them and they thought they were looking at breast cancer. This was happening almost ubiquitously for all women affected by PXE. This precipitated a study – we compared mammogram films from women with PXE and those without it as a control group. We learned that all women with PXE have micro calcifications in their breasts and that these are not indicative of cancer as they might be in women in general. These women therefore don't need a biopsy. We also discovered something similar for men, since several men reported discovering they had something called testicular microlithiasis; mineralization in the arteries of the testicles. Again, the concern that this was pre-cancer or a cancerous condition precipitated biopsies for these men. We then did a study of 20 men with PXE and 20 controls and saw that the men with PXE too had microcalcifications in the testicles. After this finding, men did not have to be screened or have biopsies every year in order to rule out cancer. In another example, we heard from women affected by PXE that when they gave birth, their doctor was very concerned because their placenta was calcified. Again, we were able to gather many placentas from mothers affected by PXE and many control placentas and do a comparison. We determined that all women with PXE appear to have calcifications in their placentas, but the babies and the women were unaffected. All of these studies resulted from the survey and face-to-face meetings and focused on the issues that people living with PXE cared most about.

The challenges of sustainability, impact and growth

As we progressed through our journey, we began to wonder how we were going to sustain it and how we were going to assure that the work was meaningful and useful, and not just at one tiny step at a time. We began to realize that it was important for our work to include more than this one disease. If we focused on one disease, we would only gradually creep forward. Instead, we needed to be a much larger, broader platform looking systemically at what needed to be done. We began a parallel pathway, meeting with other disease groups, all of whom wanted to use our emerging model.

We started to help other disease advocacy organizations create blood and tissue banks. We also began to talk to universities that were holding such collections for common and rare conditions. Throughout 1995, we worked very hard to gather people together to build a blood and tissue bank that would be cross-condition and share infrastructure.

In 1996, we attended the tenth anniversary of the Alliance of Genetic Support Groups and as a result we began to be involved in cross-condition work in earnest. The Alliance was an umbrella organization providing technical assistance to hundreds of disease organizations. At that celebration, we met the Director of the National Human Genome Research Institute, Francis Collins (now the Director of the National Institutes of Health). We began to be introduced to many researchers, we set up visits to those researchers' labs, and also sought to understand what they needed to accelerate biomedical research.

Building an organization from the ground up

PXE International was home grown. I had never run an organization, but I had helped manage the Massachusetts Home Learning Association, and had spearheaded discrete projects throughout my life. We were very fortunate that the founder of Genetic Alliance, Joan Weiss, had written a book called *Starting and Sustaining an Advocacy Organization*. It became our bible, and simultaneous to our work we began to update it, revising sections and adding new ones. (The new version is called WikiAdvocacy and is found at wikiadvocacy.org.)

We asked around our small community in Sharon, Massachusetts and recruited board members from the clinician who diagnosed our kids and from our neighbours. We found a *pro-bono* lawyer who filed our incorporation and our tax-exempt applications with the Federal Government and the state of Massachusetts. We knew that we had to find people with the condition, and so we began using newspaper community calendars, mailing brochures to ophthalmologists and dermatologists and exhibiting at professional society meetings such as the American Academy of Ophthalmology.

These were the days of the burgeoning web – and so we asked Harvard University contacts from our community if we could add a section to their website – and received the green light! For about the first decade, PXE International's online home was at harvard.edu/pxe.

We were far too under-resourced to have an office or paid staff, and so I volunteered and we turned part, and eventually all, of the kids' playroom into an office. We hired the kids' babysitters to do data entry as we began to conduct surveys – which came in by paper before being keyed into a FileMaker Pro database that I wrote myself. It wasn't pretty – but we still use it, albeit with lots more bells and whistles and a much slicker interface.

The Board of Directors met face to face about once a month when we were all local. Eventually we got larger, and more national and international, so now have a Board that meets mostly by phone across many time zones. Some of the original Board members are still with us today.

Eventually we raised enough money to move the office out of our house and into an incubator run by Genetic Alliance for disease organizations. This is in Washington DC, and so it was only possible after we had moved our whole family there, largely to be near the National Institutes of Health and Genetic Alliance. We sustained ourselves almost entirely on donations from people affected by PXE or their loved ones, until recently when we garnered a Patient Centered Outcomes Research Institute award for engagement. The one exception is a nearly annual award we have received from Yardi Systems – thanks to the father of an affected individual alerting us to the fact that we could apply for a grant from them.

Throughout PXE International's growth and development, we remained very tightly associated with Genetic Alliance. My own work began to shift from 90 per cent PXE and 10 per cent Genetic Alliance to today when it is exactly the opposite. We looked for ways to share costs, to share ideas, to share ways of accelerating biomedical research for all diseases, and the BioBank is a good example of one concrete way we were able to do just that.

After running the PXE International Registry and BioBank from 1995 to 2002, we began to ask other disease organizations if they wanted to consider joining us in a joint venture that would increase capacity and reduce cost for everyone. We also wanted to raise the bar on standards and professionalism and knew that more good minds gave us all a greater chance of keeping this brand new field operational and sustainable. We met regularly with a number of other support and advocacy organizations throughout 2002, and some became particularly interested. I remember saying that we needed to hold hands and jump into the deep end of the pool together. After a year of meetings with 10 organizations present, we decided to go ahead and found a new organization called the Genetic Alliance Registry and BioBank. Six of the 10 organizations contributed substantial amounts of money to get it up and running. In the early years it was about US $20,000 a year per organization to run, which fell to $13,000 after about 10 years. Now it's closer to $2,000. Efficiencies in our work, as well as the falling cost of technology, have allowed such a wonderful decrease in cost.

Understanding our actions and their impact

Throughout the years from the time of our children's diagnosis to 2004, we created novel solutions to traditional problems, linking up previously adjacent parts of the system. Pat applied his creative systems thinking and construction engineering to the problems and devised a plan that we follow to this day (see Figure 12.2). We engaged in 'disruptive innovation' at every turn, even before it was a popular term. Applying the skills of both advocates and scientists added new levels of engagement to the research enterprise and we were 'citizen scientists' before that had a label. PXE International adopted aspects of academic models (rigorous science), commercial enterprises (commodification and accountability) and advocacy organizations (trust and agility), and has used them to create a new model for advancing research. I created communities of trust, in both the patient and research communities, and they have been essential and novel. The increase in individuals in the PXE International Registry is shown in Figure 12.3.

FIGURE 12.2 PXE International Strategy (Patrick F Terry)

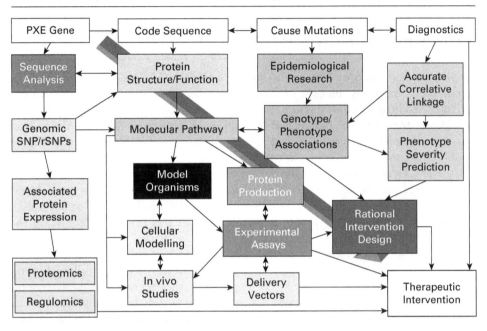

FIGURE 12.3 Growth of the Registry

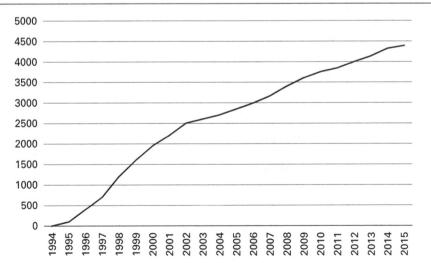

It was at the point where dozens of people were coming to sit in our living room, asking us to help them create more organizations like PXE International, and biobanks, that we decided to work for bigger systems than this one disease. At first, we did this by creating common platforms for DNA storage (the Genetic Alliance Registry and BioBank (biobank.org), or writing a manual on advocacy that later became WikiAdvocacy. Then a critical moment arrived in 2002 that opened up a completely new, unexpected opportunity.

Stepping up to the plate

By this time, I was president of the board of Genetic Alliance (renamed from the early, more narrowly focused 'Alliance for Genetic Support Groups'). Genetic Alliance had broadened its mission, and had begun to understand that the non-profit world and the world of biomedical research were changing. After all, the human genome sequence had been mapped, and nothing seemed improbable. Cures were around the corner for all of us, were they not?

In 2004, Genetic Alliance had a vacancy for the CEO position. I was fired up to find a 'world class leader' to take the organization to the next level, to blow the lid off, to create the most entrepreneurial non-profit in health. I led the Board through writing a job description for this creative and tenacious leader. I cranked up the expectations to the point where they matched my vision. I was so excited at the prospect of meeting this person, whom we would find after doing a nationwide search.

The Board told me to go home and look in the mirror. No! We had to look far and wide, there was no mirror involved. As we searched, they repeatedly told me to look in the mirror. I constantly responded that we needed world-class leadership, not me. After a few months, I saw what my reluctance was about. It was primarily fear. It was about depending on me to lead, to manifest my vision, but to do that in a transformative way that realized all of the things I was attempting to create outside of me – and to do that internally. I feared that looking in that mirror would be a symptom of pride. It was instead, perhaps, the most humble moment of my life to look there and say yes, it is me. I am the world-class leader we have been seeking.

So what of my reluctance to answer the call to become even more entrepreneurial? I found it was based on two things, one easier to deal with than the other. The first has to do with PXE International and the effect of pseudoxanthoma elasticum on my children. It is possible that my decision to work for the larger system would adversely affect them and those living with PXE. It is possible that I might not make the progress I could have on this disease if I decide to work for all diseases. Two things make this easier to accept. One is that I am convinced that if we work for the larger good, for all disease, for systems in biology, rather than silos, we will advance all causes at an accelerated rate. As President John Kennedy said: 'A rising tide lifts all boats.' The other is my children's response. At ages 14 and 12, they had admonished us that we would never have meaningful progress until we learned to 'live with disease rather than fight disease', as they did. Thus, they thought that taking charge of Genetic Alliance's destiny would be a healing step for me on that path of learning.

This leads us to the second reason for my reluctance. It is always easy to call excitedly for transformation, reformation, revolution. It is quite another thing to step up and do it. Taking the CEO position meant I would have to realize my very self. I would have to step into my weakness and lead from it. I would have to inspire by being, rather than proclaiming. With great humility and excitement, I became the CEO of Genetic Alliance.

At Genetic Alliance I have led, conspired in, and inspired, the transformation of systems. I led the coalition that promoted the Genetic Information Nondiscrimination Act of 2008 – a law that Senator Edward Kennedy proclaimed from the floor of the Senate as the 'first civil rights law of the new century'. I grew PXE International Registry and BioBank into the Genetic Alliance Registry and BioBank. Genetic Alliance established the nation's newborn screening clearing house (babysfirsttest. org). We grew from four staff when I joined Genetic Alliance to more than 22, and were named Washington DC's Best Place to Work in 2010. I can wax lyrical about our accomplishments but, as amazing as they are, they are not the measure of my effectiveness as an entrepreneur. This is one of the many things that I've learnt along the way.

Lessons learnt

1 *The 'hero model' is not my friend.* During these years, I mistakenly thought that the hero model, and later the rejection of the hero model, was the key to what it meant to be effective. In my hero model years, I purported to be able to take care of everything. I could shoulder the burden of the 7,000+ genetic conditions, and the millions of people affected by them. I could also be the one to empty the trash and buy new pens (not to mention configure the servers, install new computers, book everyone's travel, come in earlier and stay later than everyone else). I would achieve the goals we set for unprecedented transformation of the biomedical research and services sectors by brute force and elbow grease! I gradually, and then with greater speed and clarity, began to see the arrogance in such a hero model – an ego that thought I had to do it all. This model of leadership was blocking the talents of those around me, removing me from identifying with the system so much that it was outside me. A good example of this is WikiAdvocacy. It is a terrific compendium of information for anyone leading a disease advocacy organization. Very few people contributed to it, however. When I asked someone who had a hand in developing Wikipedia what they thought the problem was, they said: 'It's too well done. When a resource is so well written, so complete, the community doesn't feel capable of contributing to it. They also don't feel a need to add to it. You will do it. You will take care of them.' Wow, what a wake-up call! I believe advocacy overall is burdened by this model and must break it down if it is to be effective in the networked age. I began to vigorously reject the hero model, and instead create an entirely collaborative model of leadership. In this period, lots of staff and our Council blossomed, but they will tell you that they felt a vacuum of vision and leadership. In this period, staff became hungry for direction. I learned that not everyone has vision, or leadership, and that a balance of these things, in different quantities, made up our vibrant and hardworking staff. The Council and staff learned with me. Some of them

have been with Genetic Alliance throughout my entire time, approaching a decade, with many others for five years or more.

2 *It is true that culture eats strategy for breakfast.* The practical change that I focus on these days is what we are calling the 'movement'. My work, that of Genetic Alliance, PXE International and the handful of other non-profits I direct, is to contribute to this much larger force emerging in the world of health. The day of organizations working, leading and directing from the top down is over. We are called to be boundary-less, to work with one another sharing as much as possible, without regard for credit or acclaim. It is time for each of us to fully realize our role. It is time for individuals participating in research to move from being subjects to engaging as participants. It is now time for each component of the health systems (or lack of systems) to claim a place.

3 *The movement needs leaders who know their place as part of the whole, the we.* Ordinary people can join these leaders in the network age, finding their agency. A vision of working together, creating a movement towards reclaiming health, is emerging in many sectors. Ideas like public access to publicly funded research, rather than locking information up in journals requiring subscriptions, are ripe and sweeping nations. In 2013, the United Kingdom announced that all biomedical articles funded by UK grants would be made open access within six months of publication. The National Institute of Health has a similar policy, and other science funding agencies in the United States are considering the same. Major funding agencies have to boldly lead and determine that data sharing should be the norm. Everyone should have the opportunity to share their clinical data from their medical record or clinical trials. Systems are being created to enable cultural transformation of the biomedical enterprise. It is our hope that we can create paths into the new land of collaboration and accelerate the discoveries we need to alleviate suffering in our loved ones and beyond.

4 *A time to be grateful.* My family is thriving and entrepreneurialism is woven into its fabric. My husband Pat has founded numerous companies and non-profits. Our daughter, Elizabeth, has just finished taking PXE International to new levels as the Executive Director and finished the two-year Teach for America Corps commitment. Our son Ian is balancing high tech (web development) with organic sustainability in a farm he co-owns with us to bring us all healthy food. As he is fond of quoting from the sage Vietnamese Zen master, Thich Nhat Hanh: 'Without mud, there is no lotus'. We are learning that daily. My greatest challenge these days is the same as it has always been, but always new. It is myself. I must release myself to be big, to be sure, to be humble, to be *one* with others, to be free, to belong, to give freely and to not hold back. I am thrilled to be on this journey and grateful beyond words for my companions on the path. Life is far too short to do anything but go for it. I know that all of this is a great gift in my life, and for the world.

Discussion questions

1 In 1999, Sharon Terry patented the ABCC6 gene. Does that gene patent still stand or did the 2013 Supreme Court ruling banning the patenting of naturally occurring genes negate it?

2 Have other parents or sufferers created registries and blood and tissue banks?

3 Is it ethical to have a support group act as the gatekeeper for the data of people with a specific disease?

4 What do you think are the pros and cons when comparing bricks and mortar disease advocacy organizations (incorporated charities) with Facebook groups and other less traditional movements?

5 What are the pros and cons of Sharon Terry working for all diseases rather than just PXE? Is a narrow focus better than spreading a wider net? What could be the impact on her work and the work of the organization?

6 What do you think about the 'hero model'? How are you a hero? Does it impede others or yourself from having more impact? How strong a role does the ego play?

7 Biomedical science has been the purview of MDs and PhDs until the last few decades when ordinary citizens began to delve into the field. What do you think about the pros and cons of such entrepreneurism for this area of science? Can you give examples of either benefits or harms of citizen entrepreneurism in other sciences, perhaps astronomy, electronics or ornithology?

8 Developing treatments for diseases costs about US $1B and takes 17 or 18 years. It has a 95 per cent failure rate. How is this field ripe for disruption and what would you recommend to ensure more effective use of funds?

9 Finding treatments for rare diseases is just as expensive as common ones, but benefits far fewer people. How should society make decisions about what conditions/diseases to work on? Should people with rare diseases pay more for treatments?

10 Scientists often tend to study popular and safe topics, genes, proteins and so on. What could be done to encourage more entrepreneurial risk taking?

11 What difference does it make when the innovator has a vested interest in the problem, as Sharon did? Does a personal attachment to a problem lead to more commitment and drive, and a potentially better outcome?

Further reading

You can find more material to do with this chapter at www.koganpage.com/socialentrepreneurship

Wikiadvocacy for those who want to start or sustain an advocacy organization – www.wikiadvocacy.org [accessed 10 December 2015]

Terry, S, Learning genetics, *Health Aff (Millwood)*. 2003 Sep–Oct; 22(5): 166–71. PMID: 14515892

Terry, S, Terry, P, Rauen, K, Uitto, J, Bercovitch, L, Advocacy groups as research organizations: the PXE International example. *Nat Rev Genet*. 2007 Feb; 8(2):157–64. PMID: 17230202

Genetic Alliance – www.geneticalliance.org [accessed 10 December 2015]

PXE International – www.pxe.org [accessed 10 December 2015]

13
Power to the people: reengineering democracy

GOVRIGHT – TARIK NESH NASH

ABSTRACT

Since the advent of the internet, information is being processed so fast and societies are changing so quickly that governments are unable to keep up. This case study looks at the journey of a social entrepreneur who realized that the classical channels between governments and the people were becoming obsolete and new ones needed to be invented. Growing up in a family of activists, Tarik Nesh-Nash started applying his IT skills to build platforms for citizen participation in his home country of Morocco right at the time that the Arab Spring emerged.

In early 2015, Tarik co-founded GovRight, an international organization dedicated to bridging the gap between governments and the public, helping to contribute to building more inclusive participatory decision-making models. He launched Legislation Lab, a platform for citizen participation in the legislative process that has already been solicited in approximately 20 countries as of late 2015. Legislation Lab is now being used in Chile, Iraq and the United States to help engage citizens in the drafting of local and national legislature and has been recognized by the United Nations as one of the innovative solutions to support the newly announced Sustainable Development Goals (SGDs).

My personal journey

In the Moroccan context, the Arab Spring is marked by the date of 20 February 2011. On that day, I was marching on the streets with hundreds of thousands in the city of Tangier. Contrary to the impression given by media reports, the protesters were not only young people. I personally was marching with my father, mother, aunt and my 21-year-old brother.

The media loves to glorify events and invent heroes. However, history proves that evolution takes longer than a walk on the street. Morocco is no exception. The impetus for change had been brewing for decades.

My father, Dr Nesh-Nash, spent a lifetime doing humanitarian work and advocating for human rights. His Red Cross stories in Sudan, Somalia, Kosovo, the Philippines, Vietnam and El Salvador ingrained in me a strong drive to do good. I still remember travelling with him to the southern Spanish port of Algeciras where he was advocating for better treatment for the thousands of migrants transitioning from Europe to Morocco. At the time, he created the Transit Operation in partnership with the Spanish Red Cross with the aim of providing decent conditions for the travellers.

My grandfather, Ahmed Elmaddarsi, was jailed more times than he remembers for resisting French colonialism in Morocco and Algeria, and for fighting despotism after independence. Today, while the Arab Spring is celebrated, the reality is that it's more of a continuation of the sacrifices of multiple generations. While the struggle for justice and dignity continues, the process and the means evolve over time. In our era, technology enables unprecedented possibilities for accountability, transparency and participation.

Events, and individuals like my father and grandfather, have deeply shaped my values and my perception of the world. Back in 1991, when I was just 13, I remember discovering books about peace, identity and religion such as *The First Civilizational War* by Mehdi Mandjra and later *The Clash of Civilizations* by Samuel Huntington. That same year, the fall of Baghdad in the first Iraq war was a bitter reminder of the burning of the city seven centuries earlier by Hulagu Khan. My mother simply explained to me how 'the most educated win'. I started taking school far more seriously from that point.

I studied computer science and mathematics in Morocco and later moved to Seattle to join Microsoft as a software developer. At Microsoft, I adhered to the company's motto of 'Empowering People'. I witnessed how our work as 'techies' had a direct impact on the lives of millions. I enjoyed the work, the people and the city. I also continued my learning by taking night classes to earn a master's degree at the University of Washington.

After five years and several promotions later, my life in Seattle became comfortable. Yet, my passion was not fulfilled. I felt that I should be doing more than help build the next big programming language. I believed my work should strive to have a direct impact on the poorest and neediest of people. In 2006, I made the bold decision to join the International Committee of the Red Cross (ICRC). My bond with the Red Cross goes back to my childhood when I volunteered with the Moroccan Red Crescent, and continued later in the United States where I joined the Seattle Chapter of the American Red Cross to volunteer as an interpreter/translator delivering family messages to the refugee community. Joining the ICRC was a largely unpopular decision among my family, friends and colleagues due to the danger of the work, but the voice in my head was too loud to ignore.

My one-year Red Cross mission was as a protection delegate in northern Iraq where I was responsible for assessing detention centres and refugee camps. During this challenging time I witnessed the contrast between the degree of the suffering of the victims and the warmth and the optimism of the population – between the importance of humanitarian work and the limits and deficiencies of our actions. I had the incredible opportunity to learn about the fragility of human life and the value of small gestures such as smiles and eye contact. These small elements of human courtesy and kindness were things that I had totally ignored as a computer geek. While the experience has left me with scars of despair and hopelessness, more importantly it created an even stronger drive to contribute to a better world.

During my brief mandatory breaks, I took time out to visit the region. I particularly hold fond memories of the beautiful city of Damascus, another symbol of Arab civilization. I enjoyed identifying the architectural ties between Damascus and Andalucia in Spain, or Fes and Tetouan in Morocco. Thinking about the situation in Syria today, it feels like yet another tragedy for humanity.

Though I felt I could work for the Red Cross for a lifetime I realized that I could be more valuable leveraging my IT skills to help people, rather than doing pure fieldwork myself. I was lucky to receive a call from human resources at Microsoft asking if I was interested in taking on a programme manager position in Beijing, China. I was excited to be embarking on this new challenge and I was particularly curious about the lessons of the growth of the Chinese economy that could be adapted in developing countries.

The culture shock was considerable. China abolished my long-held beliefs in the universality of western values. The contrast between Chinese collectivism and western individualism, for example, was striking. The search for harmony in the community was socially more important than any self-centred success. Another notable observation was that democracy and development did not necessarily go hand in hand. China was a living counter-example of the belief that the western liberal democracy is the prevailing model, a theory widely publicized in Fukuyama's book *The End of History and the Last Man*. I also witnessed the energy and compassion of the general public for the victims of the Chengdu earthquake in 2008 which highlighted to me that there are often more commonalities between humans than differences. My Chinese experience raised more questions than it answered, but it definitely built a case that the path to development does not mean following the steps of other countries. Innovation in governance models may have better impact.

In late 2009, I felt it was time to walk the unpaved path of social entrepreneurship. I decided to move back 'home' to enjoy the comfort of family, the beauty of the city and to focus on my passion of using technology for development. I was planning to tackle Morocco's health, education, and other key social sectors through IT when I quickly realized that a more important fundamental step was necessary.

For these institutions to be truly effective, citizens would first have to demand change, and then hold governments accountable for the results. Many people would have to learn new roles, and we would need the development of a generation equipped to safeguard the transparency of government, constantly pushing the boundaries to ensure efficacy. At the core of this was the need to build new communication channels between citizens and the government. My IT background was perfectly suited to build this platform, but before I started I decided to go to law school to get a better understanding of the political processes that could facilitate this kind of accountability.

Identifying the problem

Current political processes developed at a time when the internet did not exist. In this modern age, citizens expect more information, transparency, accountability and participation.

In 2011, there were street protests in more than 88 countries around the world, driven by the failure of traditional leadership and the fecklessness of institutions. Politicians seemed unwilling or unable to look beyond the next election and, as a result, they often refused to make hard choices. In the United States, the Occupy Wall Street movement came up with the slogan 'We are the 99 per cent' to demonstrate how most of the population did not, and still does not, feel well represented. This movement mushroomed out of a growing discontent with the increasing wealth inequality in the United States. Additional fuel was added to the fire when the federal government bailed out corporations and their executives during the financial crisis leaving taxpayers to foot the bill. Many people in the United States see the rules and laws being written by lobbyists and the well-connected. In Spain, the movement *Indignados* (Outraged) came up with the slogan 'Real Democracy Now!', also as a result of their feeling under-represented. However, despite this, the reality is that in both the United States and Spain, democratic rules are applied properly. Elections are fair and transparent and the elected majority gets to rule.

The protests had a bigger impact in the Arab world. Citizens here had historically had no voice and had often been treated without dignity. The protests became so powerful that they brought down dictators in Tunisia, Egypt and Libya and rattled regimes in Syria, Yemen and Bahrain.

These examples raise fundamental questions about the governance model and the relationship between the public and their government. Nowadays, using the internet and mobile phones, citizens' interactions and reactions with each other can be almost instantaneous. When people make a call, send a text message (SMS) or post a message on social media, they expect a response almost immediately.

However, citizens are not able to communicate this easily and quickly with their representatives. Nor are they able to contribute to legislative decisions affecting their lives except in instances such as referendums, elections or signing a petition. There is a huge communication gap between people and their elected officials. One example is the authoring of laws. A law is, in a way, a contract between citizens and their government. It defines the rights and obligations of each party. It defines how much freedom we give away in order to live in peace and stability. But who gets to set the terms of this contract? Who should write the law? How much should citizens be involved in deciding how they are governed?

FIGURE 13.1 Tarik presenting Legislation Lab at the Solutions Summit during the General Assembly of the United Nations. Legislation Lab was selected as an innovative solution to support the Sustainable Development goals related to 'Justice and Peace'

Used with Permission (Copyright: United Nations Foundation, Diane Bondareff)

In most countries, citizens have very limited influence and few opportunities to participate in the law-making process. The most likely case would be a referendum, where one will get to vote either yes or no on a proposal detailed in a whole document.

But even this is problematic. If citizens only get to vote yes or no, how can they express their opinions if they like one part of the law but not another? How can they propose an improvement to a text they already approve? How can citizens become more interested and involved in drafting legislation that is in the best interests of the general populace?

There are many other questions too. How do we guarantee that the citizen's voice is reflected in the law? Should citizens abide by laws that they do not have access to or they do not understand? Is it even possible for citizens to be aware of all the laws? If citizens do not like a law, what processes can they go through to force government to change it? If citizens do not approve of their deputies, should they be kept waiting for four or five years before they can vote to replace them?

You can imagine the difficulties in setting up a system to collect public feedback a few centuries ago, during times when horses were the main mode of transportation. Today things are different, and we live at a time where interconnectivity is ubiquitous. Technology has disrupted and improved the fields of medicine and trade, among many others. Technology should also be at the forefront of improving political processes for the betterment of society.

How I tackled the problem

Access to legal information

I founded a tech start-up 'Software Centre' and launched my first experimental project, 'Juriste.ma' in 2010 as the first Moroccan platform to provide citizens with access to legal information. It was built on the premise that people needed to know their rights and obligations in order to become active citizens. There is an expectation for citizens to be law abiding, but hardly any person today knows enough about these laws, which is what is shocking to me. Even lawyers and law professors have difficulty tracking law texts in archaic libraries and thick legal tomes. The platform positioned itself as a free public encyclopedia of Moroccan law, court decisions and documentation. Using a simple keyword search, the user would receive the requested information in a few seconds.

Evaluation of the project was mixed. While the platform was popular among law students, it was not sufficiently attractive to the general public. Two quick conclusions were drawn. First, the lack of an official source of legal information is a structural impediment for the realization of empowered citizens. Second, law education is hard and requires more effort and innovation to bridge the legal illiteracy of the average citizen.

While I was busy with this legal civic education project, I joined the National Council of the Moroccan Organization of Human Rights to advocate for the respect and protection of human rights in the country. Then, something happened. It was the Arab Spring.

The Arab Spring

For a long time, experts had been predicting a popular uprising in the Middle East and North Africa. It was not a question of if it would happen, but rather when. All Middle Eastern and North African countries have been plagued for some time with socioeconomic challenges – including poverty, corruption and high unemployment. These problems were exacerbated by widespread violations of human rights, despotism, impunity and the control of the economy by the political elite.

In Morocco, the confusion of power (legislative, executive and judicial) under the authority of the king, as well as the control over the economy, was a systemic failure of governance. Additionally, corruption was so endemic that it was limiting progress in all sectors of society.

If there is one term that might explain the roots of the Arab Spring it is *Hogra* – the contempt of rulers towards the people. *Hogra* is a feeling of a loss of dignity, and once someone loses their dignity they feel less than human. It was an expression of this loss that became the catalyst for the Arab Spring.

It all started in December 2010 in a small city in Tunisia where a street vendor was pushed around, humiliated and slapped by an official. In a shocking reaction to his pain, he set himself on fire in a public square. This act catalysed an intensive campaign of civil resistance that quickly spread around the country. This action ultimately led to the ousting of the long-time President. But change did not stop in

Tunisia. A wave of protests and riots spread to other neighbouring countries. Rulers were forced from power in Egypt, Libya and Yemen, and reforms happened in virtually all areas within the region.

In Morocco, citizens welcomed the fall of the presidents of Tunisia and Egypt. In an attempt to drive change at home, Facebook users called on citizens to organize street protests in different cities across the country.

Crowdsourcing the Moroccan Constitution

On 16 February, I contacted Mehdi Slaoui Andaloussi, a Moroccan friend and ex-Microsoft colleague, to join me in building a site for crowdsourcing the drafting of a new Moroccan Constitution. We both believed that the best outcome of the emerging, growing change would be a new social contract that protected citizens' rights.

On a historic day, 20 February saw massive street protests spontaneously organized by the youth in various cities throughout Morocco. Slogans called for 'Change of the Constitution', 'Change of Government' and 'Fighting Corruption'. This signalled the start of the Arab Spring in the country. Protests were held weekly.

During that first week, Mehdi – based in Seattle – and myself in Tangier, spent countless hours preparing the new constitution platform. Our work was just one of a growing number of examples of the power of technology to enable remote collaboration.

When the platform was ready, we started looking for partners to help take it to the public. I contacted a number of civil society organizations and media outlets, but all the requests were turned down. So, we decided to hold onto the platform and wait for the right time to launch.

On 9 March, King Mohamed VI of Morocco pledged constitutional reforms and promised a reduction in the monarch's power and free parliamentary elections. He called for a greater consultation process with different actors. This was our moment.

The next day we launched Reforme.ma as a citizen initiative to crowdsource the drafting of the constitution. The platform enabled citizens to read through the constitution and vote for or against items in every single article, and even to make proposals and comments about the articles.

Quasi real-time statistics were published to highlight the demographics and the most prominent articles under discussion – including the most popular articles, the most accepted articles, the most rejected and the most controversial ones. Within a two-month period, there were 200,000 visitors and more than 10,000 comments. To put these numbers in perspective, this is larger than the membership of any political party in Morocco.

Interestingly, in the initial stages, the buzz was limited to the virtual (online) world. Traditional media outlets such as television and radio did not report on the platform, a phenomenon that for us questioned the independence of the offline (traditional) media. However, once the international media started publishing articles and broadcasting news about the website, the effect trickled down and the national media began reporting citizens' usage. Eventually, media outlets like television and radio ended up having a considerable impact in increasing traffic to the site. Thanks to the number of visitors and the considerable media coverage, I was invited by the Constitutional Drafting Committee to submit and present our findings.

FIGURE 13.2   Reforme.ma. Citizens could vote up/down and make comments in every article

Image courtesy author

Our report contained two sections: a purely statistical analysis and a qualitative analysis of the users' orientations. The statistical report contained analytics about the users and indicators on the most engaging articles. A segment of our online community analysed all the comments and proposals as part of our preparations for the qualitative report.

The project was successful beyond expectations. On one side, the mere fact that thousands of citizens took the time to read segments of the text of their constitution was a huge leap forward, particularly when compared to the previous constitution in 1991 where people voted without being given any practical means to be informed about its content. This time around, the Drafting Committee officially received information on citizens' orientation. In other words, citizens indirectly participated in the drafting process. Looking back, around 40 per cent of the internet users' recommendations are now in the new Moroccan constitution (which was finally voted on in July 2011.)

This project was also a turning point at a very personal level. Although the results were exhilarating at such an early stage, I was reaching a low point. I had been working on projects with no financial return and consuming my personal savings, and I found myself with no option but to ask for a loan from my family.

Another concern was security. While I was not personally targeted, I was advised to keep a low profile and avoid the spotlight. However, my biggest personal realization was seeing a light in the dark, realizing that change is possible. I came out of this experience more determined to continue work on citizen participation. Unfortunately, there was little time to think strategically about future work. As soon as the constitution referendum ended, the general elections were organized.

Marsad.ma: crowdsourcing election monitoring

Historically, elections in Morocco have largely been perceived as rigged. Corruption and false results moved people to become sceptical and apathetic towards the whole process. In order to influence change, I thought citizens needed to have more control over the process. My inspiration came from similar initiatives like the use of Ushahidi's mapping technology in Kenya. In order to regain trust in the electoral system, citizens should be able to monitor all phases of the electoral process. That was the goal of my next project – Marsad.ma. *Marsad* means 'observatory' in Arabic.

Using this new platform, citizens could monitor the legislative electoral process during November 2011 and report irregularities via SMS, the internet, Facebook or Twitter. The reports were then analysed by an expert team at the Moroccan Organization of Human Rights. The analysis was important to establish the veracity of the information. It was based on a triangulation with other sources of data including reports from media and field observers on the ground. The validated reports were published on the website and in a map form.

In another exciting outcome, the platform received 80,000 unique visits and 15,000 reports. After validation, 1,500 reports were published including one image

FIGURE 13.3 Marsad.ma used Ushahidi and FrontlineSMS technologies to engage citizens on reporting elections irregularities

Image courtesy author

reported by a citizen that tells of the use of religious symbols by a candidate. Under Moroccan law, the use of religious symbols is not allowed since religious-based political parties are outlawed. This one image was instrumental in causing a rerun of the elections in the city of Tangier. Yet, despite the general success of the election monitoring platform the experience was not without its challenges and mistakes. In one instance, the platform published a video of a candidate distributing money and alcohol in an indecent manner at a party. We received a call informing us that the video was fake and unless we removed it immediately, we would be sued. We could not verify the authenticity of the video and, as a result, had little choice but to remove it.

Marsad.ma represented my transition from working alone, to a model of partnership and collaboration. In this project, the work with the Moroccan Organization of Human Rights enabled me to leverage their team of legal experts, observers on the ground and their wide network of contacts across the country. I learned that partnership not only provides better results by leveraging additional expertise, but it also brings support and the safety net needed to work on these types of potentially controversial and widely impactful projects.

At this point, an important opportunity came my way that would lend our initiatives more recognition, resources and much needed financial support. I was successfully nominated for recognition as an Ashoka Fellow. This news was a timely boost for the team's morale and helped us continue to move forward.

Citizen participation on the fight against corruption

After the elections, things began to calm down, and I felt it was time to move my focus and energy from being reactive to begin dealing with important events, to be more proactive and work on more structural problems. I believed the highest priority was corruption. Corruption, in my opinion, is the root of all evil. In February 2012 I reached out to the leading anti-corruption association – Transparency Maroc, a member of Transparency International (TI) – and proposed a platform to enable citizens to report corruption cases.

Mamdawrinch.com, which means 'we will not bribe' in Moroccan dialect, was an improvement from the first Marsad.ma site, going beyond elections. Citizens could report corruption cases that would then be investigated by the Transparency Maroc team before publication.

I was invited to join the board of Transparency Maroc, which gave me the opportunity to be educated by some of the most respected intellectuals in the field of governance and accountability. With their help I am still learning to analyse governance dysfunctions from different angles – politics, law and culture – and the need for an integrated approach to tackle it.

I also learned that the fight against corruption could not be won overnight, and that it would require long-term strategies. Mamdawrinch's evaluation is mixed. On one hand, it received considerable online buzz nationally and internationally. However, the impact on eradicating corruption is not yet evident. Most of the reports received related to petty corruption, yet the real fight is major corruption at regional and national levels. Unfortunately, Mamdawrinch did little to uncover these kinds of stories.

Good governance

While thinking about the challenges of good governance from a different angle, it occurred to me that there was a need to strengthen and monitor parliamentarians. Today, the parliament works in a silo. Despite citizens becoming increasingly used to real-time communication via the internet and social media, they only have a say about the make-up of their parliament every four or five years through elections. Because of this, a new idea called Nouabook was born.

Nouabook.ma enables citizens to identify their representative publicly and ask them questions directly. The elected officials can use the platform to respond publicly to the questions, creating a feedback loop in the process. A dedicated civil society organization called Simsim is running the project, and so far around 15 per cent of the representatives use the platform to engage with citizens. This is quite an encouraging outcome in a country with little history of citizen–politician dialogue.

From these accumulated experiences and mixed results, it became obvious that success would require more trial and error and more innovation. Neither the NGO, nor private sectors were naturally set up to manage social innovation. Civil society was focused on field impact, while the business world focused on financial profit. There was a need for applied research and experimental methodologies. So I created a new academic organization to complement our existing work.

FIGURE 13.4   Nouabook.ma: Citizens can search for politicians and ask questions

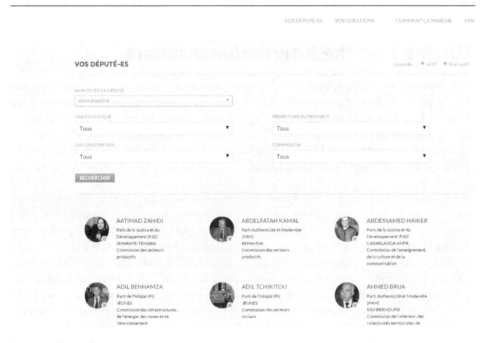

Image courtesy author

Research projects

I joined Mundiapolis University in Casablanca where I founded the ICT4Dev Research Center. Its purpose was to focus on the use of technology for development. Applied research, unlike basic research, aims to identify new solutions to a real problem with the objective of having a real impact in the field. The new organization would work in synergy with the other actors and fill the gap in exploration. Within this framework, I had the freedom to experiment with concepts, apply for grants and even partner with officials. As a representative of the university I could also sign Memorandums of Understanding (MoUs) with Ministries to gain access to information and explore with students different methodologies for citizen participation – from budget transparency to environmental assessment.

In one particularly interesting case, I remember approaching the Ministry of Finance as a member of Transparency Maroc to request financial budget data. The official response was not positive. Then, I made the same request in the name of the university and I was presented with the data. At the university, we explored working on the transparency and accountability challenge from a budget perspective. We launched Floussna.ma, a platform that uses simple visualization to communicate key budget data to the average citizen. The goal was to raise awareness among citizens, the media and politicians of key budget information beneficial to engaging in more meaningful discussion. This project is still a work in progress.

We have also set up a partnership with the Ministry of ICT to promote and reuse open data. Students would be able to build applications that made use of this existing data as a showcase of the importance of openness, and as a means to advocate for more access to more data.

Moving into the international sphere

The internet is a village, and all of my projects had some international exposure which led to further opportunities. The Juriste.ma project, for example, opened the door to join Freedom of Access to Legal Information, an international academic movement that promotes the use of ICT to publish legal information. This network enabled me to meet people like Pompeu Casanovas from the Autonomous University of Barcelona, and Tom Bruce from Cornell University, who have been very supportive of my work.

But, up to this point, the most internationally recognized project has been Reforme.ma – which resulted in an invitation for me to support similar initiatives in Egypt by Stanford University and in Libya by the United Nations Development Project (UNDP). As with these two projects, which built their own platforms, the general trend in my experience with civic platforms has been the reinvention of the wheel. Considerable financial and time resources are spent to build identical platforms.

Fortunately, I then met Heath Morrison, who happened to be struggling with the same concern. Based in Kiev in Ukraine, Heath is an American with a strong background in the technology sector who has shifted his focus towards applying technology to international social causes and initiatives. I met Heath at the International Anti-Corruption Conference in Brasilia, Brazil in 2012, where he was presenting an online platform that promotes transparency in the health sector in Ukraine. We had long discussions on how much energy is spent solving problems that have already been solved elsewhere.

We then happened to be invited by Transparency International to collaborate in the building of a generic platform to enable any individual to build a citizen corruption reporting site in a few clicks. In essence, to build a generic and improved version of 'mamdawrinch'. We spent hours on Skype discussing and collaborating on how to build a platform that would be useful for any country, in any language and in any context. This resulted in a wider discussion about how best to build generic scalable online platforms for civic participation, and it became the starting point for the creation of a new organization dedicated to building crowdsourcing platforms for citizen participation that have the potential to be scaled internationally.

At this stage, one of the key questions we had to address was our legal structure. We had two choices – a non-profit organization or a traditional for-profit company. We turned to reports, literature and consultations with friends, and in the end decided to develop a for-profit entity with the goal of becoming a legally-recognized social enterprise. The rationale for our thinking was based on the following factors:

● innovation is best promoted in the competitive environment of a start-up;
● financial sustainability is important to enable the building of a long-term strategy and to avoid a constant search for donors;
● scalability (ie a project that aims to be applied internationally);
● hiring – it is much easier to hire the best people as a start-up rather than as an NGO.

In February 2015, we created GovRight. Based on the belief that there is a divide which results from mutual misunderstanding between government and the public, our mission was to reduce the gap by both empowering and equipping citizens with user-friendly technologies to enable them to become active, informed participants in the legislative process through three main routes:

● Access to law: the publication of law documents and data in a format that is modern, accessible, and designed to be shared and integrated.
● Civic education: applying educational methodology and technology to empower citizens to better understand the function and effects of the legislation in their country.
● Participation: creating opportunities for citizens to voice their knowledge and opinions on the purpose and implementation of legislation.

Work started with our teams in Morocco and Ukraine on our first project, Legislation Lab.

The birth of Legislation Lab

Legislation Lab is a platform for encouraging public awareness and discussion of upcoming legislation. It was inspired largely by the experience of Reforme.ma as a participatory model to collect citizen feedback.

Six months after its launch, Legislation Lab has already garnered a significant amount of recognition. We have been contacted by organizations in more than 20 countries and received enough funding and grants to cover our first year's operating costs. In partnership with a group of engaged Chileans, we launched LaConstitutionsDetodos.cl ('Constitution for everybody') in March, 2015. The goal of the platform is to raise awareness and promote public dialogue about the Chilean Constitution. Fortuitously, the site going live coincided with the Chilean President, Michelle Bachelet, announcing preparations for a large and open consultation process for the new constitution. This Chilean platform remains operational today.

In Kurdistan, Iraq, the regional government announced the preparation of the regional constitution. Invited by the United States Institute of Peace (USIP) we met local civil society organizations to discuss how best to engage citizens in the constitutional dialogue. Three local NGOs decided to work together to use Legislation Lab to open a dialogue on the text of the draft constitution. In one particular case, the Coalition of Iraqi Minorities proposed changes to the articles relating to minority rights and reached out to the marginalized communities for feedback. This was an innovative approach to deal with the difficulty of the tyranny of the majority. More than a thousand interactions were recorded and prepared for submission to the Kurdish Parliament.

A more minor and, unfortunately, less successful project was with the New York City Council. Council member Ben Kallos used Legislation Lab to invite the city's online community to co-draft a bill to prevent landlords from discriminating against tenants with housing court records. It is estimated that the so-called Anti-Tenant Black Lists hold hundreds of thousands of names of would-be renters, and they are often used by landlords to deny future housing to potential tenants based on discriminatory information. The legislation would allow tenants to file a complaint with the New York City Commission on Human Rights and fine landlords if a violation is discovered.

Unfortunately, there was little engagement on the platform, and a deeper root-cause analysis needs to be made. However, without that we can still draw a few conclusions:

- Citizen engagement at the local level may require a different communication strategy than those used at the national level.
- It is harder to engage citizens in what are perceived as mature democracies. In transitional contexts, citizens are more eager to have their voices heard.
- The Legislation Lab platform needs to evolve to better highlight the content of local bills.

While it is always a joy to receive international recognition, the real measure of success is our impact on citizens and legislations. And we are still far from streamlining our process and understanding. Today, we are just scratching the surface of a huge opportunity to make legislation and law a 'commodity', and I am committed as ever to continuing to contribute to a better world.

FIGURE 13.5   GovRight co-founders spending summer of 2015 at the Legal Information Institute at Cornell University. From left to right: Sarah Frug, Tarik Nesh-Nash, Tom Bruce, Heath Morrison and Craig Newton

Photo courtesy author

The mechanics

Determining the right organizational structure has been a continuous debate in each of our projects. This is where we ended up:

GovRight

TABLE 13.1   GovRight Organizational Structure

Project	Ownership
Access to legal information (jurist.ma)	Software Centre (business)
Constitutional crowdsourcing (Reforme.ma)	Citizen initiative
Corruption fighting (Mamdawrinch.com)	Transparency Maroc (non-profit)
Election monitoring (Marsad.ma)	Moroccan Organization of Human Rights (non-profit)
MP-Citizen Dialogue (Nouabook.ma)	Simsim (non-profit)
Budget Transparency (Floussna.ma)	Mundiapolis University (academia)
Legislation Lab (legislationlab.org)	GovRight (business/social enterprise)

The choice of organizational structure reflects the mindset of the project's mission:

- We use the business organization model when there are financial profit expectations.
- We use the non-profit organization when there is real social value but no expectation of financial returns.
- I use academic and research centres where the project is still exploratory and its value is not yet evident.
- I use the social enterprise model when there is a combination of sustainable business model and social impact.

As of late 2015 I am the CEO of Software Centre, a private tech company, a board member of Transparency Maroc in the civil society space, and head of ICT4Dev Research Center at Mundiapolis University in the academic sector. I am also the CEO of GovRight LLC, an international social enterprise based in the United States. I reflect sometimes that I am spending too much energy on too many fronts. However, on the other hand, this diversity and knowledge does give me the flexibility to launch different projects using the most appropriate organizational set-up. From my wider experiences to date, I am learning to focus on having a larger impact by building sustainable and scalable solutions.

Funding and sustainability

Funding was a challenge that I had to learn to manage between my personal passion and financial constraints. Looking back, I usually went through three distinct phases.

- Initial phase: cost sink
  My first projects had no revenue model. They were built with the sole purpose of having a social impact. I had to use my personal savings, or in some cases work on side projects to reduce the losses. Obviously this model was, and is not, sustainable (financially, at least).

- Second phase: break even
  Once I hit a financial barrier, I became more conscious of avoiding losses. I decided to work with civil society organizations and request sufficient funds to cover the costs of the project. This model allowed me to break even and to continue following my passion. However, it required finding the right NGOs with similar visions and sufficient funds for bringing projects to fruition, all of which took additional (and sometimes considerable) effort.

- Third phase: return on investment
  To overcome my dependency on NGOs, we built a social enterprise which encapsulates both the social mission and the need to provide some degree of financial return.

  GovRight, for example, was bootstrapped by the personal investment of the two founders and by selling related products and services to customers. GovRight's initial investment was about $30,000 and the break-even point happened eight months after its founding. Legislation Lab has a 'Freemium model' where it is free for anybody to use, but there is a paid version which provides more customized and richer functionality for more serious, heavy users. The current model is allowing the organization to grow organically.

Marketing

Given our limited resources, we are betting on a three-pronged approach to marketing:

- Face to face: In the last few years, I have been invited to more than 20 countries to promote concepts of online citizen participation. The audience is usually made up of civil society organizations (CSOs), academia and public actors. This is usually our opportunity to highlight our work and share it widely with a range of different stakeholders.

- Online marketing: We publish a weekly blog post to share news about our work, supported by e-mail newsletters and various social media channels such as Facebook and Twitter.

- Customer satisfaction: A happy customer is the best marketing tool you can have. Our reputation by word of mouth has been our most successful strategy.

Impact

It is important to have clear impact indicators to help ensure your work is heading in the right direction. In the case of Legislation Lab, we defined our indicators at three levels:

1 Legislation Lab usage:
   - number of requests: to track the number of potential customers who are interested to learn more, or to test the platform;
   - number of deployments: to measure the number of instances where Legislation Lab was deployed.
2 Legislation Lab deployment usage:

   For each deployment, we track its impact and use by:
   - number of unique visitors to the site;
   - number of interactions (votes, comments and proposals).
3 Deployment impact

   Beyond deployment, we measure the impact of participation on the final law:
   - comparison between the recommendations of citizens and the final content of the law.

Lessons learnt

1 *Follow your passion.* You may need to go through a rollercoaster of financial and/or social pressure, but the pleasure of working on what you are passionate about is immeasurable.
2 *Find a co-founder.* Finding the right co-founder may be hard, but find the right person and you set yourself up for a greater chance of success. In my case, my co-founder has kept us focused on our existing commitments rather than stretching to engage in new ones (which I would naturally do). It is often said that the path to entrepreneurship is long and lonely. If you have a choice, engage other trusted partners along the way who will bring complementary ideas, skills and values to the table.
3 *Act local, think global.* It is great to have the best ideas, but unless they are executed and have an impact, they cannot be considered a success. First, focus on making sure you have an impact, and then you can work on taking the concept to scale.
4 *Technology is not enough.* We often get excited about building cool technologies. The reality is that impact may require less technical innovation and more social and project management.
5 *Take good care of your health, your family and your friends.* This is easier said than done, but a healthy balance is critical for everyone.

FIGURE 13.6   Dashboard of the Chilean constitution discussion
(www.laconstituciondetodos.cl)

<< Constitución de Chile

✓ 134   ✗ 192   ☰ 1   ✎ 44   ○ 167

Votos   Votos   Links de   Cambios   Comentarios
favorables   negativos   interés   sugeridos

Contribuciones en Artículos

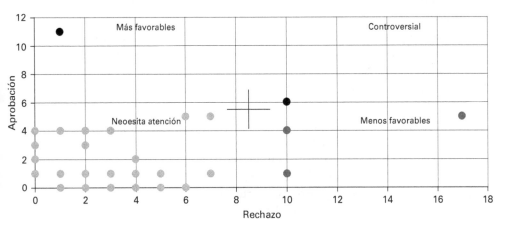

Demografía de las contribuciones

Indicators include demographic data and participation weight for each article (Image courtesy author)

Discussion questions

1 How much of a role did technology play in the Arab Spring? What do you think about the use of the terms 'Facebook Revolution' or 'Twitter Revolution' to describe its role? Would the Arab Spring have happened without technology?

2 'Technology can be a double-edged sword and be an enabler for organizations working towards open government and democracy, whilst enabling those governments to monitor citizens and civil society.' Discuss.

3 How important is it to build open platforms that anyone can take and deploy for their own use, in their own country?

4 Is it an advantage or a disadvantage that many of the social media platforms used to engage citizens are commercial, for-profit ventures based largely out of the United States?

5 What was it about Tarik's background that gave him the skills, drive and vision that were so useful – and critical – to him in his later career?

6 Drafting legislation is complex and often beyond the understanding of many citizens. What techniques can be used to make it more relevant, and that might encourage people to engage in the process?

7 How crucial are the growing movements for open data and open governance to the future of democracy? Are we overplaying their importance? What evidence do we have that they work?

Further reading

You can find more material to do with this chapter at www.koganpage.com/socialentrepreneurship

TEDx talk: Rethinking democracy through technology – www.youtube.com/watch?v=A2P19zK6t1M
Ashoka profile: www.ashoka.org/fellow/tarik-nesh-nash [accessed 12 December 2015]
Govright blog: govright.org/latest-news/ [accessed 12 December 2015]
Legislation Lab: http://legislationlab.org/ [accessed 12 December 2015]
Protest: http://content.time.com/time/person-of-the-year/2011/ [accessed 12 December 2015]
Brownlee, J, Masoud, T and Reynolds, A (2015) *The Arab Spring: Pathways of Repression and Reform* Oxford University Press
What Went Wrong: The Clash between Islam and modernity in the Middle East, Bernard Lewis https://en.wikipedia.org/wiki/What_Went_Wrong%3F
The Wisdom of Crowds, James Surowiecki https://sivers.org/book/WisdomOfCrowds

INDEX

NB: Abstracts, discussion questions, further reading, lessons learnt and references are indexed as such. Page numbers in *italic* indicate figures or tables.

CPSIA information can be obtained
at www.ICGtesting.com
Printed in the USA
JSHW011118030822
28854JS00005B/65

9 780749 475918